T5-CQB-665

THE PITTSBURGH THEOLOGICAL MONOGRAPHS

New Series

Dikran Y. Hadidian

General Editor

9

"TO SAVE THEIR HEATHEN SOULS"

Voyage to and Life in Fouchow, China

Based on Wentworth Diaries and Letters, 1854-1858

"TO SAVE THEIR HEATHEN SOULS"

VOYAGE TO AND LIFE IN FOUCHOW, CHINA

BASED ON WENTWORTH DIARIES AND LETTERS, 1854-1858

Edited by

Polly Park

Foreword by Francis West

PICKWICK PUBLICATIONS

Allison Park, Pennsylvania

1984

Library of Congress Cataloging in Publication Data
Main entry under title:

"To save their heathen souls".

   (Pittsburgh theological monographs. New series ; 9)
   1. Wentworth, Erastus. 2. Wentworth, Anna M.
3. Missionaries—China—Correspondence. 4. Missionaries—
United States—Correspondence. 5. Missions—China—
Fu-chou shih (Fukien Province)—History—Sources.
6. Fu-chou shih (Fukien Province, China)—History—
Sources. I. Park, Polly. II. Series.
BV3427.A1T6 1984   266'.76'0922 [B]   84-4247
ISBN 0-915138-66-2

TO PETER

CONTENTS

CONTENTS

FOREWORD

"They came here to do good. And they've done very well." That is an old joke about missionaries around the Pacific islands and, no doubt, in many another area of missionary enterprise. Polly Park's excellent edition of some of the family's papers shows the other side of the story, not as a piece of pious hagiography but as the missionaries themselves saw it at the time. In the diaries, letters and related papers of Erastus Wentworth and his wife Anna, Methodist missionaries from Connecticut and Pennsylvania to China in the mid 19th century, we can see the dedication which led those who believed themselves to be "saved" to risk physical discomfort, sickness, and death to bring the heathen to salvation.

The value of such an edition as Polly Park's is clear. In these papers we can discern the characters, the hopes and the fears of those who went out to deliver a heathen land from error's chain. Writing to their own contemporaries, not to us, these missionaries were not consciously putting a gloss on their own experiences. They were trying to tell it as it was. And this is manna to any historian.

What either or both of the Wentworths wrote at the time is not, of course, the complete picture. As Mrs. Park makes clear in her introduction, in any human testimony you have to allow for the limitations of the writer and for their tempering the wind to their reader's sensibilities. But what we have in these papers is an immediate account of their writers' experiences and a conscious desire to tell the truth, not to deceive.

Many, perhaps most, of the assumptions of the Wentworths and their correspondents we would not these days share. The idea, for example, that those who are not called by God to salvation shall without doubt perish everlastingly is not one that modern Western man and woman readily acknowledges, although militant Islam reveals still the power of the idea. Nor would we share their belief that there is an imperative duty upon Christian men and women, even at the risk of our own lives, to save souls. Plainly Anna Wentworth believed that there was.

Still, it is not simply the beliefs of those of our great grand-parents' days which are of interest in this book. It is the things they take for granted as part of life. They take for granted sickness and death in a way we do not. They take for granted the insecurity of life in this world. Their expectations of happiness in this world are much less than ours. As the Editor points out: this had its price. The young Anna Wentworth, sent back by her widowed father from China to West Chester, fashionably educated in Philadelphia and at Vassar, died in 1933 having to command the love and attention that she so much desired but had not received because of her parents' sense of duty.

Beyond the personalities who speak for themselves in this book, there is the additional fascination that these were missionaries to China: a fabulous empire in decay. Erastus Wentworth was an acute observer, and his letters record a view of China. They also begin to explain the origins of that American connection with China which runs through later history.

Polly Park's book will interest anybody with a curiosity about the past, but it can also be read for pleasure: a family observed with sympathy, but also with a shrewd eye for character and incident.

Francis West, F.R.H.S.   F.A.H.A.

Dean of Social Sciences
and Professor of History,
Deakin University
Geelong, Victoria,
Australia

PREFACE

THE DISCOVERY OF THE WENTWORTH LETTERS

On Monday, January 20th, 1975, two days after my mother-in-law's funeral, her three children gathered at her house, "Cloverly Farm", in West Chester, Pennsylvania, for the purpose of choosing her belongings. The occasion was made doubly sad by their awareness that an era had ended. "Cloverly Farm", which had been purchased by their grandparents Richard G. Park and his wife Anna (Wentworth) in 1882 as a country estate was soon to be put on the market for sale. Four generations of Parks had known and loved that beautiful rural estate with its 100 acres or more of rolling green countryside, its forests, fields, streams and acres of mowed lawns dappled with the shade from venerable oak, maple and beech trees.

The party moved indoors to the lovely old colonial farm-house made of field-stone with its paneled dining-room and spacious sitting rooms where sunlight gleamed through deep-set paned windows onto polished wide-oak floors. How lifeless it all seemed now.

Room by room they moved through the first floor, then the second floor, each, in turn choosing those things that they wished to keep. Finally they climbed the stairs to the large attic which covered the major portion of the house where a number of miscellaneous items had been stored over the years.

While passing a cedar-closet, Peter's attention was drawn to a package lying on the floor of the otherwise empty closet. The package was neatly wrapped in brown paper and tied with string. On the front was marked WENTWORTH LETTERS. He called it to the attention of the others.

All were aware that the letters were those of their great-grandparents, Erastus and Anna Wentworth who had gone out to Foochow, China, in 1855 to serve as Methodist missionaries. All had heard the tale many times, about their grandmother's birth in Foochow, how soon after the birth the young mother had died and the baby was later sent back with her Chinese nurse to America to be brought up by her grandparents, the Joseph J. Lewis family of West Chester, Pennsylvania. A joint decision was therefore made on the spot that the letters should go to the West Chester Historical Society. The following day Peter flew back to our home in Canberra, Australia.

A year later "Cloverly Farm" was sold. On hearing the news of the sale, Peter's first thought was of the letters. Had they been taken to the Historical Society, or were they still lying on the attic floor perhaps to be swept out later by the new owners?

He telephoned, immediately, to our eldest son, Peter Jr., in Washington, D.C. and asked him if he would drive up to "Cloverly Farm" and see if the letters were still there and if so, to mail them over to us for a reading. He had long since regretted his hasty decision to turn them over to the Historical Society without recording their contents for the sake of our children and grandchildren.

A week later the package arrived in a large, padded mailing envelope. The letters were in a remarkable state of preservation considering their age and the long sea voyage that most of them had withstood from China to the United States in the mid-19th century. Although originally folded, each had been carefully opened out and laid flat, no doubt by the loving hands of the recipients. This was important, for had they been left folded, time would have caused those folds to turn brown in color obscuring much of the writing.

Anna's letters, which began from her early childhood days, were written on very fine paper, either pale blue, gray, or white in color. Most sheets were embossed on the top left side with the maker's name and either Paris or London beneath it.

Erastus' letters were written on larger double-folded sheets of a slightly darker blue with a white embossed sailing ship with the name, "John Butler" above.

The strong emphasis of the day on good penmanship was evidenced by the extraordinarily even hand-writing without blotches or spelling errors. In fact, there was a remarkable similarity in the hand-writing of both, his being only slightly larger and bolder than hers.

Even a brief glance at the contents convinced me that "some day" those letters should be typed up for the family. However, after struggling to read only a few, it was obvious that the task would be a painstaking one requiring months of work with the assistance of a magnifying glass.

That "some day" didn't come until five years later, in 1981, when I put everything else aside and tackled the project "head on". I wasn't far into the letters when I realized the value of this first person account both to the general reader and to the student of Chinese history.

The better part of another year was spent in research in order to write a complete Introduction and Epilogue to the book. When the whole was completed I sought the opinion of two writers of biographical history. Both encouraged publication. The rest is history.

Polly Park
Red Hill, Australia

福 州

ACKNOWLEDGEMENTS

I would like to thank all of my children and their spouses, Peter G. Park, Jr. and his wife Joy, Thomas P. Park and his wife Catherine, Lewis W. Park and his wife Elspeth, and Mary P. Keightley and her husband David, for their advice and support throughout the development of the book. I would particularly thank Peter and Joy for the enormous amount of research they have done for me at Harvard University's Widener, Yengching, and Divinity School libraries and other libraries on America's East Coast and for attending so promptly to numerous other matters pertaining to the book.

I am deeply grateful for the information received from Maggie Holtzberg at Wesleyan University's Olin Library, from Brenda Pehle (Director of Alumni Relations) at McKendree College, and from the West Chester Historical Society. I wish to thank the National Portrait Gallery in Washington, D.C. for permitting a photograph to be taken of a charcoal drawing in their collection of Joseph Jackson Lewis and to my brother, Richard E. Pearson, for discovering the whereabouts of the portrait and making the necessary arrangements for having it photographed.

My very special thanks to Professor Francis J. West of Deakin University for first reading the manuscript and offering suggestions and alterations to the Introduction, and for his kindness in taking time from his busy schedule to write the Foreword to the book. My thanks, too, to Victor Crittendon for reading the manuscript and encouraging its publication.

I am grateful to Ella L. Aderholdt for the time she spent in researching words in those faded letters that appeared almost indistinguishable.

The long and arduous task of bringing the book to fruition has been made considerably easier by the consistently pleasant association that I have had with my publisher, Dikran Y. Hadidian, a man of gentle ways and kind persuasion.

To my husband, Peter, I owe everything.

Polly Park

And I will set my glory among
the heathen, and all the heathen
shall see my judgment that
I have executed, and my hand
that I have laid upon them.

Ezekiel 39:21
King James Version

INTRODUCTION

Erastus Wentworth D.D. (1813-1886) of Stonington and Norwich, Connecticut, was born in that early 19th century era of Protestant religious revival in America when eminent preachers stumped the countryside bringing the word of God to the people wherever they found them. In thunderous and lengthy sermons they sought to convert the non-converted with the promise of eternal salvation as a reward for commitment to the teachings of the Bible.

Prominent among these evangelistic Christians were the Methodists, the newest great Protestant religion of all, founded in England in the 18th century by John Wesley. Wesley had never intended that his religion should be separated from the Anglican church and he remained an Anglican himself throughout his life. To him, it was simply a matter of carrying the words of the Bible to the people in the hope of bringing a little light and a purpose for living to the wretchedly oppressed masses at a time when the new industrial revolution had brought an almost slave-like existence to the working classes in England.

By the 19th century the movement had spread across the Atlantic to America where it gathered great momentum with its personalized appeal for salvation by conversion. Each new convert sought to convert the soul of another. Tracts were distributed on street corners and camp meetings held in open fields where preachers from far and near stirred the minds of their listeners.

This radical departure from the heretofore structured church worship appealed enormously to the young seeking new and different ways from their elders. The informality of camp meetings where individual tents were set up with each church congregation pegging out its own site in the open field, provided them with a picnic-like atmosphere for socializing while the emotional words of the preachers and the witnessing of mass conversions provided the drama.

It was at such a camp meeting in Norwich, Connecticut, that the eighteen year old Erastus Wentworth first heard the fiery Methodist preaching that was to stir his young mind and to change the course of his life. After due consideration and preparation he, too, would join the vast number of other converts to the Methodist faith.

Erastus Wentworth was born in Stonington, Connecticut in 1813. He was the eldest of 12 children born to Erastus and Mary (States) Wentworth. Seven of the twelve children lived to maturity.

His parents were devout Congregationalists, an outgrowth of the Puritan faith of which his ancestors were members. Erastus Wentworth was a direct descendant of Elder William Wentworth of Alford (Lincolnshire) England who in 1620 had sailed for America with a small band of other Puritans in order to freely practice their austere faith. Elder Wentworth's signature appears along with 33 others who formed the government of Exeter, New Hampshire "on Friday the fourth of October 1639".

Erastus Wentworth (Sr.) was a respected member of the Stonington community and was elected as its representative in the State Legislature. Later the family moved to Norwich. In the surrounds of that lake and forest Connecticut countryside the younger Erastus developed an absorbing interest in nature, observing the habits of the wild animals of the fields and forests, the flora, and the natural characteristics of the land. His interest in natural history was to remain with him for the rest of his days.

He was a brilliant boy with a questioning mind. At an early age he was reading on such diversified topics as natural history, classical history, religion, poetry, science, and the arts. His interest in music was apparent from an early age when he taught himself to play the melodeon.

A year after his conversion to the Methodist faith he entered the Cazenovia Seminary in New York where he studied for two years before entering Wesleyan University in Middletown, Connecticut.

At Wesleyan he was active in the Missionary Lyceum (an undergraduate society of which he was a founder and subscriber to the originial constitution). The Lyceum held gatherings and debates and its members corresponded regularly with foreign missionaries. It was Erastus himself, along with two fellow members who proposed the following resolution to the President of the University who, in turn, presented it to the Methodist church:

APRIL 20th, 1835---"Resolved that it be recommended to establish a mission at some favorable point in China---- and that Missionaries and a printing press be sent forth immediately."

Although the resolution was adopted by the church that same year and the funds subscribed for by the Methodist church, it was not until a decade later that the first Methodist missionaries sailed from America to Foochow, China. The printing press was not purchased until 1861 when Wentworth, himself, on a three month visit to Hong Kong and Canton bought "one of Hoe's Washington presses" and had it shipped to Foochow with a Cantonese foreman to operate the machine.

After graduation from Wesleyan University in 1837, Erastus Wentworth was appointed teacher of Natural Science at Gouveneur Wesleyan Seminary in New York. The following year, at the age of 25, he married Mary Alexander of De Kalb in northern New York State.

In 1841 Erastus and Mary moved to Poultney, Vermont where he accepted a second teaching appointment in Natural Science at Troy Conference Academy. In that same year their first child, James Lemuel, was born. It was this same James, or Jimmy, who was later to accompany his father and new step-mother, Anna Lewis, to China.

In 1845, a daughter, Frances Caroline was born but died soon after. In that same year Mary Wentworth had contracted tuberculosis.

In 1846 Erastus Wentworth was appointed President of McKendree College in Lebanon, Illinois. He writes: "The position was readily accepted, though at a pecuniary sacrifice, as a providential opening to get a consumptive wife out of cold Vermont into the milder Mississippi Valley. A move which doubtless prolonged her life several years.

"My allowance was less than three hundred dollars a year on which I laid up money, while I ran in debt at Dickinson on a salary of a thousand. Our neighbors, the prairie farmers, were especially liberal to the new professors who preached every Sunday in their school houses, bringing in corn and 'side meat' more than we could possibly make use of. One brother put into my log crib forty bushels of Indian corn for five dollars. 'I give you corn,' he said. 'I only charge a bit (12 1/2 cents) for hauling it.' We had a cow and her keeping, pigs, poultry, and a vegetable garden which it was next to impossible to protect from the wolfish hogs that ranged the woods, and made no bones of forcing pickets and could scale a six rail fence with the agility of a racoon. Lovely were those years in that broad college campus with its sunlit lawns, its graceful swells, its huge trees, the home of contemplation and retirement, yet made lively by the shouts of students with their games of 'shinney' and foot ball. Cottages nestled among the trees, as cosy, if not as handsome, as those provided for the accommodation of the guests at Saratoga."

In reflecting on his years at McKendree College he writes: "The next four years were the busiest of a busy life. I was constantly preaching, lecturing, teaching, writing, dedicating churches, attending camp meetings, conferences, conventions, and conducting a weekly paper, The Lebanon Journal, the modest bud which at length bloomed into the full flowered and richly flavored 'Central Christian Advocate'."

Jimmy, too, must have looked back upon those four years as the happiest of his childhood. He was five when they moved to McKendree and nine when they left. From then on he was to experience an endless series of personal tragedies.

In 1850 the family moved to Carlisle, Pennsylvania where Erastus took up his new appointment as Professor of Natural Philosophy and Chemistry at Dickinson College. While there, he received the degree of Doctor of Divinity at Allegheny College.

Soon after their arrival at Dickinson a third child was born, William Strafford, but like the baby before, died soon after. Mary Wentworth's health deteriorated rapidly and the following year she died. Jimmy was eleven when his mother died. Already he had witnessed three deaths in his family.

Father and son remained at Dickinson for two more years. In 1854 Erastus accepted a missionary appointment to Foochow, China.

Four months before sailing to China he was invited to preach at a camp meeting outside of Philadelphia during which time he was a guest in the house of the Joseph Jackson Lewis family in West Chester at the specific request of Mrs. Lewis, a convert to the Methodist faith. It was the Lewis' first meeting with Wentworth and his brilliance and wit made a marked impression upon the family especially their daughter Anna.

Anna was 26 and Erastus 42 at the time of their meeting. Even the most imaginative novelist could not have envisioned a more providential meeting for both.

Anna's dedication to the work of the Methodist church had not wavered since her conversion to the Methodist faith at the age of thirteen and her subsequent acceptance into the church a year later. Her friend Annie Kelly describes that moment: "Some-one came to me saying Anna wanted me. I found her whole counte-nance lighted up with the blessed change, and while tears of joy bedewed her face, she exclaimed: 'O Annie! Help me to praise the Lord'. And then in the beautiful words of the Psalmist, her full heart found utterance: 'Bless the Lord, O my soul, and all that is within me bless His holy name!' "

From the pen of another friend we are told: "The mission-ary spirit showed itself very early. I can remember many conversa-tions about the heathen, and her earnest desire, if she grew up, to become a teacher among them. She carried a missionary subscrip-tion for a long time. Many a trudge through the snow and rain we have had together, while she collected the monthly contributions for poor old Mr. B. I remember, too, her devoting her afternoons to the care of the sick children of a poor woman who was anxiously inquiring after the way of life, that she might attend church. While others of her own age were taking amusement in the plays of girlhood, Anna sat in the room of squalid poverty, soothing fretful children by her gentleness and pleasant stories."

The same friend describes Anna's character during her years at boarding school in nearby Wilmington, Delaware where she attended Wesleyan Female Collegiate Institute.

"As a scholar she was without a peer in college. In every department she excelled. When compositions were read, however listless and forced the attention that had been given to previous readers, Anna always commanded a universal attitude of interest, a brightening, intelligent eye, and responsive appreciative glances. In recitations she was rarely at fault. In matters legitimately within the province of reason, what shallower and less carefully trained minds received with unquestioning faith she refused credence to, unless sustained by a sufficiency, if not an opulence, of evidence. Authority made a thing probable, but not certain to her.

"Loving music with all the earnestness of her nature, it is not wonderful that she excelled as a performer. Her music abilities were the pride of the whole school."

Anna graduated in 1847 with the highest honors in her class and thus was chosen as Valedictorian of the day.

Her mother's illness required that she remain at home for five years during which time she was extremely active in church work. In writing to her friend Annie Kelly near the end of those five years at home she states: "I am not satisfied with my idle life. I am not needed at home, and feel as if I ought to make myself useful in the world. Something almost compels me to go."

In 1852 she accepted the position as an assistant teacher at a girl's boarding school in New Market, Maryland. She remained at the school for only a year when she contracted typhoid fever. Writing to a friend, Mollie Turner, she states: "I don't know why the Lord spared my life. I felt ready to die then. I had not a care or anxiety about the future; but it must have been that I might glorify Him by a more devoted life, or perhaps I am to suffer for Christ. You know I have never had much trouble. I feel under such obligations, and as if I were living so much beneath what God requires of me."

This same recurrent theme of searching for guidelines to her future through misfortune as well as favorable occurrences is found in so many of Anna's letters. On her commitment to God she was absolute, but she agonized continually over which fork in the road she should take in order to fulfill that commitment.

Much of her indecisiveness was no doubt due to the strong, decisive nature of her father to whom the family turned for guidance on even the most seemingly inconsequential matters. In a letter written to her father while teaching at the New Market school she confesses: "I wish you would write and let me know what you would like me to do for I cannot choose for myself."

Her father, Joseph Jackson Lewis, was a prominent lawyer. He was described as "rugged in appearance, gruff in manner, intensely egotistical, yet his ability was recognized by all, and at the age of forty-eight he enjoyed the largest practice at the Bar". Lewis was later to become Commissioner of Internal Revenue in Abraham Lincoln's Cabinet. It was Lewis who introduced the income tax to America. The Lewis family were Quakers, however, because of his marriage to Mary (Miner) Lewis, a recent convert to the Methodist faith, he was not permitted to attend Quaker meeting. After her death he was re-instated in the Quaker faith and allowed the full rights of membership. It was one of Anna's deepest regrets that her father had not been converted to the Methodist faith.

The mutual admiration shared by Erastus Wentworth and Joseph Lewis was evident from their first meeting and is recorded by Anna in a letter written to her younger brother, Charlton, then a student at Yale: "I don't think I ever saw father so much pleased with a guest. I have suspected his interest in camp meeting was somewhat connected with his interest in Dr. Wentworth." At the time of that meeting Lewis was fifty-three and Wentworth forty-two, only twelve years younger than his father-in-law to be.

---

*   Wilmer W. MacElree, **Sidelights of the Bench and Bar of Chester County.**

The very qualities that Anna admired most in her father, his forthright manner, his wit, his decisiveness, his brilliance were all contained in the person of Erastus Wentworth. Her father's obvious approval of Wentworth could therefore have played an important part in her decision, only a month after their first meeting, to accept his proposal of marriage and to accompany him to China.

In a letter to her friend Annie Kelly she explains her feelings: August 30th, 1854 ---"Yesterday morning Dr. W. left us, and I have had two days to review the strange events of the past few weeks. Who could have believed that so short a time could have so changed all my prospects and plans? Judging from the dictates of human wisdom, it seems most rash to allow so short a time to decide matters of so great moment . . . But as I try to bring a calm judgement to sit upon my decisions, I cannot find anything to regret. And why should I regret it? Have I not many times asked the Lord to direct all my paths? And shall I not believe that he will do it? Have I not for years asked, 'Lord, what wilt thou have me do?' And when by his providence he seems to have laid a noble work before me, shall I refuse to enter upon it? Rather I will thankfully acknowledge the goodness that has chosen me for a post of such exalted honor; and while I feel in the depths of my nature my unfitness for the work, I will implicitly confide in the wisdom and grace that are able to ordain praise from the weakest of his creatures. I know it is a great undertaking, and I want to be able rationally to count the cost, and yet not to harass myself with needless fears. There must, of course, be privation and toil. I must leave friends, who have seemed almost as necessary to my life as the air I have breathed; but my heart goes out in thankfulness to God, that while he has called me to leave much, he has given me a strong arm and a noble heart to lean upon. In this I recognize a pledge of what he will do for me. Already he has given me an earthly guide, and counselor, and teacher, and I feel sure that all his influence will be to exalt and ennoble me, and make me worthy of him and the cause to which we have consecrated our lives."

By his own admission in a letter to his father-in-law written June 15th, 1858---three years after Anna's death---Erastus states that he "set about a second marriage as a duty", to which he adds "its fulfillment brought unexpected pleasure". It is important, however, that we understand the circumstances that demanded such a hurried marriage.

In practice, the church desired their missionaries to be married before leaving for unknown years in "heathen" lands. Only occasionally did they permit single men and women to carry the Christian message abroad. In their judgment a lonely or frustrated missionary could not perform the same service to the church as one who had his family with him to set an example of Christian family life to the "heathen". Coupled with this was the underlying fear that a single man might seek to co-habit with the "heathen" thus bringing disgrace upon the church. How different this viewpoint was from the Catholic church whose celibate missionaries, who had been in China long before the arrival of the Protestants, actually lived in the towns and villages with the Chinese people whom they had come to convert.

The marriage of Erastus to Anna can, therefore, be seen as a mutually satisfying contract for both. For Anna, Erastus provided a strong rudder for her floundering ship and an opportunity to carry out the missionary work that she had desired for so long. For Erastus there would be the companionship of a young, intelligent, and very dedicated missionary wife, and a mother to his fourteen year old son, Jimmy, who would accompany them to Foochow. There was the certainty, too, of approval from the home Mission. The fact that this seemingly cooly, calculated arrangement blossomed later into a much deeper relationship was no doubt surprising to both parties.

The wedding took place on October 31st, 1854 in the library of the Lewis house in West Chester. In the month long honeymoon that followed they farewelled their friends and relations in New York, Connecticut, Massachusetts, New Hampshire, and Pennsylvania.

Another month of frantic packing and farewelling followed. Then on January 8th Erastus, Anna, and Jimmy boarded the bark STORM in New York for the six month journey that would take them to their new home in Foochow, China.

Anna kept a daily diary throughout the long and harrowing voyage where often, in rough seas, she was forced to sleep on the floor of the tiny cabin despite the continuous leakage of water through the door which kept them in a permanent state of wetness for days on end. The sea-sickness that they both encountered from the start remained with them for most of the trip punctuated only by short respites of calm and sunny weather. At times she admits to an overwhelming feeling of depression and loneliness. "I cannot help asking why I have been brought here & only just now, mental suffering should be added to physical", she records.

When editing her diary after her death, Erastus explains to the Lewis family: "You recollect that for the first five weeks out, when she most needed society, I was so sick as to be very little else than a burden to self or anyone else---I do not wonder the poor girl complains so often of 'loneliness'."

After a welcome 2 1/2 week stopover in Singapore where

they met other missionaries, they sailed for Hong Kong arriving there on May 24th where they were the houseguests of Mr. and Mrs. Johnson. Mr. Johnson was the only American Missionary in Hong Kong at the time. In a detailed letter written to her mother, Anna describes the missionary life in that more sophisticated colony while expressing the hope that life in Foochow will be simpler and less socially demanding.

On June 7th they boarded the SPITFIRE (an American clipper ship) which carried them on their final journey to the port of Amoy. There they transferred to a smaller boat which took them thirty-five miles up the Min River to the city of Foochow where a warm reception awaited them from the small band of resident missionaries.

It seems strange to us today, that in all of Anna's letters and diaries there is not a mention of her pregnancy which must have added considerably to her discomfort during the whole of the journey. Their baby, Anna, was born only two months after their arrival in Foochow, only weeks after she had contracted the dreaded dysentery. In an undated letter she alludes vaguely to her physical state when she writes to her parents: "I am almost afraid to tell you how much I like Fuh Chau and its missionaries and particularly "Olive Orchard", our snug little home, because I may meet with difficulties and inconveniences after a while, of which I shall be sure to write, and you will think I am disposed to be fickle."

Towards the end of September her physician, Dr. Welton, pronounced her case hopeless. The calm way in which Anna accepted this startling pronouncement is recorded in a lengthy letter written by Mrs. Maclay (the wife of a fellow missionary) to Anna's mother after her death.

"When we found that she was failing I greatly desired that she should come to our house where I could constantly be with her, and bestow unremitting care in nursing her. I invited her to come, but she said she was too much of an invalid to go away from home then, but when she should get better she would like to accept my invitation. I reminded her that I wished to aid her in getting better, and for that reason I hoped that she would at once conclude to come. She steadily declined my invitation, however, until one Sunday morning, when I promised her so much that she was at last inclined to yield, and said, 'It is very tempting--you do almost persuade me to go. I will talk with Dr. Wentworth about it.'

"Feeling satisfied that she would come to our house, I immediately returned home and prepared a large retired room for her reception, and in about 2 hours after she was conveyed to our house in a Sedan chair. I was greatly pleased with this change for I did not doubt in the least that she would be benefitted by it and recover. But my hopes were soon blasted, for her physician soon came and announced to her and to us that she could not live. When this trying announcement was made to her I was not in the room but on going to her bedside shortly after, she said to me with a great look of discouragement, "Why do so much for me? It is of no use.'

"I assured her that I had great hopes of doing her good. She did not tell me in reply what the physician had said but so far as I could discover she was entirely unmoved, and tranquil, and I did not suspect that he had mentioned to her the alarming symptoms of her case. During the remainder of the day and night she seemed very comfortable and after spoke of it, saying she was so glad she had come over to our house."

During the week that followed Anna expressed a wish that her baby (then two months old) should be brought up by her mother, and made detailed plans for her own funeral. On October 2nd, 1855, she died and was buried in the Mission Cemetery on the hillside overlooking the river.

Two months after Anna's death, on January 16th, 1856, Erastus Wentworth commenced his own daily diary which he sent in monthly packets to the Lewis family in West Chester, Pennsylvania.

In writing his diary to Anna's parents, Wentworth has the interests of both in mind. For Mary Lewis, a practical down-to-earth woman and a confirmed Methodist, he tells of the daily problems he encounters in bringing up his baby daughter, the demands of her Chinese wet-nurse, the cost of running the household, how and where fresh food and milk is procured, the problems that other missionary wives encounter in bringing their children up in China and his duties to the church.

But for Joseph Lewis, an avowed Quaker, he allows his pen to fly with uninhibited commentaries combining both wit and sarcasm of the people and the life-style of both Chinese and foreigners in Foochow. Nor is he above poking fun at his own Methodist colleagues as well as those of the English Church of England Mission.

His keen observations of the people, written through the detached eye of a journalist, his marvelous descriptions of the natural and man-made scenery of that beautiful mountainous city of Foochow and its environs, make a unique contribution to the reader's knowledge of mid-19th century life in that southern region of China. Unlike the mass of publications written by missionaries of that period, the majority of which were slanted towards winning new converts to the religion by painting a saintly glow on missionary life abroad with the added hope of obtaining the necessary funds for the continuance of the missions, Wentworth's diary and letters allow us to see the life and the people--warts and all.

We are surprised at what very little attempt was made by the missionaries of the Protestant faith to make closer contact with the Chinese whom they had come to convert to Christianity. In most instances their only intimate knowledge of the Chinese people was with the servants employed in their households. While they were quick to set up 'chapels' (usually rented rooms in the towns where sermons were preached and tracts distributed to the curious who wandered in from the street) and to build churches (three were built in Foochow before the first Chinese convert offered himself for baptism), the direction was from the beginning one-sided. In short they were saying: "We will supply the churches, the literature, the sermons and the information on Christianity in the hope of converting your "heathen" soul--but you must come to us, we will not go to you".

To become a Christian, the Chinese, in effect, had to give up all that had been dear to them; their family and friends (for once having been converted to the Christian faith they were no longer accepted by the family and community), their idols (a survey of the convert's house was always made before the ritual of baptism was performed to ascertain that all idols had been removed), and very often their jobs as well. Is it any wonder, therefore, that conversions were so slow in coming?

The missionaries, on the other hand, accepted these sacrifices as a normal state of affairs. For, after all, hadn't they saved the soul of the "heathen" from eternal damnation?

Success was measured in numbers. If one could report to the home mission that one, three or five had been converted in a period of several months, one could be assured of a continuance of funds for the running of the mission.

Even the doctors sent out to care for the health of the missionaries and of the natives, as well, had a duty to use their influence to convert "the heathen". Ellsworth C. Carlson in his book **The Foochow Missionaries 1847-1880** (published by East Asian Research Center, Harvard University, 1974) describes the practice of three doctors sent to Foochow between the years of 1847-1856:

"All three of these men were more concerned with ministering to spiritual than to physical needs. Although they responded to calls for medical help, their way of work reflected their primary concern for 'souls'. Collins reported that White talked to his patients 'In regard to the interest of their souls'. When Wiley took over the Methodist medical work in 1851, White interpreted for him and preached to the patients who came to the dispensary. For a time Welton worked rather closely with Johnson in the latter's chapel; Welton attended to the people's physical needs, while Johnson handed out tracts and preached. One of Welton's letters tells of being called to the house of a mandarin to attend his wife; after prescribing medicine, he talked with the family for a time and offered copies of the New Testament and some tracts. Subsequently he wrote that he 'made it a point of conscience to give all of his patients tracts or copies of the Scriptures'." [p. 63]

It was this same Dr. Welton who had informed Anna of her impending death, no doubt with the thought of allowing her the necessary time in which to make her spiritual preparations before departing this world for another. He could not have been unaware of the shock, the fear, and the disappointment that such a dire pronouncement would have made on his young patient. Therefore, we can assume that this spiritual motivation far out-weighed his concern for her physical reaction.

Foochow was one of five port cities opened for foreign trade and residence by the treaties of 1842. The city lay thirty-five miles inland from the coast which afforded it some protection from the coastal skirmishes that regularly took place between British ships wishing to unload their cargoes of opium in exchange for the tea of the district and Chinese soldiers who at the request of the Emperor were ordered to prevent the unloading of the opium on the Chinese shores.

Foochow was the capital of Fukien Province, an educational center where the important annual state examinations took place. Its estimated population at the time of the Wentworth's arrival in 1855 was somewhere between six and seven hundred thousand people. It was a city of rare beauty with its mountains crowned with splendid Pagodas and the winding river below with its long stone bridge stretching from the mainland to the heavily populated island beyond. So mountainous was the region that only human transportation was possible.

The cultural shock that the missionaries encountered upon their arrival in China was enormous. Most had had little or no preparation for the problems they would encounter in dealing with the Chinese people. The vastness of the population, the poverty, the sickness, the corruption, the stealing that they witnessed daily only served to re-inforce their belief in the "rightness" of their own Christian life-style and the necessity for imposing that life-style and religion upon the "heathen".

Even those who might have wished to make more intimate contact with the Chinese people succumbed to the general disapproval of the Christian community who kept a close watch on their colleagues.

It was the duty of all missionaries to immediately set about learning the Chinese language for the purpose of carrying the Christian message to the "heathen" in their native tongue. A bare three weeks after her arrival in Foochow, Anna writes to her father: July 4th, 1855--"I have just been having a sitting with our long-tailed, long-nailed Chinese teacher. First I recited a lesson of just a yard and a half of Chinese radicals; then got from him the proper pronunciation of some household phrases I have been picking up, and afterwards learned to count as far as one hundred. At the end of the lesson, which was rather a lengthy one, he rose from his chair, bowed very politely, put two fingers to his mouth to represent chop-sticks, I suppose, and gave me to understand that he wanted to go to his dinner."

Their tutors very often provided the missionaries with their only source of knowledge on the social and political conditions in China. Wentworth's references to his tutor are contained very often in his letters.

The chasm between "the heathen" and "the foreign devil" thus widened, with the missionaries living side by side in a cocoon-like existence and socializing only with themselves and the other foreigners in the region, while the Chinese increasingly regarded them with contempt, or at the least, suspicion. Often the missionaries were forced to take up temporary residence in the homes of English merchants dealing with opium trade which the Chinese government vehemently opposed, thus in the eyes of the natives aligning them with the merchants by association.

The chasm was widened, too, as the missionaries gradually bought up prime pieces of land for the building of their increasingly "comfortable" houses. Wentworth writes: "Foreign building is very monopolizing--English and Americans have claimed lot to lot until they have compassed the whole hill--not used for sepulture-- & are hardly restrained from setting their residences over the bone-patches of past generations. Indeed a spirited dispute is going on now about a piece of ground--perhaps as large as your home lot--lying between the wall of the British Consulate & a time honored banion shaded temple to the East--It is claimed by different parties & probably owned by the dead--yet the foreigners have bought it for a billiard room! The Chinese--like the American Indians--have been crowded off the foreign quarter & yet we are not content."

Erastus Wentworth's monthly diaries to the Lewis family

xxix

in West Chester, Pennsylvania end on July 28th, 1856 when he writes: "I am hourly sensible that the golden chain which bound my interests & affections to yours has been snapt asunder. That only a little silver link remains--so frail that the slightest touch of disease might part it & leave as we were of yore--Our universe is one of motion. The probability is that no two particles in it occupy the same relations to it & each other for two successive instants together. How then can we expect permanency in our relations. From the changeable we pass to the changeless- Even here- memory immortalizes mortality & imparts durability to the passing & transient. One of the brightest portions of my shifting panorama was that illuminated by the presence of our darling Anna. The brightness- like that of a painting by the Old Masters- was enhanced by its solitariness & the darkness which surrounded it- It has dwindled to a star- Another guiding lamp to Heaven."

In December of the same year he sent his two children Jimmy aged fifteen and the fourteen month old baby "Anna" back to the United States to their respective grandparents. The baby was accompanied by a Chinese nurse.

However, his correspondence with the Lewis family was not broken altogether. On April 8th, 1857 he writes to Joseph Lewis concerning monument for Anna's grave and answers Lewis' questions concerning "Fuh Chau Beggars".

On April 25th of the same year he writes of his "impatience" at hearing of the safe arrival in America of his children and tells of the dangerous situation in China with the country over-run with banditti and "resistance to a foreign power".

On March 8th, 1858 his letter to Joseph Lewis is largely taken up with answering the accusations of his father-in-law who wonders why his deceased daughter Anna, was not sent to the better climate of Shanghai at the inception of her illness, his pleasure on hearing about his baby- the sad memory he has of their parting, the life of the missionaries and the state of the Empire.

His final letter to Joseph Lewis is written on June 15th, 1858. Although couched in witty sarcasms one senses his feelings now, of isolation from friends and family in America and his loneliness. In it he mentions the arrival of three ladies whom he describes as "good looking- well educated & well instructed housekeepers but have the misfortune to be measured by superior standards" and concludes by stating: "I may conclude to give attention to the matter in the fall- but it is too hot to think of it at present."

For the enlightenment of the reader the following character assessments by two intimate friends of Erastus Wentworth are taken from his obituary for the class of 1837 at Wesleyan University (in part only). First a layman's view.

"Among our earlier alumni there have been few of more varied attainments, or of more striking personality, than the late Dr. Wentworth. His work was done in widely different departments-- as teacher, college president, preacher, missionary, editor,--but he carried into all these departments something of the versatile brilliancy, intensity, and peculiar individual force that belongs only to genius. Dr. Wentworth was a man of very wide reading, especially in polite literature, and of highly cultivated literary tastes, a pithy and brilliant writer; and eloquent, though somewhat uneven preacher; an incisive but kindly critic; a most genial companion, with a peculiar and unfailing vein of humor. Such a combination of abilities all in such high degree, is rare; and in Dr. Wentworth they were all subservient to a steady and devoted Christian purpose. He had the elements of a great man."

(From the pen of an old friend, Rev. B. K. Peirce D.D.):

"He was a man of marked intellectual ability, a powerful preacher at times sweeping an audience in his discourses with astonishing force. He could be terribly sarcastic, but had the tenderest of natures; he was eminently witty, and had a rare gift of caricature. His private letters were often amusingly illustrated. He was a genial companion of rare conversational powers. He was a true man, and had a wholesome abomination of all shams. He had a very picturesque and epigrammatic style in writing, and was a broad, general scholar. He was a good man, prayerful, devout, without distrust in the divine plan of salvation or in the providence of God. He was not surprised when death came, but readily accepted his call, and trusting confidently in his Saviour passed peacefully behind the clouds into the open vision of Paradise."

Polly Park

ANNA M. WENTWORTH

LETTERS

MRS. ANNA M. WENTWORTH.

West Chester
August 1st 1854

Dear Charlton,

        Mother wants to know whether you will be able to get
us tent poles near the ground. Will you please see & let us know
as soon as possible. Any of your camp going brethren can tell
you what will be necessary. We cannot get a tent here and are
obliged to have one made but as there will be 4 or five of us
we will need one good-sized & airy. We want side poles so as
to make it in the form of a mearkee- mother thinks it should
be about 12 ft long and I expect that is all she will make it unless
you should decidedly agree with me that 15 would be a much
better length. The strips of muslin that she will make the tent
of will be 30 ft or 10 yas long- you can judge from that what
will be the necessary height of the standing poles- the cross poles
must of course be 12 ft long. If you can get them will you please
bespeak all the poles that are necessary at once and have them
ready by the Monday morning before the meeting begins- Our
tent is to be sent with the baggage from Ebenezer Church and
will be on the ground on Monday evening. Mother would like right
well to be there at the same time and thinks if it would be convenient for you- she would like you to come up this week and take
her to Newark on Saturday- Then she would rest over Sunday
and go to the ground the next day to see after our boxes and
select a place for our tent. Please let us know by return of mail
whether you can do so-

        I have just read to mother what I have written and she
says upon second thought particularly as next Sunday will be our
Quarterly Meeting- she thinks she would rather not spend next
Sunday at Newark- and that it will suit her still better if you
can be on the ground on Monday morning when the Ebenezer
baggage arrives, take care of our boxes and choose a pleasant
place for pitching our tent. Mr Culver will be there as a committee
from West Chester but we would like of course that you should
attend to our things. Then Mother will go down with us by railway
on Wednesday. Do let us know about the poles at once- if you
cannot get them we must try to have them made & sent from
W.C. [West Chester] & it should be attended to at once- but it
will save us a great deal of trouble in the transportation if you
can get them near the ground. I am sorry to trouble you about
these things because I know your time must be very much occupied

3

but you know we have no one else to look to for assistance- and we hope when we are once there to make it up to you in some degree, by giving you something of a home & so making you more comfortable than you would otherwise be.

I dont know exactly who will be going from W.C. but I think about 20. We will be with the Ebenezer people and of course our tents must be pitched with theirs. At home we think & talk of little else. Father seems as much interested as any of us and is continuing ways of making us more comfortable- Is it not strange- He intends too if possible to spend Sunday with us on the ground. Oh Charlton if that day <u>should</u> be blessed to his conversion! And why should it not be! Why should we not pray that it may be so.

We have written for Aunt Sarah Miner to come down and go with us but in this sickly season I suppose she would hardly leave grandfather-

Dr. Wentworth who has been spending a few days with us left us this morning. He has been for four years Prof. at Dickinson College and as perhaps you know has been lately appointed missionary to China & goes out in December. He is very singular but one of the most interesting men I ever met. A real universal Yankee genius. He has promised to return next week to spend a day with us and then accompany us to Red Lion. I dont think I ever saw father so much pleased with a guest. I have suspected his interest in camp meeting was somewhat connected with his interest in Dr. Wentworth-

I had a long letter on Friday from Robert Thompson in which he announced his own marriage on the 13th and Miss Dixon's on the 12th of this month. It is a right pleasant newsy letter; His only description of his wife is that she is very much like me! Now aint that complimentary from a groom on the honey moon. He wishes to be remembered to you and says he means to try to write to you very soon. If you have time do write him a line of congratulation on his marriage- I know it would please them all that you should do so.

With sincere affection

Your sister Anna

4

My dear friend, [Erastus]

By this time I suppose you have left Sandy Hill and are again on the wing. Would that you could follow the birds on their Autumnal flight! Surely all natural instincts are against Northward migration in September. I read mother parts of your last evening's letter. "I go North on Monday." "Dear me!" she replied, "I should think he was north of everything by this time. If he does not soon turn round he will have gone as far as Wm. Frost's man who travelled so far the North Star was south of him." You know Dr. Kane is on another Arctic expedition- pray dont take it into your head to join him. The Almanac says Sept. but we are having summer weather- on Sunday the thermometer stood at 94 in the shade & we felt the heat the more from the cool days we have had of late. We had three services in our church, it being our regular communion day. Mr. Karson preached in the morning- the first time for six or seven weeks- It was one of his best sermons- at least so everybody said- for my part I heard but little of it- I lost all of firstly, and much of secondly & finally, thinking of Mr. Gibson and trying to forgive him for putting off his wedding so long, I am afraid I did not go to church in a very christian spirit that morning- and what is worse I came back no better than I went. But the poor man must be married of course and of course there is nobody else in all the state of New York that can tie the knot matrimonial but you. So I must just be content to wait patiently till he is quite done with you & shall graciously permit you to return to me. But seriously Dr. Wentworth, dont you think it a little strange that he should have made so great a change in his arrangements without letting you know of it- it might have been difficult as you were travelling constantly but I am right sorry that your return must be delayed so long.

Joe returned to school on Sat- a day earlier than was necessary for the sake of getting a good room & Annie Gallison joined her yesterday. Mr. Gallison has, I have no doubt, sent her there for the express purpose of breaking up any China plans that he might have feared were forming. Poor deluded man! I am afraid he has made a grand mistake if that was his object- for Mr. Loomis never lets a spark of missionary zeal come within his influence without fanning it into a flame- and Mr. Peirce I am convinced could not find a more able advocate. I consider

5

it in very good hands- Joe told me in confidence before she went away that she intended to go back to school very meekly without a word of opposition but that as soon as she heard of your return to West Chester she meant to have a very bad attack of quinsey or something that would be equally effectual in bringing her home. I have no doubt she will come if she wants to for she is a privileged person and does pretty much as she pleases at all times.

I spent part of last evening with Annie Marshall- You remember her, dont you?- our little friend who has been suffering so long with sprue disease- She had heard of my new plans and the few moments we were alone spoke of them most enthusiastically. She thinks it "perfectly splendid" and says she cannot feel a bit sorry that I am going. Her weaker minded sister has been crying bitterly about it & thinks it very strange Dr. Wentworth could not have taken somebody else. How thankful I am to anybody who will talk to me cheerfully and hopefully about it! Even father has concluded to make the best of it and talks right freely and pleasantly. I think you would have laughed if you could have heard the reports at the breakfast table yesterday morning. Let commenced by saying she was just as tired as when she went to bed. Dr. Wentworth had haunted her dreams so that her sleep had done her no good. Mother had not rested well because the whole Chinese mission with its responsibilities & perplexities had been weighing on her mind all night and father reported that a long sea-voyage had interrupted his rest so much that he was obliged to take a nap on the parlor sofa after coming down stairs. For my part I had to make the unromantic confession that I had dreamed nothing at all- had slept delightfully and felt remarkably bright & well- Do you remember a list of "wants" you showed me once but that I did not take time to read? If it would be of any use to Mother I wish you would send it to me. I will copy it & return it if you wish at once. She is very much in need of something as a guide. She is going to the city this afternoon to attend to some of Enoch's wants & says she thinks she had better order me a set of chop sticks as they will be the most indispensible articles of household furniture. Do not fear to write too often- There is no danger- Indeed I am very grateful to you that amidst the hurry & fatigues of travel and the pleasure of meeting old friends you have so often remembered me. I feel the need of your letters and shall continue to look for them anxiously. I was sorry I could not write to you at Sandy Hill but your first was not received till Saturday night. I wrote Mon. morning before breakfast, but just missed the early mail & had to keep it till afternoon. I shall now have to wait for another letter to know where to direct to you next.

Much love to dear Jimmy- Truly Anna

West Chester
Sept. 29th 1854

Dear Charlton,

I hope you have seen Mr. Karsner in your parts and have needed no line from me to say that he did not return to W.C. on Wednesday- It was because I thought it almost certain you would do so that I did not write yesterday. I still hope you may make an arrangement with him that will keep him in Newark and allow you to spend next Sunday with us- it would be so pleasant to have you there then. If you cannot I stress you will find a substitute for Sunday 15th so that when you come up week after next you will be able to stay with us over that day-

We are having beautiful weather- beautiful for anything but particularly for pic-nics & I am half crazy to get into the woods. We were to have had one yesterday but allowed some trivial matter to interfere- and to-day we have engagements that will keep us at home- To morrow I hope Providence will smile upon us and that the obstinancy of Mother and Dr. Wentworth will not prove more than my zeal can overcome. There are crowds of delightful associations connected with that old Brandywine pic-nic ground and I feel that I cannot go away without spending one more day under its beautiful trees.

Last evening Mother was invited to take tea at the Darlington's- I felt first in the mood of "teasing" and so sent Mrs. D. word that Dr. W. and I would be happy to accept an invitation of the same kind- The invitation came & we of course promptly accepted it. We sat down to an excellent supper but first as grace was said a message came to Mother that Judge Conrad was at the office and would take tea with us. Mother of course left her undisturbed coffee & rushed up home to prepare for the honorable Mayor- We took our supper comfortably and then followed with Mrs. D. & Henry close behind to pay our respects to his honor- and you may be sure looked slightly bland upon being introduced to Mr. Jesse Connard- now Judge of some petty court in the far West- Wasn't that a take in?

To-night we are to go to Judge Bell's and have the promise of being introduced to Mr. Ray- if this promise will come- I anticipate some fun from hearing the Dr. talk to him. Of course a modest person like myself would not venture to say a word.

7

Last night I victimized the poor Dr. dreadfully- took him out after ten o'clock & made him walk till almost twelve- He has been sleepy ever since & I suppose will hardly recover from the effects of it for a week to come. I sympathize with him deeply- but indeed I must have somebody to walk with these beautiful nights-

Poor Joe is not to come home for two or three weeks yet. I am sorry both for her & for myself- I suppose it is better because when she once comes home she will not want to return to school till we are "clean done gone".

I have broken the point off my gold pen and am obliged to write with this outrageous stub one which must serve as my excuse for sending this miserable scratch to a dignified clergyman.

With truest affection- your sister Anna

My dear Mollie,

   I came home from the city in the evening's car after spending two days in the most fatiguing business of shopping. How glad I was to find your letter waiting for me, I cannot tell you. I had waited long and anxiously for it and at last had almost despaired from hearing from you at all. As I rode in the cars this afternoon I said to a friend who knows you better than you know him that I thought your silence unaccountable & I had resolved to write again in a day or two hoping by perseverence to draw a letter from you. From the tenor of your letter I think you have not received the last one I wrote in which I urged you very much to come to West Chester this Fall- I wrote in perfect ignorance of your whereabouts and directed to Portsmouth supposing if you were not there the letter would be forwarded at once- Did you get it? I was and still am exceedingly anxious you should come to see us before Christmas but a letter dated Oak Bowery almost puts a death blow to my hopes.

   Do you remember the promise we made each other when we were in school- that which ever of us was married first should have the other for bridesmaid? I have not forgotten it & I had still hoped that the promise would be redeemed. I should have written several weeks ago to claim the fulfillment of it- but that it had been so long since I had heard from you that I did not know where you were & indeed whether you still felt enough interest in me to care whether I needed a bridesmaid or not. But now that your kind letter has come my old wish has revived more strongly than ever- Can I have it gratified? Will you now two weeks from to-night stand by my side in that capacity? I can scarcely hope it both because you are so far away and because it is so late to give you notice. Still I can only say it would be a great pleasure to me if you could be here. When I knew that I should be married this Fall my first thought was to send for you- but I had had no answer to my last letter and I felt such an uncertainty as to where you were or what you were doing that I did not feel that I could write to you of all my plans till I had heard from you- So I wrote urging you very much to come & see us without telling you why- but I think you have not received that letter. I suppose it is but fair dino Mollie to take it for granted that you know nothing of the new life that seems opening before

9

me so I shall tell you all that I think will interest you. <u>Dr. Wentworth</u> is one of the three missionaries appointed last Spring to China- and to that far away land dear friend I now look for my home. It seems strange that it should be so & I can scarcely realize it yet- and it seems stranger still that with all my preconceived notions of the subject I should marry a man whom four months ago I knew only by reputation. How little we know what is before us in life! Our prudent plan is to have an old fashioned evening wedding on the 24th of this month and start the next morning for the North. We expect first to visit Dr. Wentworth's sister in Northern New York and his father who lives in Connecticut & come home by the way of Wyoming valley where you know I have a great many relations. We will probably be gone two or three weeks and after that I shall stay at home preparing for the voyage & for life in China till orders come from the missionary board to sail. Do you remember Mollie the letter you wrote me about this time last year in which you spoke of your desire to be in the missionary field? I have thought of it so much lately and wished constantly that you could be of our party. Do you still think of it Mollie? Are you still waiting to be sent? Why not offer yourself just now to our missionary board & go out with us to Fuh Chau? I do not think there is any other part of our work so interesting and surely there could not be a wider field anywhere. And yet I do not think I would want you to go unmarried. I am afraid you would be neither as happy nor as useful. But it is not strange that knowing your interest in the subject my heart should have turned to you as soon as I had decided to go & I still hope that after while if not now- Providence will lead you to China & that we shall yet work side by side there. I wish (I have wished it many many times) that you were right here by my side that I might tell you all I have thought & felt on the subject. Sometimes I feel & see so clearly my entire unfitness for the place that I am afraid I am doing wrong to accept a position that I will probably disgrace. But then I know that all my ways are in the hands of the Lord and I feel so perfectly convinced that it is not a way of my own choosing but one in which the Lord has led me that I think I may safely trust that He will make all things work together both for my good & that of the mission. I know it will be a great treat to me to leave home but I shall not go in my own strength & I believe that Arm on which I lean will support me- and that even in China the promise shall not fail as the day is, thy strength shall be.

West Chester
Oct. 30th '54

My dear Aunt Sarah,

For two weeks we have been hoping & expecting to see some of you in West Chester but now that it is impossible for you to be here in time for the wedding I hope you will not make your visit till after we return home! Lettie has been so anxious to be present at the ceremony & I so anxious to have her that we decided to wait till she was able to be brought down stairs. She has been recovering so fast that a few days ago uncle Dr. thought we might safely count upon having her brought down on Tuesday (to-morrow)- We are to have as few as possible so as to have no more excitement for Lettie than can be helped- Uncle Dr., Lettie, Mr. Butler, Cassy, Mrs. Bell & Cars, Mrs. Darlington and Sarah Lewis, Cousin Abby & Mr. & Mrs. Harsure- are the only invited guests. Charlton is to bring Rep. Scott up to-night and we are to be married about 8 1/2 o'clock, have breakfast immediately afterwards & then take a carriage in time to meet the morning train to Downingtown- We are to go on to New York to-morrow, thence to Troy, Sandy Hill, Boston, Stonington, Norwich & Wilkesbarre by the 17th or 18th but I will write you again when we know exactly when.

I am so sorry you cannot be here tomorrow- I had so hoped to have somebody from Wilkesbarre. But we shall spend three or four days there, longer if possible, and then our plan is to bring you and Aunt Ellen down to be present at the grand party that will follow & help with the "packins"-

With love to grandfather Aunt Ellen & all

Aff your niece Anna M. Lewis

11

West Chester
Dec. 2nd 1854

Dear Aunt Sarah,

Dr. Wentworth wrote to you the day after we marched
home to announce our safe arrival and I intended to write in a
day or two after but company & the "packing" have so constantly
occupied my time that I have not been able to find the convenient
season till now. The party came off on Thursday evening and
was I think more pleasant & social than such parties generally
are. Among the guests were the Rev. Mr. Wood & his wife who
went out to China with Bp. Boon, nine years ago and spent one
year in connection with the Episcopal Mission at Shanghai. At
the end of that time Mr. W's health failed and they were obliged
to come home. But they could tell me many interesting things
about the voyage & country. It is encouraging to find that although
they met with many difficulties they are anxious to go back &
looking forward to the time when they may be able to do so.
Friday we did little but not from the fatigue of the journey &
party. Saturday our friends began to call and kept us almost constantly occupied for several days. Monday evening we took tea
at Uncle Dr's- Tuesday at Mrs. Hidgson's- Wednesday at Mrs.
Lewis'- Thursday at Mrs. Darlington's & last night there was
an evening party given for us at Judge Bell's. This morning we
had expected to go to Harrisburg to see Mr. & Mrs. Cookman
& Mrs. Colder, but last evening cars brought Mrs. Keen & Lizzie
Longacre from Phila. to spend the day with us & we were obliged
to postpone our visit. I wrote to Mrs. Colder last week asking
for some information & received in return a very pleasant letter.
She gave me a sketch of the place of one of the mission houses
which on paper looks comfortable and much more commodious
than I had expected. Yesterday we received a dispatch from New
York saying that a vessel will sail for Hong Kong on the 15th
of this month and asking if we would be ready. The Dr. answered
that we would & we even expect to go on or about that day.
It makes it seem very real to have a day appointed for sailing
but we knew the summons must come and are only thankful the
time is as long as it is. You have heard of course of Mary Park's
death- it must have been a great shock to you as to all of us.
How will her husband bear it? I still hope to see Aunt Ellen before
I leave- wont she come down at once? Dear Aunt Sarah wont
you relent & let me have your daguerreotype? If you knew how
very much I wished it I believe you would. Best love to grandfather
& Aunt Ellen.

With truest love- your niece Anna M. L. Wentworth

12

Dear Charlton,

We now expect to leave West Chester the day after Christmas. You will certainly spend that day with us as well as the day before, will you not? Do try to be here on Sunday- it will be so pleasant to spend one more Sunday together. We do not know what day the vessel will sail- possibly not till the latter part of the week- but Dr. Wentworth thinks we will be obliged to go on Tuesday because of the uncertainty and to make some purchases.

Dr. Wiley came home with Dr. Wentworth on Tuesday and staid with us till this morning- He is a very agreeable man & I am delighted with the prospect of having him in Fuh Chau in the course of the next year. He has almost determined to return & Dr. Durbin & Bp. Jones are anxious he should go- so I suppose the matter is almost settled. He told us many things about our new home- the people, houses, conveniences of living, etc. that brightens the picture greatly. There will be trials & annoyances of course but I think there will be many compensations & upon the whole I look to it very hopefully.

Mollie Torrance is here, not less brilliant, but far more lovely & winning it seems to me than ever before. She is anxious to see you- will be here I suppose till we leave & probably go onto New York with us. Try to come on Saturday Charlton & stay with us till we go then go with us to New York- I write in great haste- Dr. Wentworth is first sending some letters to the office & this must go with them- besides Mother is talking to me all the time about "packings". She is going to the city this afternoon to buy the last bundle & then the boxes will be sent to New York. Did you know our piano was burnt in the fire in Philadelphia in which Walker was burnt out. We loose it entirely.

With love and affection your sister

Anna M. L. Wentworth

13

My dear Father,

We left Singapore Monday morning May 7th & commenced our voyage up the China Sea. At the time of year when the monsoon is just changing we could expect nothing but light & variable winds & warned by all who knew, we made up our minds to a long passage & settled down to our old routine of sea life. The first ten days justified our expectations- we made from 20 to 100 miles per day & were thankful for that speed- but on Friday the breeze began to freshen & grew strong every hour till Saturday night we were driving before a fierce gale. The first swell of the sea made me sick & in a few hours Dr. Wentworth and Jimmy were both stretched in their berths. It was nothing compared with our first experience- but sea sickness can never be pleasant & surrounded by the dreariness and desolation of a storm, must always form a melancholy chapter in one's reminiscences. The most dismal feature of the scene is the <u>wetness</u> of everything. The waves dash water through the crevices of the doors "fore & aft"- The rain streams through the skylight & trickles through the roof till chairs, boxes, books, shoes- in fact everything that belongs on the floor or is thrown there by the rocking of the vessel might join in the chorus "I'm afloat, I'm afloat". I was not literally quite afloat but I lay all day Sunday on the floor of my state room on wet pillows & a wet blanket & with all my clothes soaked with water. It would have been useless to change my clothes to lie down again on a wet bed & to find a dry spot to lie, sit or stand on was an impossibility. The only dry lodgings I saw during those ten days & nights of storm was the pitch of the parrot on which his green majesty swung high & dry in the Captain's state-room- I often cast envious glances toward him, but he had no American chivalry & did not offer to vacate in my favor. The storm though not pleasant at the time was not without what Dr. Wentworth calls its compensations. It left us a good breeze that has been filling our sails ever since & while I write this evening (6 o'clock) the high mountain of Hong Kong is just looming into sight. Our pilot- a small round faced, merry looking young Chinaman is already on board & we expect to anchor this evening before the city. It has been a day of great excitement to us all. The nearing coast of China brings of course many thoughts both sad and pleasant. We are glad to find our long voyage drawing to a close & hope that in a few weeks more we will again be amidst something like home comforts- But the very surroundings of that home must leave to remind us continually how far we are from the old home that has been so long & so dearly loved, and we cannot as we look for the first time on the blue shores of the strange land, help looking back with steady yearnings to those that nearly 5 months ago faded in the twilight & wondering when, if ever, those will be the nearing & these the fading hills. Our voyage has been a pleasant one & fills a kind of parenthesis in life that I think we shall refer to with pleasure. Its greatest peculiarity perhaps is its entire freedom from care- No house keeping, no company, no interruptions of any kind- almost no responsibility. There are few situations when one can have his time so completely at his own command as at sea. That of itself I enjoyed & it may be in the busy life and amid the cares of my new home I may sometimes look back regretfully to these long leisure days.

May 24th Thursday morning--

Last night we sat on deck till after ten o'clock enjoying the fine moonlight & talking of our new home in the land on which our eyes were for the first time resting- I had intended to sit up till we had anchored but as the wind lulled & seemed to promise to keep us several hours in getting in I concluded to go to bed upon the Captain's promise to call me as soon as we entered the harbour. Dr. Wentworth laughed at my "absurd fancy" & laid himself away on his shelf with strict injunctions that he should not be disturbed- but the event proved- (should any proof be needed) that curiosity is not wholly confined to one sex- for the first sound of the Capt's voice brought the Rev. Prof. from his perch- & though I had slept in my wrapper to be ready for the call, he had donned his gown & mounted the deck before I could get my feet into my slippers. I soon followed. Hong Kong lay before us & the bold high hills of China closed us round. The harbor is entirely land-locked- two or three miles across in each direction- and surrounded by high volcanic looking mountains which are for the most part covered with grass left entirely destitute of trees. This gives them a strange appearance- more like huge moss covered rocks thrown together in heaps than anything else I can compare them to. A long line of lights marked the city of Hong Kong & the cheery crowing of numerous cocks welcomed us to this land of Cochius & Shanghais. Our vessel will remain here a day or two to get our own freights & then go up to discharge her cargo of rice. Dr. Wentworth went ashore after breakfast to reconnoiter, get lodging for us & see what hope there is of a conveyance to Fuh Chau- & I must get at "the packins" & do what I can toward getting ready to leave the ship-

Wednesday June 6th--

I had meant dear Father to have written you a few lines every day of our stay in Hong Kong- but with bathing, walking,

15

napping- visiting & receiving company and the constant demands
made upon my time by our chatty and agreeable hostess I have
let the days slip away scarcely knowing what has become of them.
But Dr. Wentworth's missal will give you a record of each day
& with that you will scarcely want further news. We have been
looking for a day or two for the Frigate Bird from Whampou in
which we expected to take passage to Fuh Chau- But this morning
two hours ago one of the English missionaries bound to the same
port came in to say that the large American clipper ship Spit
Fire Capt. Aery- would sail for Fuh Chau tomorrow morning &
would take us for $25 apiece. Dr. Wentworth sent for the Capt.
immediately, engaged our passage & made arrangements to go
on board at seven tomorrow morning. It is an excellent opportunity
for us & we hope to have a comfortable & speedy passage- We
will have the English missionaries Mr. & Mrs. Macow & Mr. Fernley
for fellow passengers & as the vessel is large- 1700 tons- I think
we will probably have more pleasant quarters than in the little
barque that brought us out. We took tea last evening at the house
of Bp. Smith- had a pleasant evening & heard some sweet music-
The Bp. himself was the performer & really played on his fine
parlor organ with a great deal of taste & skill. Except his pius
music I did not see much in "my lord" that was interesting. His
appearance is effeminate & I guess he is wanting in good common
sense but his wife is a delightful woman & as I spent most of
the evening chatting with her I enjoyed it very much. She asked
me about the articles of household furniture we had brought from
home- Seemed to think we were wise in providing as much as
we had & particularly congratulated us on having an iron safe.
They have one & think is has been a great security to them. Mr.
& Mrs. Macow have come out from England without anything
but the small articles they have brought in trunks- Some persons
say "What a pity! They will be put to so much trouble & expense-"
others "How ridiculous! They ought to have known better." From
what I am told by the missionaries here I am disposed to think
that while we have brought everything that is necessary there
is very little that is superfluous. Just the articles we have provided
seem to be the ones most expensive & most difficult to procure
here- Thanks to your generosity & Mother's care I have all that
is necessary or desirable. I hope to date my next letter from my
new house.

With true affection

your daughter Anna

Hong Kong China
May 28th 1855

My very dear Mother,

It seems altogether natural that my first letter written on Chinese soil should be addressed to you- You who love China so well & whose prayers & influence & example have been the instrumentalities through which a good Providence has sent me here. How strange it seems that I should really be here-so many thousand miles from you & the dear home in which one year ago all my thoughts were centered, & surrounded by those who have always seemed so far away almost to be inhabitants of another world. But here I am, very thankful to have been preserved through so many perils & to feel our long voyage drawing to a close & to have the prospect before us of a quiet home after our long pilgrimage. Yes, and thankful to be here- for even while I feel most painfully the separation from home I can appreciate the privilege of being here & feel that I would not exchange my lot for any other. We have been most kindly received by Mr. Johnson the only American missionary in Hong Kong, & his little Dutch wife is as cordial & kind as we could desire. Mr. Johnson has sold his own house and while a new one is building lives in a rented house which is smaller & more inconvenient than the one they left. Still by putting up a bed in the library & fitting up a little room at the back of the house for a dressing room they have managed to accommodate us, & Jimmy is provided with a bed at Mr. Taylor's next door. We are sorry to crowd Mr. & Mrs. J. but they do not allow us to feel like intruders & we find ourselves very comfortable here. The change from ship life is pleasant. Airy rooms with high ceilings, decent & comfortable beds and good color water, besides their excellence have something of the charm of novelty to us. What I particularly enjoy is the abundant supply of water. The dressing room Mrs. J. has fitted me is a cool shady little room off the verandah, & there I go three or four times a day, these warm days, to wash from head to foot & luxuriate in the cold water. The few days since we have been here have been very warm & I feel the effect of the heat in an indisposition to do anything. It will be very easy to fall into lazy habits in this climate- but that is one of the things I shall have to guard against- By early rising & frequent bathing I hope to be able to make some good use of my time. Indeed it is to the virtues of cold water I look for my physical salvation in China. Already I am sure it has done me a great deal of good. You know I was always a good deal of a hydropathic and for this enervating

17

climate I am sure it is just the thing, and now that I am so far from dear uncle Dr. I must take more pains to keep well as far as I can. So far, I have been remarkably well & with the watchful care of my careful husband and the blessing of heaven- I hope I shall be able to retain my health under this Southern sun. There is nothing I dread so much as breaking down into a weak helpless invalid useless to the mission & a hindrance instead of a help to the Dr. An early death would be much preferred.

I have not been out of the house except to church yesterday & once for a ride since I have been here, so I cannot give you much of a description of Hong Kong or of the style of living outside of the Johnson's family. Here they live much more in the American style than at Mr. Keasbury's though in some respects they adopt the habits of the English by whom they are surrounded. Mr. Johnson is a very pleasant man- a gentleman in every aspect and with a very cordial manner. His wife (his second- all the men here have their second, third or fourth wife) is from Holland but when you imagine a little Dutch woman I am sure you see a very different figure from our hostess. In personal appearance Mrs. J. reminds me more of Mrs. Lucy Darlington than any one I know at home. She must be considerably younger than Mrs. Darlington but her style & figure & the upper part of her face are very similar. She has been here but four years but already speaks English with singular accuracy & seems to have an excellent command of the colloquial Chinese. French & German are equally familiar to her. Mr. Johnson says she frequently sits down & writes a pile of letters to different correpondents in four languages without hesitating a moment in going from one idiom & script to another. I believe she belongs to an aristocratic Dutch family & certainly has been highly educated, but I tell her she has the gift of tongues for besides the attention she has given to Chinese, she has learned more English in four years than most foreigners learn in twice the time. I suppose she has a fortune of her own or at least that her parents are wealthy for I am sure her wardrobe is not sapphire out of Mr. J's salary. Neither here nor at Singapore have I seen a wrapper or anything like a house dress. Mrs. Johnson's morning dresses are all of lawn small figured & smart but very nicely made & trimmed. Her afternoon dresses are lawn & muslin flowered tucked or embroidered- and besides these I have seen in her wardrobe quantities of elegant dresses, silk, fine muslin, & that could be a prize to any lady in Philadelphia. She took me to her wardrobe the other day to show me a particular material- a kind of silk tarlatan or gauze of which she had three all handsomely made & this morning she bought of a Chinese who came to the house another of the same kind. It seems to me there is no end to the number of lawn dresses I have seen in her room all handsomely made & apparently nearly new. All the ladies here dress a good deal- I suppose it is the influence of European society and I hope to find in Fuh Chau when Americans are in the majority- a simpler style of dress and indeed more simplicity in their mode of living altogether. Certainly we cannot afford to live so & for my part I should not wish it. Here I suppose a certain style of living is almost necessary- I can see that at a port so much frequented as Hong Kong one of the most important services rendered by the missionaries is to make a pleasant place of a sort for officers of the Army & Navy & other transient visitors & so in some measure counteract the influence of other foreign residents. But to do this they must be persons of affluence & education & be able to practice a liberal & elegant hospitality. Some of the most pleasant acquaintances we have made have been among the officers of the Vandalia & Powhatun, two of the vessels of the Japan expedition which are lying here. They call almost every day & sometimes three or four drop in at tea time & spend the evening. We have now been here a week (I should have dated this page, Thursday the 31st) and I believe we have had some of them to tea every evening since we have been here. They always stay for evening worship, join in the singing and are chiefly [of a] religious bent, or those whose education & inclination had to seek & enjoy religious society. Mr. Johnson says that three or four of the officers of our Navy have made a profession of religion in Hong Kong. He takes a great interest in them- talks to them very seriously & induces them to attend the social evening prayer meetings at his house. In this way & by throwing open his house to them & bringing them in contact with religious people of refinement I have no doubt he does a great deal of good. I am afraid from what I have said of Mrs. Johnson you will form a very wrong estimation of her. Though she dresses very handsomely & is a very careful house keeper- weighing & measuring everything that comes into her house & giving out with her own hands every article that is used in her kitchen she is by no means neglectful of other duties. She has 12 Chinese girls in her house whom she supports & educates out of her own private purse. She has a Chinese teacher for them & a Chinese woman to attend to their clothing & take care of the little ones. Still she superintends everything herself & until the last six months when her health has been very delicate she has spent three or four hours every day teaching. She came out with Dr. Gutzluff four years ago after his last visit to Europe, for the purpose of establishing on her own account a school for females. They arrived here in January. But she found everything so entirely different from what she expected, was so unkindly treated by those from whom she had expected to receive every assistance & as a single woman met with so many difficulties in establishing a school that she determined to return home in the April steamer- but before Spring Mr. Johnson who had been a widower three years persuaded her to remain & in April they were married. The following September she commenced her school & for three years attended to it constantly herself. She is very much interested in it & still spends a good deal ofher time with the children. Three of them have been converted and when Mr. Johnson tries to persuade her to give up the school on account of her health- she replies- "How can I give up my children? Three have already been converted- Can I give up my school?" I believe she is a right-minded Christian & is doing a great deal of good here- to many others as well as the members of her school- but she has too much to do & her health is fast breaking down. Most ladies here find housekeeping as much as they can attend to in this enervating climate. It is a very different thing from American housekeeping. The most vigilant care is necessary to keep mould, rust & insects from destroying everything in the house- everything that is brought in must be weighed & measured & all table supplies must be given out from the pantry with your own hands- the washing is done out of the house & each article must be counted both when it goes & returns- so you see the care of even a small establishment is a pretty heavy duty. What kind of a housekeeper do you think I will make with all my careless habits? We shall see! Necessity may make me careful & economical but it will be a hard lesson for me, won't it Mother? We hope to be able to reach Fuh Chau by the middle of June. I am very anxious to get there and be settled. We are most kindly treated here and are very comfortable but we have been so long knocking about among strangers that it will be very pleasant to be alone again & I feel it is time I had the quiet of privacy of a home- It seems unfortunate that at a time when there is so much to be done I should be so unfitted for any extra exertion but Dr. Wentworth insists that I shall have nothing taken from the boxes at present but what is absolutely necessary for our present use. I am afraid that many of our things are already spoiled and that others will be ruined during these warm months, but there will be a great deal to do when they are unpacked that no one can do but myself & I suppose it is better I should have it all the Fall, when, if my life is spared, I hope to have more strength for such an undertaking.

Last Sunday morning we all went off to the Vandalia where Mr. Johnson was to preach. As soon as I heard there was a vessel of the Japan expedition in port, of course, I thought of Nathan Marshall, but it seemed so impossible that I should find him just in this vessel that happened to be in port at the time, that I said nothing about him till we got on board- During the service I searched among the congregation for a familiar face but my seat was where I could see but a part of the audience & I could recognize no one- but after service I asked one of the officers if a young man by the name of Marshall was connected with their vessel- He said Nathan Marshall was their surgeon's steward- did I know him- would I like to see him? Of course I did know him & would like to see him- So he was sent for at once and we had a good talk of home- Did it not seem strange that I should meet a West Chester boy the first Sunday I spent in China. He is very much improved both in appearance & manner

& I think when his mother sees him she will not regret the sacrifice she made in parting with him so long. He says his health has been perfectly good & he certainly looks much better than I ever saw him at home. He is considerably stouter & his color is much better and altogether he is very different from the thin pale faced boy that left W.C. two years ago. Yesterday afternoon he called to see me & brought Mr. A's last letter to read. He sat an hour or more & then accompanied us all to the parade ground to hear her Majesty's brass band perform. I am very much pleased with him- his manners are easy, quiet & gentlemanly & I think his voyage has done more to educate him & make a man of him than many years at home. I have invited him to come & see us as often as possible while they are here & hope he will do so. How glad I am to hear Annie is better & has a prospect of being quite well again. I hope I shall hear of her constant improvement. Please give my love to her & to Mrs. Marshall & Carry.

Thursday morning June 7th--

It is now half past seven- In two hours we expect to be on board the "Spit Fire"- horrid name- is it not- & at ten o'clock hope to weigh anchor & set sail for Fuh Chau. Six hundred miles still lie between us & the city we are seeking, & there is still time for accidents & much room for groans between us & it- but we say thus far the Lord hath led us on, & trusting to the same guiding hand, hope in a few more days to be brought safely to our journey's end. Wont you be glad to hear from us from our own home dear Mother? I know you will and wont we be glad to write from a quiet spot where we may rest for a little while at least- I think when I see Fuh Chau I shall feel like Noah's dove when she spied the green olive branch- Still our journey has been a very pleasant one- and even these delays have given us the opportunity of seeing many things we should have been sorry to miss & of making friends whose acquaintances will be valuable to us. It is a great convenience as well as a great pleasure to have friends among the missionaries at other stations & I should not think it desirable to sail direct to the final destination. I have not seen the vessel in which we are to go but she is an American Clipper & is said to be a fine ship & well finished.

Mr. & Mrs. Macaw and Mr. Fernley go with us & we shall have a good opportunity of becoming acquainted with them. I hope I shall like Mrs. Macaw better. What I have seen of her has not given me a favorable impression- but if pity is akin to love I shall come very near loving her- for I certainly think her greatly to be pitied. They have brought with them nothing for housekeeping but the little articles that could be stored in trunks & everybody predicts they will have great difficulty in providing themselves in Fuh Chau. As there are no other ladies connected with this mission she will not feel that she has any special claim

21

on those who are there. Of course the ladies will do all they can for her, but she is sick & not one I am afraid to make many friends & as they are to live in a part of the city three miles from the other mission houses I think she has a sad prospect before her. I think it probable- however they may be entertained at the British Consul's & if so may be made very comfortable. I congratulate myself upon being so well & abundantly provided. I believe every article the different missionaries have mentioned to us as desirable to be brought from home we have in our boxes & we have little or nothing that can be got conveniently here. Almost every lady I have met has asked me if I brought a dinner & tea set- China ware being a thing that cannot be bought in China & which house-keepers seem to have especial difficulty in getting from home. Mrs. Johnson received by our vessel some articles to replenish her dinner set that she had sent for by Mr. & Mrs. Colder & had been waiting for more than a year.

We took tea last night with Mrs. Pustaw the wife of a wealthy German merchant and had an opportunity of seeing high life in the East. It is an elegant house & we had a delightful supper- but I had been packing all afternoon & was too tired to enjoy anything but Mrs. P's fine piano on which I played the greater part of the evening. They have had it eight years & it is still in good order & excellent tune. Dr. Wentworth wanted me to have these two pages for him to fill- but going off three or four days earlier than we expected has hurried him with his letters & I was so sure he would not have time to write that I have filled them myself. Our early departure will prevent me too from writing letters I had intended to have ready- particularly to Let & Cousin Carry- Thank Cousin Carry for her kind letter & tell her I hope to write her by next mail. How sad it is to hear of Cousin Anna Maria Stout's death! How can she be spared- She was so active & well & bright when I saw her last. I can scarcely realize she is gone. And Mrs. Bennet too is dead! She will be greatly missed- It struck me painfully that our first two mails from home should bring each the account of the death of one we left in health & strength. Give my love to dear Mrs. Darlington and to all the sweet children at home. Pray for me a great deal my darling Mother. I need your prayers very much in this strange land.

With heartfelt affection

your daughter Anna

My dear Father,

        Instead of the long letters I had expected to write on
my arrival in Fuh Chau, I am afraid I shall have to make one
short and hasty one answer. By some strange arrangement, the
mail we had expected to send in July is advertised to close to-day
at noon, and I have only time for a few lines to assure you of
our safe arrival and kind reception, and must leave the many
little particulars I would like to write for another opportunity.
I wrote you from the vessel Spit Fire, dating my letter, I think,
the day we went on board. That was Thursday morning the seventh.
Mr. Johnson, who went on board with us, took leave of us directly
after dinner; but in consequence of heavy rains and light winds
we did not get out of the harbor till Saturday afternoon. All Saturday it rained, and all Sunday. Monday, which was my birthday,
it seemed as if the flood-gates above us had given way, and the
water fell in sheets. In the afternoon it was necessary to fasten
down the sky-lights and shut every shutter to keep out the driving
rain. All the week the rain continued almost without cessation,
and it was not till Thursday morning we saw the first gleam of
sunshine. The rolling of the vessel made all sea-sick, and you
may imagine it was an uncomfortable time. It was probably, too,
a time of more danger than any other we have passed through.
For an entire week we tossed among rocks and sandbanks, without
a single observation of the sun to tell where we were.

        On Thursday morning the sun came out and the Capt.
found that we were but forty miles from the mouth of the river
Min. A few hours sail brought us to the first sand-bar, where
we anchored to wait for a pilot. The navigation of the river is
very difficult, especially to vessels as large as the Spit Fire,
and our captain, besides being naturally a very cautious man,
was part owner of the vessel, and not disposed to run any risks;
so we came up slowly, just as wind and tide favored and did not
come in sight of Kianpai Pass, four or five miles from the mouth
of the river, till some time on Sabbath day. Word was immediately
sent up to the city announcing our arrival, and early the next
morning, about three o'clock, we were aroused by the arrival
of Dr. Welton, the Church of England physician and missionary,
who brought a boat large enough for Mr. and Mrs. Macaw, Mr.
Fernley, and ourselves; and also letters to us from Mr. and Mrs.
Maclay, giving us welcome to China, and an invitation to come
immediately to their house. The gentlemen got up to receive

Dr. Welton, and consult about leaving the ship. The English party decided to leave after an early breakfast. At eight o'clock we bade our friends "good-by", and sat down in our cabin to a quiet day alone. We lay at anchor all day without any wind; but about four o'clock were surprised to see a steamboat, having a tea-laden vessel in tow, come puffing down the river. Captain Aery went immediately on board to secure her services, and by five the next morning she was churning and puffing at our side.

One of the most pleasant and exciting things in our whole voyage was the passage from Kianpai Pass to Pagoda Island. The scenery on the Min is exquisitely beautiful, and the enjoyment of that, added to the home-like scream of the steam-pipe and puff of the engine made the trip, in spite of the drizzling rain, which, by the way, we did not condescend to notice, extremely pleasant. Mr. Clark, one of the house of Russel & Co., to which the vessel was consigned, had a comfortable boat, well cushioned and covered, waiting at the island, and was polite enough to offer us a passage to the city. We came up very comfortably in less than three hours, were met at the landing by Mr. Maclay, who brought us immediately to his house. Here we were surprised to find our English friends, Mr. and Mrs. Macaw, and Mr. Fernley, so worn out and exhausted by their trip of the day before, that they had not been able to go to their own house at the English consulate. They had been nine hours getting up the river in a small, close boat, without cushions and but ill protected from sun and rain, and with no food but a sandwich they had carried with them. Mrs. Macaw was burned almost to a blister, and was sick from fatigue; and the whole party were too weary to think of going three miles into the city, and had come up to Mrs. Maclay's for a night's lodging and a day of rest.

Mr. and Mrs. Maclay received us cordially, and I believe were really glad to see us . . . They have had the house on the hill, the "Olive Orchard House" as it is called, put in repair for us, a verandah thrown across the front, and the house well cleaned. The few articles of furniture Dr. Wentworth wrote from home about are ready, and for two or three months they have had a cook and table-boy in training for us, that we might have as little trouble as possible at first. There is some furniture too belonging to the mission, which they have had in use, but which they place for the moment at our disposal. After Mr. Gibson has come, and we are all settled, it will be divided equally among the three families; but it will be a great convenience to have the use of it while we are having others made, and will enable us to get into our own house sooner than we would otherwise do. . .

On Monday it rained all the afternoon, so that it was impossible to go over to the house. Of course I was extremely anxious to see it, but for that day was obliged to be satisfied with Dr. Wentworth's report. He went over immediately after dinner, and came back with a woeful story. The garden was much smaller than he expected, and overrun with weeds; the house was dark and gloomy, and the rooms small and inconvenient. In everything he was disappointed; was sure I would not be satisfied with it, and thought we could only live in it while another was being built. I only laughed at his pitiful tale, and told him I did not believe a word of it; reminded him that a man knew nothing of the difference furniture made in the apparent size of a house; and that a day when the rain was pouring in torrents was rather a bad time to judge of the cheerfulness of a strange place. So I reserved my judgment for a sunnier day. The next morning was bright and pleasant, and directly after breakfast I put on my bonnet, took the Dr's arm, and, accompanied by Mr. and Mrs. Maclay and Jimmy, started to see the new home. We passed through Mr. Maclay's back yard into what he called Avenue "B", a street eight or ten feet wide, running between two high stone walls, and neither graded nor paved. At the distance of about a square we turned into Avenue "A", and after walking nearly the same distance, entered through a double gate the "Olive Orchard". Perhaps the doctor's report was a good preparation for me, for everything certainly did look smaller in reality than on Dr. Wiley's paper; but after examining everything, and taking into account the difference care and furniture would make, I was more than satisfied with the whole establishment.

The grounds I find are well laid out, and besides the pretty olive grove at the lower end, has many valuable and well-grown plants in it. I think a dozen Chinamen, under my direction, will soon make a different looking place of it. The greater part of the yard is in front; back there is only room, between the verandah and the high stone wall, for a walk and a wide flower bed. A flight of stone steps leads to a gate in this wall, which opens on the beautiful hill on which are all the burial grounds. There is a fine view from this hill, and it is the favorite morning and evening walk of all foreigners. The situation is certainly a beautiful one, and seems to me the most desirable I have seen. From the front of the house we have a view of the river, with the island and the massive bridge; and of the city on the other side, and the noble mountain range beyond. The river itself is enough to reconcile one to any inconveniences in the house; but I do not believe we shall find any.

Your daughter

Anna L. Wentworth

(Quote from 'The Mission Cemetery' in regard to Anna)

"On the fourth of July we have a fragment of a letter written to her father, which shows her already engaged in the study of Chinese. She says: 'I have just been having a sitting with our long-tailed, long-nailed gentlemanly Chinese teacher. First I recited a lesson of just a yard and a half of Chinese radicals; then got from him the proper pronunciation of some household phrases I have been picking up, and afterward learned to count as far as one hundred. At the end of the lesson, which was rather a lengthy one, he rose from his chair, bowed very politely, put two fingers in his mouth to represent chop-sticks, I suppose, and gave me to understand that he wanted to go to his dinner.' "

"On the sixteenth of July, on this same sheet, Dr. Wentworth wrote that Mrs. Wentworth had been in the hand of the physician ever since the date of her letter above, and was still unable to attempt further correspondence. She had been quite reduced by an attack of the disease so fatal to foreigners in China."

(Anna's last letter written to her 5 year old sister, Willie)

Fuh Chau
August 2, 1855

My Dear Little Willie,-

I wonder what you and Allie are doing at home this pleasant morning. I wish you could be here to play in the beautiful yard around sister Anna's house, and to hear the birds sing in the trees. I don't think you ever heard so many birds in your life. For an hour or two early in the morning, they sing so loud that if you were in the yard you could hardly hear each other talk. It is a very nice garden and has some beautiful flowers in it; but I think you would like, better than anything else, a fine large grass-plot at the bottom, shaded by great large trees. I hardly ever go out and look at it without thinking what a nice place it would be for you to play, and how Mary Ellen would enjoy setting out her table and getting supper under those beautiful trees. O how I would like to have you three children come to see me, and hear your merry voices through the house and garden. But I am afraid you never can, it is so very, very far."

26

(Portion of letter [undated] written by Anna to her mother soon after her arrival in Fuh Chau, published in 'The Mission Cemetery'.)

"My Dearest Mother,-

"I write you at last in our own home. My writing desk stands on a low center-table in the middle of our parlor, and the light shining on my paper is thrown by the same bronze lamp round which our happy family circle has so often gathered at home. It was unpacked and filled this morning, and is now shedding its rays on heathendom for the first time. . .

"I am almost afraid to tell you how much I like Fuh Chau and its missionaries, and particularly 'Olive Orchard', our snug little home, because I may meet with difficulties and inconveniences after a while, of which I shall be sure to write, and you will think I am disposed to be fickle.

"Yet in this letter, notwithstanding its cheerful tone, there are references to debility and disease, for which she had been under medical treatment."

*   *   *   *   *

(Baby Anna born Aug. 12th 1855 - In late September the Doctor told Anna she could not recover.---Anna L. Wentworth died Oct. 2nd 1855).

Enoch Lewis

Joseph J. Lewis from his
daughter Anna - Fuh. Chau -
Chain - October 2nd 1855.
" Tell him to keep it on his
Office Table. "

Lewis Wentworth Park March 23, 19

ANNA M. WENTWORTH

DIARY

January 1st to June 24th 1855

Anna's fragmentary Journal kept in pencil in pocket Diary

January 1st to June 24th 1855

[Comments by Erastus Wentworth]

Jan. 1st- Left home Saturday Dec. 30- Parted with my father-whether I shall ever be permitted to see his face again- God only knows- Reached N.Y. Sat. eve. accompanied by Mother & Charlton, Mollie Turner, Dr. W. & Jimmy. Sunday morning Mulberry Street- Evening Watch Night- Madison Street. To-day visited ship- Small but has an air of comfort-

Jan. 2nd- New York- Mission Rooms- visit from Mrs. Peck in the afternoon- Went to Mrs. Palmer's meeting- disappointed in Mrs. P. nothing particularly winning or interesting about her-

Jan. 3rd- Visit from Drs. Kidder & Durbine.

Jan. 4th- Spent at Dr. Kidder's house in Jersey City (Newark she means) pleasant day. Palmois mistook Dr. Palmer for Professor Lephan. Enjoyed the music very much. The girls sing sweetly together. I played, but indifferently, on the piano, but enjoyed myself much.- Wonder when I shall touch one again? (see April 24th)

Jan. 6th- On shipboard- at work packing and unpacking making what arrangements we could for the comfort of the voyage-

Jan. 7th- Mother & Mollie & I attended communion in at Mulberry Street Church- It was a very solemn time- I knew it was the last- (the last she ever attended on earth, I think).

Jan. 8th- Sailed at 12 o'clock- Barque Storm- from N.Y. bound for Singapore & Hongkong & China. Mother & Mollie left us at 5 in the pilot boat- that surrendered the last link that bound me to home & former associations- Now my relations are altogether changed. May God help me to fill the new ones faithfully- The shore fades in the distance- "My native land- good night"-

Jan. 9th- Sea-sick at night- terrible thirst- (Never slaked till she quaffed the waters of the river of life- poor girl)

Jan. 10th- Sea-sick-

Jan. 11th- Sea-sick-

Jan. 12th- Sea-sick, headache- dreadful-

Jan. 13th- Sea-sick- but a little better-

Jan. 14th- Sunday- Crawled out of the cabin for the first time. Picked a chicken bone & drank a cup of tea in the vestibule where fresh air was plentiful. Sat there with great effort a couple of hours- Saw the sea for the first time- Ate a hearty dinner. Spent most of the afternoon on deck- but everything I had eaten coming up again before bed time.

Jan. 15th- Fresh- pleasant breeze- sailing ten knots an hour. Spent most of the morning lying in the upper deck propped against the sky-light- Tried to read a little but eyes too weak. Ate some dinner & a light supper- but in the evening nausea- headache & fever again. Quite a comfortable night- Awoke feeling better but still quite weak.

Jan. 16th- Still a good breeze & sailing fast. Morning in the cabin but feeling better. Afternoon tried to write a little, but found my hand too weak- Took my first walk on deck with Jimmy's assistance just before tea- At evening Dr. quite sick- sat by him till he fell asleep then went on deck. Find it very lonely here- (How often she said, "O how much I wish Joe had come with us"- You recollect that for the first five weeks out, when she most needed society, I was so sick as to be very little else than a burden to self or anyone else- I do not wonder the poor girl complains so often of "loneliness.")

Jan. 17th- Sail in sight- small schooner- to the West. Rained all morning- Read till my eyes fail- Dr. sleeps all the morning- Head too heavy to read or write- heart too heavy to sing- nobody to talk to- it is very, very lonely- After sunshine- calm- no wind- pleasant evening in the cabin.

Jan. 18th- Raining again- but warm- Lounged on the sofa in the Capt's private room- Borrowed Mr. Freeman's guitar & tried to play it. How pleasant to have anything like music. I enjoyed it so much- I am afraid I shall annoy everybody on ship-board.

Jan. 19th- Spent most of the morning on deck with a book & Mr. F's guitar- Sat there till driven down by the heat of the sun- Head better. My plan of diet seems to agree with me & I grow stronger daily. Jimmy is quite well again. Doctor improves more slowly- Afternoon wrote. Evening sewing & chatted.

Jan. 20th- Went on deck immediately after breakfast-

32

Dr. read to me Comte's **Positive Philosophy** till 1 1/2 o'clock when we were driven down by the heat of the sun- Sheep killed this morning. Now for mutton- Late in the evening ship passed with a quarter of a width of our bow westward bound-

Jan. 21st- Sunday- Little wind- Ship rolling badly. It affects my head so much that I can read but little. Am obliged to spend most of the day lying still. Am sorry to spend it so improfitably but cannot do otherwise. May the Holy Spirit direct aright the words of my mouth & the meditations of my heart.

Jan. 22nd- Lonely & heavy hearted- how long! how long!

Jan. 23rd- A beautiful sunset after which the young moon came out faintly but beautifully. The weather's beginning to be warm & I think I shall enjoy the moonlight evenings on deck very much. Felt better today than at any time since we came out.

Jan. 24th- Feeling badly not able to do anything. My head is very weak. I feel the want of society very much. It is very lonely here.

Jan. 25th- Lay in my berth nearly all day with headache- How much I feel the want of home comforts & home kindness when I am sick. I must learn to do without them- but it is a hard lesson- The Dr. read Shakespeare to us in the evening.

Jan. 26th- I am afraid I am growing fretful & reproving- I cannot help asking why I have been brought here & only just now, mental suffering should be added to physical. No doubt for some good end. Perhaps discipline for the future. God help me to trust where I cannot see.

Jan. 27th- A more pleasant day. My head feels somewhat clearer & my heart lighter- Spoke a vessel- the Golden Eagle bound for Liverpool- Sorry we could not send a letter by her.

Jan. 28th- Sunday- Vessel rolling badly- It affects my head a good deal. Read for awhile in my bible & a little to Jimmy. Afterwards took up **Judson's Life** but after reading an hour or two was obliged to put it down- Have time to think a great deal if I could only do so to profit.

Jan. 29th- No wind- Sails flap mournfully- vessel rolls from side to side making no headway- Towards evening a sail appears in the horizon. A pleasant evening on deck- bright moonlight- looked at the moon & planets through the Capt's telescope & hunted out some new constellations. Found Capella & the Kids, 30 Vini from Capt. Macey of the Whaler "Union". The jolly Capt. spent the morning & took dinner with us- entertained & amused us greatly. Wrote a number of letters to send by him, which he hopes to mail in Barbados about the 1st of March. We are all better & brighter today than we have been- I hope the Dr. is decidedly better.

Jan. 31st- (No record)

Feb. 1st- Raining at intervals all day. About 8 in the morning spoke the Dashaway from Bath, Maine- 31 days out bound for Calcutta. In the doldroms. Sails flapping- Irishman's Hurricane-

Feb. 2nd- Rain again. Not light showers- but pouring rain- passed five vessels, spoke bark "Vickery" from New York 68 days out- Crossed the equator.

Feb. 3rd- Blank

Feb. 4th- Sunday- 3 degrees south of the equator & driving rapidly forward with a stiff breeze- Jimmy distributes tracts in different languages among the sailors which I select for him. The Dr. is still too unwell to preach. He has little encouragement to do so- I cannot read much & am very solitary.

Feb. 5th, 6th, 7th, 8th- Ship rolling badly- everything not fastened to the floor is upset. Sat. 15,L. & a stiff breeze carrying us rapidly onward- Read at evening **Twelfth Night-**

Feb. 9th, 10th (Blank), 11th- Sunday- Not able to read any. Jimmy read several chapters of the Old Testament to me- but I spent a very quiet & lonely day. What will be the pleasures & occupations of heaven? An endless subject of thought-

Feb. 12th, 13th- Visit from Capt. Russel of the Whaler "Olympia" bound direct to New Bedford- We were delighted to have the opportunity of sending letters directly home- He hoped to mail them in 40 days. **Midsummer Night's Dream-**

Feb. 14th- (Has the same record as 13th!)

Feb. 15th- Pretty well to-day. My head better for the entire rest it had yesterday. Made a curtain for the Dr.'s window- mended his coat & did a little other stitching. I believe sewing agrees with my eyes better than reading. Dr. read to us **As You Like It.** Many beauties in it- Saw a whale for the first time.

Feb. 16th- Lay in my berth most of the day- Head feeling weak & light though not aching much. We have concluded "Uncle Dr." was right in thinking sea-sickness an affection of the brain. **All's Well That Ends Well.** After tea a part of Termpon's Princess- which I enjoyed very much- Later- the wind shifted South- Ship rocking badly- A sleepless & uncomfortable night.

34

Feb. 17th- Pleasant stiff breeze- ship pitching badly-

Feb. 18th- Sunday- Dr. gone to the forecastle to preach to the sailors for the first time. He has never before been able- He thinks it better I should not go to-day but I pray in my quiet room that God may crown with success his efforts to do good to those poor sailors- There seems to be serious feeling among them- Two or three have already converted through the instumentality of Mr. Freeman & Charley Nolan.

Feb. 19th- Ship reeling & any attempt to read or write or sew is sure to bring on headaches. I can do nothing but fold my hands & be patient. The guitar is a great resource for which I feel very thankful. Six weeks out to-day.

Feb. 20th- Took a lesson in perspective drawing. The Dr. is my teacher and hopes I will be able to while away some of the tedium of the voyage with my pencils. I am afraid I shall prove a dull scholar. I have neither the correct eye nor steady hand necessary for success.

Feb. 21st- The Dr. finished a sketch of our Pic-Nic ground. It is beautiful & a faithful representation of my favorite spot- I think it will be a great pleasure to me to hang in my strange house in Fuh Chau.

Feb. 22nd- Washington's Birthday. No demonstration on ship board- and so we are reminded that we no longer breathe American air.

Feb. 23rd- Planning Taylor's Seminary (a building in Fort Edward, N.Y.)- Find it difficult to get the proportions exact on so small a scale.

Feb. 24th- Dr. drawing a grand plan & view of grandfather Miner's house. I wish I could give him an idea of the view from the hill above the dam- It would make a beautiful picture.

Feb. 25th- Sunday- Charlton's birthday! 21 years old! Dear boy! I am too far away to offer my customary congratulations but God knows how fervently I invoke for him every blessing temporal & spiritual. This morning the Dr. preached in the forecastle. The first public service I have attended since Mother & I communed together in Mulberry Street & now we worship God miles apart.

Feb. 26th- Wrote a few lines to Charlton but could not finish my letter on account of the rolling of the ship. We are moving S.E. & the weather is perceptibly colder daily- Fire would be comfortable. Read **Comedy of Errors.** A most improbable story.

Feb. 27th- Weather getting cool. We are obliged to confine ourselves to cabin & state room & wear warm clothing. There is no fire & extra clothing is required to keep us comfortable.

Feb. 28th- We begin to experience some of the stormy weather we have been anticipating- rolling- pitching- tumbling- Soup served to-day in bowls- Steward & cabin boy have to hold the dishes on to the table during dinner. The milk cup upsets into Mr. Freeman's lap & Jimmy turns a somersault.

March 1st- Passed the Cape of Good Hope. It seems like a dividing point & as we shoot into Eastern waters- to sepate us from home. Read **Macbeth.**

March 2nd- Bad night- sleeping- or rather- rolling about on the floor. Waves break over the deck- the bell tolls mournfully with the swinging of the vessel. The officers are hoarse with commands. The mournful chant of the sailors, dashing waves & roaring winds prevent sleep. Saw to-day flocks of Stormy Petrels in the ship's wake. **King John- Macbeth!** Dr. reading Rousseau's **Napoleon** & much of it aloud to me. I hope I shall soon be able to use my own eyes- **Richard 2nd-**

March 4th- Sunday- Sailors at work all the morning putting up a new spar in place of one lost last week- Just as they had got it up the wind struck it & carried it away- Another was rigged in its place but just as it was set it became calm- reading in the afternoon from a "Remember the Sabbath day to keep it holy".

March 5th- Read **Life of Bonaparte** nearly all day- Strained my eyes- must rest them for a day or two.

March 6th- Rested all the morning. Sewed a little in the afternoon. Commenced a pair of slippers for the doctor, in a pattern invented for me by the Capt. I find sewing less trying to the eyes than anything else.

March 7th- I find the guitar a great resource. By taking it up when I could do nothing else I have learned to manage accompaniments quite well & to play a few tunes. With a little practice I think I could learn all that is desirable of the instrument.

March 8th- Commenced reading the German Testament. Have found in the Ship's library a German translation of the **Pilgrim's Progress,** which I want to read during the remainder of the voyage- Eyes better.

March 9th- Dear Joe's birthday- How much I want to be at home on these anniversaries- but I do not forget the dear ones there & I hope they think of me. A stormy day- sea running very high- frequently breaking over the deck, dreadful rolling at night-

March 10th- To-day the wind has lulled somewhat but the waves are dashing higher than we have ever seen them before. It is a splendid sight in the sunshine. Find no safe seat but the floor where I sit & read & sew nearly all day. Odd scenes at the table. Upsets & broken dishes frequent-

March 11th- Sunday- Too stormy for church. Spent a pleasant day in the cabin. Dr. read aloud the book of Exodus which I followed in the German bible- "Urim & Thummim"- Luther traces later "Licht und Recht"- "Light & Right". Spend the evening in singing together in our stateroom. Enjoyed it very much.

March 12th- The sea is still rolling high though the wind has abated much- Finished Tasso's "Jerusalem"- a most beautiful poem. During the day so much water dashed upon the deck that it two or three times found its way into the room door of our Stateroom- flooded the floor. Slept on the floor of the cabin braced between the side of the table. Read German Testament afterwards Chamber's **Notes on America.** Decks still so wet that I cannot go out- Have not been on deck for nearly a week.

March 14th- Sea comparatively quiet. Dining on deck- Pay my first visit to the boy's (saloon) caboose- where I make acquaintance with Otis (an honest lad from Connecticut)- Charley Kregger (an interesting German lad- who left us at Singapore- who had embraced religion on board & has recently been baptized at Shanghai) & Jack (an English boy- servant of the first mate)- Read a little of Spencer's **Fairy Queen.** Spent the rest of the evening till 11 1/2 o'clock listening to an interesting discussion between the Capt. & doctor, on religion.

March 15th- Passed St. Paul's a volcanic uninhabited island- last night & have thus lost our only chance of seeing land till we reach Anjer Point. Sixty six days under the ship's bow sight of land.

March 16th- Mate speared a porpoise under the ship's bow.

March 16th- Friday- (continued) It was between 3 & 4 ft long- an ugly thing. Had some of the liver fried for supper which tasted pretty well hot made me sick afterwards.

March 17th- Attempted a new business for me. Turned barber & cut the Dr.'s hair. I did it reluctantly for fear of spoiling it- but congratulated myself on my success- Laughed heartily at Jimmy's request that I would cut his also. The Capt. sheared him a week ago and it is not yet long enough to get hold of-

March 18th- Sunday- Read Leviticus, Half in English-half in German & a little in the Danish Testament. Danish seems very easy- so many English & German words are in it & the idiom is so much like the English. Rough weather- no service-

March 19th- To-day Charlton goes to Lancaster to attend Conference- His examination will take place to-day into tomorrow- I hope he will pass a good one. How anxious I shall be to know the appointments of the Phila. Conference (They came in our July mail)

March 20th- Weather growing warm & spring like. I feel the effects of it, headache & langour- I am afraid I shall have to give up reading again as we near the equator- Felt very badly all the afternoon & evening. A sort of dreary foreboding as if some great evil was about to befall me.

March 21st- Head feels badly. Slept heavily all the morning. How much I wish for Joe- I think almost every day what a comfort it would be to have her with me- I feel very anxious to hear from home. How long it seems to be without any tidings from those I love so dearly.

March 22nd- Weather growing quite warm- We find necessity for change of clothing. Had a pleasant day sewing in the morning- reading to the Dr. in the afternoon from Miss Pardoes' **Louis XIV.** Playing the guitar at evening- Beautiful moonlight.

March 23rd- The Dr. has commenced writing a Sunday School book which he hopes to finish in 8 or 10 days (not done yet) asks me to try my hand at it- New business for me- never attempted a thing of the kind in my life. It will be amusement for our leisure hours- (She wrote one chapter)

March 24th- Did a little sewing but read aloud most of the day in Miss Pardoe's work. It is absorbingly interesting- a good history- a good novel- a good Summary- Louis' character was a strange compound of strength & weakness- Madame de Maintenon the most estimable character depicted.

March 25th- Sunday- No church again to-day- I am sadly disappointed- Have enjoyed so much the few short & hurried services we have had that I am sorry to be deprived of them. Read Numbers with the Dr. & afterwards Madame Guyon's **Memoirs.** Comparing myself with so holy a woman makes me fear I am no Christian at all.

March 26th- Read Miss Pardoe to the Dr. nearly all day. Not feeling very well- This warm weather is so ennervating- Spent the afternoon sewing & the evening chiefly on deck in the moonlight- These nights are exquisitely beautiful.

March 27th- Finished Miss Pardoe. We have read it with great interest & pleasure- Mate caught another porpoise- I caught a glimpse of the frightful thing bleeding on the deck- I shall not want to eat any of it. Evening Dr. writes & I play-

March 28th- 13,660 miles from N.Y. & or 500 miles from Anjer Point on Letty Butler's birthday- 26 years old- I am not far behind her- How old we are getting!

March 29th- At work nearly all day making a chart of our voyage to send home- An awning was put up this morning which shelters us somewhat from the burning sun. A day to be remembered- A perfect show day in the heavens- A storm cloud that (?) one third of the horizon, a perfect rainbow- brilliant sunset- fine moonlight- distant storm & beautiful lightning up of the clouds.

March 30th- Another beautiful day- I enjoy the warm weather & so does the Dr. I hope a warm climate will agree with us both. Too lazy to work much but I enjoy everything- particularly the glorious sunsets & beautiful evenings.

March 31st- Thermometer at 90° in the shade- Winds very light- We had hoped to reach Angice (?) tomorrow but that is now out of the question. How grateful will be the sight of land again & how I long for it. Wrote a page to father.

April 1st- Sunday- A beautiful clear day though very warm. I spent nearly the whole morning under the awning on the upper deck reading. In the afternoon the Dr. read me Benson's **Life.** The evening we spent on deck in the glorious moonlight. Had hoped to see land to-day but it is almost a dead calm.

April 2nd- Land ho! Eighty four days since we watched the fading shores of America- draw for the first time our eyes to greet the land. Gradually the blue strip becomes more & more distinct till we at last distinguish the green trees & the hills. How beautiful! How refreshing!

April 3rd- In the Straits of Sunda- The shore of Java is remarkably grand & fine. The mountains are high- their heads sometimes hidden in the clouds- & their bases resting upon the water's brink. Visited by 8 or 10 boats of copper-colored-strait-haired- flat nosed natives of whom the Capt. bought quantities of fowls- eggs, fruit & vegetables. Wrote a long letter to Annie Kelly-

April 4th- Passed out of Sunda into Java Sea- Saw several vessels but spoke none. Lost the hoped for opportunity of sending letters home- Capt. busy loading the gun & examining the arms to be ready in case of encounter with pirates. Afternoon saw a Chinese junk- but she did not come near us.

April 5th- Dangerous navigation- Shoals and coral reefs all around. Heard the Capt. pacing the deck nearly all night & the frequent monstrous sound of the lead-hearers calling out the result of the soundings. To-day off Bangka Island. Fell asleep on deck about 5 o'clock & did not wake till 11. Beautiful moonlight- wind ahead- anchored-

April 6th- Anchored all night. In the morning a wind that made it necessary to beat. Entering the Straits of Gaspar. Full of shoals & rocks- navigation difficult- Commenced a little pencil sketch before breakfast- Sewing most of the day. Consequence, a head-ache-

April 7th- About 4 in the morning ran on a coral reef- No harm done. Small boats from the shore came out to reconnoiter. Capt. had the muskets to take down & loaded. Afternoon Mate & Mr. Freeman paid a visit to a ship anchored near us. Capt. - Portuguese from Hongkong- 300 Chinese on board- bound for Australia- Got off the rocks at 4 P.M. Caught beautiful fish on the reef & seemed some fine specimens of coral.

April 8th- Sunday- Dead calm all day- Sea smooth as a lake- 2 the afternoon Capt. & sailors bathing. Less dog-music than usual. Read with the Dr. Joshua- Judges & Ruth- a little in German text & finished Madame Guyon. A pleasant happy evening on deck- Thank God for these happy days-

April 9th- A heavy squall struck us at six A.M. which drove us at the rate of 10 knots an hour for some time- The ship rolled badly & made me sea-sick- Stay in my berth sleeping all the morning. Eight days since we enter in the Straits & still 200 miles from Singapore-

April 10th- Not a breath of air- Sea calm as a lake- Spent the morning on deck drawing from Harper's- Sewing all afternoon- Quite tired. Evening on deck. A little breeze blew us to the East but we made nothing- "We take it calmly - but not cooly" says the Dr. The temperature of the thermometer is decidedly high. Slow progress.

April 11th- Took a lesson in Trigonometry before breakfast- studied it all the morning & part of the afternoon- Then after washing & dressing drew till tea-time. Sea still calm. Eight days since we left Anjer & still 200 miles from Singapore-

April 12th- "Dead Clams" as the Capt. says- Still we spend the days very pleasantly & as long as water & provisions last we have no reason to complain.

April 13th- To-day the Capt. orders the steward to make no more soup because it takes so much water which is getting very low- Only one more cask & when we begin on that, we will be put on allowance- Still every day we hope for a breeze-

April 14th- Calm, calm. Still 20 miles South of the Equator- made but seven miles yesterday- House-cleaning & berth scouring in the morning- In the afternoon wrote to Mother. Weather oppressively warm- Not a breath of air & thermometer at 90° in the cabin.

April 15th- Sunday- Still calm. Spent the morning on deck reading. Read 1st book of Samuel & the "Super annuate". Borrowed Mrs. Palmer's **Entire Devotion** & read it in the cabin. In deed I do want to be a pure-hearted Christian- Why am I not? Crew Sabbath-breaking as usual- Were in swimming in our wake. Dr. suffers all day bug with face ache- Shark take- 7 ft long- 5 rows of teeth- five others seen-

April 16th- No swimming in our wake- Dr. suffers all day bug with face ache- No breeze- but the moon will change at 3 this P.M. & we hope for a change of weather. We begin to look anxiously for Singapore- Fresh provisions have nearly given out- the water is low & our clothing spoiling with mould- this warm weather requires frequent changes & we will soon need washing done-

April 17th- The moon proved true. About 9 last evening a breeze sprang up which has blown steadily ever since- Sailing all day at 5 knots- Spoke the "Hound-Mystic"- 9 days out of Hongkong- bound to Havana with 700 Chinamen- 1500 miles in nine days & we 60 in 11 days!

April 18th- Anchored in Singapore Harbor- What dressing & preparation for visiting & visitors- Numbers of boats come off- mostly Malay- Two white men- Delighted to be once more so near the dwellings of man & to feel the throbbing pulse of life- We sat on deck after tea watching the lights on shore sniffing the land breeze & listening to the sounds that floated over the water with indescribable pleasure-

April 19th- Received our first letters from home. Father, Mother, Charlton, Wayne, Letty, Joe- sister Abby & the other father. God bless them all for their good kind letters. They are like apples of gold in pictures of silver. How I enjoyed them & how I cried over them- 30 long days to wait for others- Consul Bradley called on us.

41

April 20th- Busy writing letters for the mail that is expected tomorrow. Cannot go on shore- Dr. goes & finds much that we will enjoy. Boarding is high & we have concluded to remain on the ship. Mr. Freeman embarks on an English vessel for Shanghai. I shall miss him & his guitar.

April 21st- Still busy writing letters. Singapore looks beautifully from the distance. When the mail is gone will take a nearer view of it- but I must write till the last moment- Mr. Freeman has gone- the Capt. has gone ashore & we are alone but we have a good table & think we shall enjoy ourselves much. Sent 25 pieces of clothing to the "dobey" to beat out.

April 22nd- Sunday- For the first time in 106 days set foot on land & for the first time on Asiatic soil. How delicious to see the green trees- smell the landbreeze- & hear the twitter of birds- Went to service in the English Church- To the eye all was strange- to the ear all familiar.

April 23th- Sent off our mail- Letters to father- mother- Letty- Wayne- Charlton- Joe- Enoch- Mary Ellen- Allie- Willie- and Sarah Miner- Annie Kelly- father Wentworth- sister "Champ" & Dr. & Mrs. Miller- Mr. Keasbury called invited us to his house. Beautiful moonlight ride on the shore.

April 24th- Went on shore to dine & spend the night at Mr. Keasbury's. He has a beautiful place which he calls M Ti'o two miles from town. This house is spacious- his school of Malay boys interesting- his wife a lady- and everything delightful. For the first time since I left America touched a piano & for the first time in my life slept under a mosquito curtain.

April 25th- Awoke at Mr. K's to the music of birds- How sweet & home like it sounded- "Tiffin" at 8. Spent a pleasant morning in the school- at the piano & with Mrs. K. After breakfast at 12 rode back to town- called on Mr. & Mrs. Wright at the Institute & then went on Shipboard.

April 26- 27- 28- Spent on Shipboard-

April 29th- Sunday- My darling little Willie's birthday- Five years old today. I wish the dear child was here that I might give her 55 kisses. May God spare her to see many birth days & keep her pure & beautiful in character unspotted from the world. Went to church in the morning & read the rest of the day.

April 30th- Dined with Mrs. Wright at the Institute- Met there the little party of Singapore missionaries- Mr. & Mrs. James- Misses Cook & Wright & Mr. Keasbury- Dr. W. entertained them with an account of our German missions & African missions. For the first time- sat at the table with two black men-

May 1st- Went on shore at 6 A.M. & rode for some time over the beautiful, level, well shaded roads that encompass Singapore. Found ourselves unexpectedly at Mr. Keasbury's- called & took "tiffin".

May 3rd- Dressed- pic-nic costume expecting Mr. Bradley to accompany us to one of the islands near- but business prevented him & afterwards we thankfully accepted an invitation to tea with Dr. Curtiss. Had a pleasant evening at his house & good play on the piano & a beautiful row home by moonlight.

May 4th- Went to breakfast at 10 with Miss Cooke. Saw her interesting school of Chinese girls & enjoyed her piano. Called a few minutes at Mr. Bradley's rooms- returned to the ship by 4. A call from Dr. House- 9 years a missionary in Siam- homeward bound. Shall I ever turn my face toward home again? retrace this lingering journey- God knows and he will direct- O my dear-dear- home.

May 5th- Not feeling well- Lying in my berth most of the day- but towards evening packed our carpet bags & went to spend the night at Mr. K's. Spent the evening singing sacred music which dispelled my home sickness. Still my heart yearns toward home-

May 6th- Sunday- "Who killed cock robin"- When we returned to the ship after service Mr. K's Malay chaplain found all our pretty Java sparrows gone. I suspect foul play.

May 7th- Left Singapore- Visit from Dr. House before breakfast who carried with him a budget of letters to father-mother- Letty- & others. Sea sick all the rest of the day.

May 8th- Vessel motion affects me still- shall be over it soon- Spent part of the day on deck writing but not very well.

May 9th- Commenced an oil painting!!

May 10th- Quiet & pleasant afternoon- painting & reading Comte.

May 11th- Feeling quite miserable- lying all evening on the floor reading **Middle Kingdom**. Afternoon "oil painting" which progresses finely- Breeze in evening.

May 12-13-14-15-16-17-18-19-20-21-22-23-24- Arrived Hongkong- Got out of bed. Went on deck to see China at 2 A.M.-

thought of Willie's "Stare Prow"- a vast amphitheater of mountains & a long line of lights- After breakfast Dr. went ashore. 2 the afternoon Mr. Johnson came & took us to his house-

May 23 to June 18- Reached Fuh Chau at 1 o'clock P.M. 5 months & 10 days from N.Y. How thankful I am that the voyage is over. It will be so delightful to <u>rest</u>. Kindly received at Mr. Maclay's. Rain pouring. Cannot go to see our house to-day. Dr. goes over. Reports rather unfavorably but cannot judge on so dull a day.

June 24th- Sunday- The first day in our own house. How delightful it is to be here- I have a feeling of <u>rest</u> that is indescribably pleasant- I think we shall be very happy here & I hope very useful- May God bless our household & make it the abode of peace & love- (with this beautiful benediction the journal closes . It was not until a longer struggle with the winds & waves of this troublesome world that the dear sufferer entered upon the "<u>rest</u> that remaineth for the people of God.")

LETTER

Erastus Wentworth, Sr.
December 6th 1855

LETTERS OF CONDOLENCE FROM FUH CHAU

November 20th 1855 - April 27th 1856

CUM-FA-MEW LANDING-PLACE, HONAN.

THE CREW OF A GUN-BOAT IN CANTON RIVER AT PRAYERS.

Dear Madam

Your very interesting and welcome letter of the 1st instant came to hand in due time, and has been faithfully read & re-read, and we are a thousand times obliged to you for giving us the intelligence so promptly, we have been looking forward to that event with no small degree of anxiety, and are very thankfull to learn that it has turned out this favorable. We shall hope to hear erelong that Anna is up and doing well- I congratulate you and Brother Lewis on the birth of the first grand-child, and hope you may live to have many, though, so far as I am concerned I should like to have a good share of boys, so as to keep up the name of Wentworth as I esteem it Honorable-

We have had several letters from them, one by ship Phaton, date July 16th which came to hand Nov. 29th. Today we got a package of letters by ship Lotus dateing up to July 28th, so we are indebted to you for the latest intelligence, also for the first intelligence of their arrival at Fuh Chau, in your former letter- In regard to sending the Journal it will be perfectly safe to send by Mail, your direction of letters is correct and they come safely. We should like well to see it- Would it be a good plan to have it put in print?

I join with you heartily in your last remark in your letter, relative to some personal intercourse in our families before the passing of next summer- and hope you may some of you visit up here and that I might take a trip to Norwich with you- I think now if we are spared that some of us will visit you next summer, but more of that hereafter-

Mrs. W. & daughter Abby join with me in our best respects to you, Mr. Lewis & family.

Respectfully Yours

E. Wentworth (Sr.)

47

My dear Mrs. Lewis,

As Dr. Wentworth has invited me to write you, respecting the last hours of our dear Mrs. Wentworth, your lamented daughter, I esteem it- a very great pleasure thus to do.

We all were very glad to welcome her to our missionary circle, not for a moment thinking, that like a ray of sun light-she would shine upon us, and then be gone forever, <u>but</u> <u>so</u> <u>it</u> <u>was.</u> Still we who were with her and witnessed the happy hours of her departure were constrained to say, even in this <u>very</u> mysterious providence Our Heavenly Father "Seeth all things well".

I was with her only occasionally during the first of her illness, when watching with her I learned that bathing was very refreshing and soothing to her, especially during the most restless part of the night which was between the hours of three and four A.M. She enjoyed it so much that at one time when bathing her an hour elapsed without either of us being aware of it. She often said I shall remember this kindness, if ever you are sick.

About ten days before her death I went to see her, after speaking to me, she said softly, I have been waiting for you to come and bathe me, I bathed her with vinegar and water and she expressed herself very much refreshed, I, that day, thought for the first time that she would not live, not so much from her weakness, though she was very much emaciated and very weak, but from the manner of her conversation, which seemed to me to come from a soul near the Heavenly King- Now such a happy expression of countenance and such peaceful sayings, to me very plainly whispered, 'I am almost home', and I often during the day turned away to weep, that one so lovely and so beloved, must be taken away so soon. During the day she was very much troubled with nausea, as she had been for a long time, especially when she lay on her side, moving in the least was usually followed by vomiting, consequently she was obliged to keep on her back, which after a time became very wearisome, during this day I gave her beef tea from a spoon once an hour, & for a change thin custard just a spoonful at a time, she was enabled to keep it down some of the time, by gently rubbing her stomach with the palm of her hand.

She at this time enjoyed her full powers of mind, though

it was evident from her conversation that she was fully convinced the time of her departure was very near. She conversed about you her dear mother, her husband, her motherless child, and about death, with great calmness, unweakened judgment and the deepest love. Once she said, "if mother could only have been here to nurse me," and immediately added, "everyone has done all they could"-

At one time her babe was brought to her, before looking at it she asked, "Is this my babe?" Being informed it was, she kissed it- and gently pushed it away saying, "Go away dear baby, go away dear baby: I must not love you now," and when it was taken away she said to me, "Oh! how hard it is to give up my child." A day or two before her death when bathing her feet, she asked if she might put them in the basin. When told she might, she put them gently down into the water saying "River Jordan". The next day when giving her some drinks she said, "This will not quench my thirst, nothing can, until I drink from the river of life that flows out from the throne of God, then I shall never thirst again."

When watching with her she asked cannot you read some to me from the Bible? I then read one of the Psalms. After having finished she said, "How excellent", then said, "Will you read some from Revelation?" I then read part of the last chapter and she exclaimed how I long to drink from that pure river.

I said to her the day before her death, the physician speaks a little favourably of your recovery, she replied, "I do not want to stay, I am ready, I am waiting to go." At another time of the same day she said, "how long to wait, but the Lord knows best."

I cannot describe to you the sweet peace she enjoyed, it was indescribable, it was glorious. The day before her death I think it was, she requested to have the hymn sung, "Jesus Lover of my Soul" and joined in the singing. I can assure you I shall never forget that lovely scene. There she lay, her head reclining near her husband, her hands clasped together . . . her eyes raised to heaven, and her countenance beaming with unearthly pleasure and peace, could you her dear mother have seen her then, even a mother's bleeding heart would have been constrained to say, "Go beloved child, earth is no longer a fit dwelling place for thee."

Early in the evening of the night of her death, we moved her a little, to relieve if possible her wearied body. After being moved she said, "how comfortable". Late in the evening I took her some drinks but found she could not swallow. As I was going away with her drink, she looked after me so wistfully that one sitting near requested me to return, and I think she then took two swallows. Soon after she said very distinctly, "Open the door". These were the last words I heard her say, her breathing for a time was heavy, after that it became easy, and she passed away as sweetly as a child going to sleep.

I assisted in dressing her for the grave. We clothed her in the garments she herself had selected, her under garment was one, as she had informed one of the ladies her own dear mother had made herself, her outside dress, was one of the bed gowns with plaits in front- with a very newly washed collar. I cut off her back hair as she had desired and combed her front hair as near as I could after the manner I had seen her wear it when well. She was so lovely in her sickness that even her body after the Spirit had departed seemed exceedingly precious to me. I printed a farewell kiss on her cold cheek: praying in my soul that all her relatives especially her dear mother might have sufficient grace given them, to be perfectly resigned to the early and unexpected death of this lovely daughter.

I cannot say to you do not mourn. It is your privilege thus to do, but I would ask what more could you have asked for your daughter, that God in his infinite mercy did not give her? He gave her the greatest of all gifts, even enough of his Holy Spirit to enable her joyfully to lay down her life for his glory.

Though buried in a heathen land, she is just as near the ministering angels that watch over the dust of the saints, as though buried in her own native land- And may we not hopefully rejoice that at the last day her glorified body will ascend to eternal bliss, with a host of ransomed spirits from among the poor benighted Chinese, for whom, in the providence of God she so joyfully laid down her life.

With Kindest love to all your family

I am affectionately

Your sympathizing

friend

Sephin N. Doolittle

50

Fuh Chau
Jan. 23rd 1856

Dear Mrs. Lewis-

Accompanying this is an interesting letter from Mrs. Maclay of Anna's last hours. Perhaps in her anxiety to vindicate the reputation of Fuh Chau for healthfulness she has over estimated the effects of the voyage & she even intimates that she had the consumption or its seeds in her constitution before she left home! She speaks confidently of its being "ulceration of the bowels" whereas Dr. Welton only said he "<u>feared</u> ulceration of the bowels".

Anna had two sinking turns on Saturday 29th- one about one o'clock or thereabouts, the other at evening- in each of which I thought her departure at hand- Mrs. M. thought her wandering in mind all day Tuesday & excited Anna's feelings once by intimating that she did not know what she was saying- whereas- although her powers were failing & she said of her own mind "it was difficult to steady it" scarce did not forsake its throne permanently earlier than four o'clock P.M. & even then she knew everybody & everything that was passing-

Mrs. M. says the final struggle commenced at 11. I was administering medicines every half hour, watch in hand & noted the instant of every change.

We shifted her from the bed at 9- Obstructed breathing accompanied by a low moaning distressing to hear, but of which the Dr. said she was unconscious- as her hands lay motionless- commenced at 9 1/2- She revived so far as to speak incoherently at 10 1/2 and at 11 all was over- I mention these things for the sake of accuracy in her obituary- should it be published- A writer must select & arrange with due discrimination-

Truly yours

E. W.

[Dear Mrs. Lewis,]

It was not long after Mrs. Wentworth's arrival in Fuh Chau when we became acquainted with the state of her health, which, taken in connection with our past observation and the extreme heat of the season could not but excite in us very serious apprehensions. We noticed however her calm temperament, her persevering prudence in diet, and, as medicines somewhat availed we trusted that she would soon overcome the difficulty and long be spared to labor in China. Nor did we relinquish the hopes thus fondly cherished until within a few days before her death. It was no less a surprise, than a grief when we learned that her disease had taken the serious form of ulceration of the bowels. I with others had supposed that she was gradually recovering her strength, and that she would soon be entirely well. How changed our feelings then, when we found that she had begun rapidly to fail, and, that her physician entertained but little hope of her recovery! It was a very painful thought that we must so soon part with one whom we had learned so much to love and who seemed so eminently qualified to live and labor for the heathen. Can it be? Must she be taken away? was the constant enquiry of our hearts- until death itself convinced us of the sad reality- and it was only because we knew that He who did it was "too wise to err, too good to be unkind," that we could in any degree become reconciled to the bereavement.

When we found that she was failing I greatly desired that she should come to our house where I could constantly be with her, and bestow unremitting care in nursing her. I invited her to come, but she said she was too much of an invalid to go away from home then, but when she should get better she would like to accept my invitation. I reminded her that I wished to aid her in getting better, and for that reason I hoped she would at once conclude to come. She steadily declined my invitation however until one Sunday morning, when I promised her so much that she was at last inclined to yield, and said, "It is very tempting- you do almost persuade me to go. I will talk with Dr. Wentworth about it." Feeling satisfied that she would come to our house I immediately returned home and prepared a large retired room for her reception, and in about 2 hours after she was conveyed to our house in a Sedan chair. I was greatly pleased with this change for I did not doubt in the least that she would be benefitted by it and recover. But my hopes were soon blasted, for her physician soon came and announced to her and to us that she could not live. When this trying announcement was made to her I was not in the room, but on going to her bed-side shortly after, she said to me, with a look of great discouragement, "Why do so much for me? It is of no use." I assured her that I had great hopes of doing her good. She did not tell me in reply what the physician had said but so far as I could discover she was entirely unmoved, and tranquil, and I did not suspect that he had mentioned to her the alarming symptoms of her case. During the remainder of the day and night she seemed very comfortable and after spoke of it, saying she was so glad she had come over to our house.

The next morning, as myself and her Chinese woman were preparing herself and the room for the day she asked me for something to drink. I prepared her some water with brandy to which having tasted she said, looking me in the face with a sweet smile, "There'll be no thirst in Heaven- Almost a year I have been suffering with thirst"- And then fixing her uplifted eye upon the wall as if in sweet meditation, she repeated slowly and with much emphasis, "The water of the river of life- and Giver of life"- then, turning again to me she said, "O, I feel as if I can hardly stay <u>here</u> any longer. There are so many tempting things beyond the river."

I said to her- What a blessing it is, now that you feel but little certainty- about your getting well that you have an anchor to the soul- "O, yes" she says, "<u>sure</u> and <u>steadfast</u>- entering within the veil."

In the course of the day she alluded to the trying hour of death and taking the hymn book I read to her the hymn commencing "Deathless Spirit now arise" directing her mind particularly to the lines "Not one object of his care, Ever suffered shipwreck there."

She seemed much gratified and remarked that she needed to have her thoughts continually directed to such sweet promises.

On the following morning I sat by her bed-side and read for her comfort 1 Cor. XV chap. When I had finished she exclaimed "<u>Isn't</u> it a <u>beautiful</u> chapter." You have doubtless heard how much she loved to have us sing "Jesus lover of my soul." It was her favorite hymn, and whenever it was sung for her to every word she seemed to give the most heartfelt assent-

Our usual family worship was conducted by her bed-side every day which she enjoyed very much.

About the middle of the week we were much encouraged respecting her, and I think her physician considered her symptoms Bulliaded. Our strong hopes somewhat revived hers, and as little Anna was being carried thro' the room after her morning bath, she called to the Chinese nurse saying, "Bring her here, I want to see her." She extended her arm to receive her and gazing upon the little one pressed close to her bosom, so unconscious of passing scenes, she said, "I don't know how it is, I try to give her up and not love her, and then I think I _may_ possibly get well and my heart will cling to her. I know she will be well taken care of, and better brought up than I can bring her up, so long as my Mother lives, but I think after a few years my Mother will be taken away. My brothers and sisters will settle in life and have families of their own, and she is a little _girl,_ and as she grows up into woman-hood, she'll need a _Mother's_ sympathy- and counsel" and bursting into a fresh flood of tears, she exclaimed- "O What will you do without your Mama then!" It was a touching scene, and grief for which I knew no remedy, but _Trust in God._

I recommended committing her to Him, assuring her that He would do better for her than she was able to ask or think.

Notwithstanding our strong hopes we became sensible as early as Friday that in spite of all our efforts to save her, she was fast failing.

She noticed that we spoke with less confidence about her recovery, and as she viewed her wasted frame, she said- "This seems like _death itself_ doesn't it?" I replied in the affirmative, when she remarked that it was "not desirable to get well, and go through a long convalescence." She was again thoughtful for a moment and said, "I dont like to leave my mind unsettled about these things."

On Saturday she was still weaker and after we had arranged her dress as usual for the day she complained of slight deafness. Soon after, as I gave her some medicine, she suddenly turned upon her side and rolling her eyes back said, "O if the Lord would only be pleased to take me now."

I observed a great change in her countenance, as well as difficult respiration. I immediately apprized Dr. Wentworth of the change, who at once came in and raised her up upon the pillows, she said to him "This is death"- We, too, thought the messenger had come, and during the day we often gathered about the bed expecting that she would soon leave us. She had frequent turns of oppressed breathing during the day turning her head upon the pillow first on this side, then on that. She complained of weakness and weariness more than of pain. Mrs. Baldwin took care of her during the night and at an early hour the next morning I rose and went to her bed-side. I saw that she seemed revived and remarked that I did not expect to see her with us this morning. She replied "I dont think I shall live through the day- Dr. Welton thinks that- I believe, does he not?" I proposed reading a little to her from the Bible- she answered "Yes- a little- I cant listen long." I read a small portion of the XLIII chap. of Isaiah and the CXXI Ps. When I had finished she seemed for a moment uneasy in her mind and said, "You don't think I would be cut off at last do you?" "No," I replied- "Not with such a Saviour." She said, "I <u>trust</u> Him with <u>all</u> my might but I find it difficult to keep my mind from wandering." I assured her that the Lord would take care of that- repeating also, "He <u>knoweth</u> our frame: He <u>remembereth</u> that we are dust- and as a <u>father</u> pitieth his children, so the <u>Lord</u> pitieth them that fear him." She then seemed satisfied and rested quietly. Towards evening she said to me, "I have some things that I want to say to you, but I never seem to see you alone when I have the strength to talk." I asked if she <u>then</u> felt strong enough to talk, and if I should request others to leave us alone. She said, "Yes." Having done so, she desired me to put my face close down to hers, when she said, "I dont know what the custom here is, and I thought I would like to ask you how you prepare a corpse for its burial. I stated to her as nearly as possible what had been our custom. She then told me that she thought perhaps she had things already made suitable to be buried in. "I have a chemise," said she that my mother made with her own hands, and describing it with such accuracy that I could not well mistake it, she said- "Take this- I was married in it, and I thought I would like to be buried in it". She then spoke of night-dresses made with plaited bosoms which she thought would do for a shroud and said- "Take one that I have never worn"- She gave other directions about the stockings, etc. I asked if she would have some of her hair saved for little Anna. "O yes," she says, "cut off <u>all</u> my back hair and send it to my Mother."

She then mentioned some things in connection with which she thought her friends would not have any <u>especially</u> pleasing associations, and wh. on that account, she preferred to have given "as they would be useful" to the ladies here (who, she said, had been so kind to her). She then made selections in her mind for most of the ladies, but did not quite finish because of fatigue.

Contrary to our expectations she continued thro' the night and the next day seemed no worse. She was occupied most of the day, in arranging as she had strength- her worldly affairs. I came to the foot of the bed as she was being laid back upon her pillows after the effort to write little Anna's name in her Bible. She looked up at me so very pleasantly as if she wished me to understand that she was <u>intensely</u> gratified in having succeeded in the attempt. The next morning I named the circumstance to her, and said, I did not suppose you had sufficient control over your mental powers to compose like that, even if you had the physical strength to write. She said- "Could you read it?" I replied that it was written quite well. She then added- "I did not know as any one could read it, I could not hold a glass of water when I did it."

On Monday morning we were all surprised to find her considerably revived, and we even hoped that the worst was over, and that from this time she might begin to amend- I remarked it to her but she replied with earnestness- "I want to go Mrs. Maclay"- Just as I was going to breakfast- she said- "By and by come and have prayers in the room- wont you?" Said she- "I should love to have you all come in and pray and while you were praying I should love to fly away to Heaven. Dont you think it would be delightful?"

I was with her but little on Monday as others rendered every needed assistance- On Tuesday morning I went to her bedside and saw that she was declining- She looked up at me and taking my hand in hers she said- "That hymn- 'Deathless Spirit'- has been in my mind all night- I could repeat only a verse or two of it"- I proposed reading it to her- she assented- and when I had finished the first verse, she said- "Isn't it beautiful?" I read on and she seemed to enjoy it much. After I had read it all she again alluded to the first verse and, repeating the words "Deathless Spirit"- she said- "It is a beautiful expression- isn't it?" Soon after this she became delirious and said but little during the day, except in an incoherent manner. Mrs. Gibson however came in just at dark and she recognized her and called her by name. Late in the evening, perhaps as late as eleven the fearful struggle began, and at midnight all was over. Her lifeless clay remained- but she was ranging the banks of the river whose streams make glad the city of our God- "The water of the river of life" was hers and there was "no more thirst"-

It is superfluous, perhaps, for me to add anything to you respecting her peculiar traits of character. You know them all- and knowing them- you will not wonder that we loved and valued her much both as a member of our mission and of the small social circle here.

From the first we found her all gentleness and possessed of a genuine piety and ardent missionary zeal- Her intelligence and refinement too, as well as her most affectionate regard for all around her, we could not but mark and appreciate- She was a step-mother too, and such another I never saw. One remark that fell from her dying lips was concerning him for whom it was "so hard to be left motherless twice".

She loved her Mother too- She loved dearly to think and talk of you- She loved to discover traits in others that reminded her of you- and how convulsively did she press your daguerreotype to her lips saying with triumphant faith "I think I shall see her soon". No one of her dear friends were forgotten by her in her last hours.

The sweet little Anna was with us, sharing the comforts of our nursery with my own little ones for awhile after her mother's death. I had a very good opportunity thus of becoming acquainted with her. My impression of her is that she greatly resembles her mother both in looks and disposition. Her gentleness is quite as prominent as was Mrs. Wentworth's.

As she grows older I fancy she will have the same fondness for flowers which was so manifest with her mother for she is never tired of tracing out the figures which she finds upon my de-laine and calico dresses, and she shows a decided preference to dresses of this kind, to those black and blue garments which her semi-barbarian nurses wear. Be advised she will never want for friends while she remains in Fuh Chau. She has, at present just as good care as any baby I know of, who has a Mother, and I trust she will continue to have every needed comfort.

Sensing, that in your sore affliction you are abundantly sustained by Him on whom you cast your every care, and that He will cause these afflictions which are but for a moment to work out for you a far more exceeding and eternal weight of glory, I am

Yours Very Truly & Aff.

Henrietta L. Maclay

Baltimore January 8, 1856

To the dear, bereaved Parents, Sisters
& Brothers of the late Mrs. Wentworth

Sorrowing Friends

How much do you need
sympathy & comfort beyond all that your warmest earthly friends
can offer you! But that which they cannot give "Your merciful
& faithful high Priest" can & will bestow on you.

"To him commend your cause.
His ear attends the softest prayer."

I admired the zeal of your once devoted, & now Sainted daughter
& Sister. She gave herself to the cause of her Lord & Master,
from the hallowed influence of love to him, & to the souls for
whom Christ died. A noble sacrifice! But in a good cause! She
early fell at her post, but it was not without the notice of her
Heavenly Father-How mysterious to us! Mysterious, because we
know now only in part. When we see in the light of Eternal world,
towards which we are all rapidly tending, we shall doubtless see
that all was wisely & graciously ordered. In the overwhelmings
of the sorrows produced by the demise of a beloved child, at
a point so far distant from her natal home, while in the spirit
of ancient piety, as exemplified in the character of bereaved
& afflicted Job, you say in those memorable words, first uttered
by him, "The Lord gave, and the Lord hath taken away, blessed
be the name of the Lord:" let this consideration relieve & cheer
you, the way from distant Fuh Chau, is just as direct & near
to Heaven, as from your own West Chester. You cannot but feel
fully assured that Sister Wentworth is "not lost- but gone before".
Follow on, you shall meet her again, in that happy place above,

"Where sickness & sorrow, pain & death,
Are felt & feared no more."

Let this be your motto, One tie less on Earth- One more in Heaven.
I commend you to him, who has said, "My grace is sufficient
for thee." Farewell

Yours affectionately

B. Waugh

58

April 29, 1856

To J. J. Lewis Esq & lady- A letter from Rev. R. Maclay came to hand this week which has been a long time on the way- it is dated Dec 1855- Thinking a portion would be grateful to your feelings I have caused the following to be made- D. Terry

Before this reaches you, you will have received the announcement of the death of Mrs. Anna Wentworth- a worthy and beloved Member of our Mission in this city. She died about 11 o'clock on the night of October 2nd 1855. Her death has produced a profound sensation in our Mission and has filled our hearts with grief. It seems but as yesterday that we welcomed her to our Mission and we can scarcely assure ourselves that she has really gone from us forever. We received her to our Mission-circle with a sincere and grateful joy: for we felt that she had come to this people on an errand of love and mercy. We observed too, her genial spirit and richly endowed mind, and we thought that in this land of heathenism, her presence would be to all a source of comfort and profit. We hoped that God, in mercy, would long spare her, in this field, to her family, and to the work upon which we felt assured she would concentrate all her energies. But how utterly have all our hopes been disappointed! After a residence among us of less than four months, she was taken to her reward on high. We fancied she had come to bless this people and to bless us by a life of faithful toil in the service of God, but He had ordained that she should accomplish those results by showing us how a christian can die.

Mrs. Wentworth possessed more than ordinary qualifications for the foreign missionary work, with a clear vigorous religious experience, and a worthy conception of the missionary work. She combined a refinement of mind, a sweetness of spirit and a steading of purpose which eminently fitted her for the work to which she had devoted herself. Her religious experience was very satisfactory. She seemed never to doubt her interest with Christ, her acceptance with God, or her title to a home in heaven. You received this conviction, not so much from her own statements on these points, as from observing the general current of her thoughts, and her experience during her last sickness. She felt assured that God for Christ's sake had pardoned her sins, had stamped His image on her heart and had written her name in heaven. Here were her "refuge and strength" here her impregnable fortress.

She cherished an exalted conception of the importance and greatness of the missionary work. She regarded it as the most honorable employment on earth, in comparison with which other pursuits seemed to dwindle into nothingness. The sincerity with which she entertained this view, she has given the most convincing proof: for in consequence of it she has left kindred, home, and country to carry to these ends of the earth the tidings of Salvation. From the day of her arrival to the hour of her death, her thoughts were full of this great subject. She loved the Chinese and longed to do something towards leading them to the Saviour. During the brief period when she felt able to do so, she addressed herself with energy to the work of acquiring this dialect, and preparing to labor among this people. This love for the work clung to her through her entire sickness, her waking thoughts on the subject were repeated in the dreams of the night, and plans for future labor in this her chosen field were intertwined with her visions of the glorious land "beyond the river".

Thus eminently qualified for her work in this heathen land it might seem strange that she has been so early removed but we repose with confidence on the thought that He who has taken her [torn section] wise to err, too good to be unkind. "It is the Lord" we will fall at his feet and adore. We cannot, at present, understand all the reasons for this mournful event or appreciate all its bearings: but may we not express, with profit, some of the thoughts it suggests. It certainly exerted an important and salutary influence on the religious experience of our departed sister that in obedience to the divine command, she gave herself to the work of God in China. She received great emulation in her last sickness from the fact that she had taken this step. Does she regret it now that she gazes on Him whose command she obeyed? The influence of this step on the kindred and friends of the deceased, who can estimate. Will her example be lost on the church? Is it nothing that in this age of infidel theories and Mammon worship, christianity can present such an illustration of its power? And with regard to that vast nation for whose good she suffered and beneath whose sod her mortal remains now rest in peace, will no blessing flow to any of its untold millions from this example of christian love and obedience?

We sympathize most sincerely with the Board and the Church in this affliction dispensation: and with our bereaved Brother in this Mission and with the bereaved family and friends in the United States we would mingle our tears in view of the death of one so worthy of their love. A few weeks previous to their embarkation it was our happiness to welcome Dr. Wentworth and lady to our home in Harrisburg. In conversation we seemed to live over the past and the hours sped entirely too swiftly away- A little while before we bade these precious friends a final farewell Mrs. C. remarked to Anna that she hoped they might meet again in the future & renew their delightful intercourse- To this Anna responded in a sweet & subdued manner. "No! I shall never return- I go expecting to die in China"- Then said Mrs. C. impulsively- "Why do you go?" Her beautiful answer was "it is no farther from China to heaven than from my own pleasant home in West Chester"- True- true- delightfully true- doubtless she has proven it true- On the wings of angels her disembodied spirit has mounted far above the disgusting abominations of degraded China. We gaze after her with an aching and tearful vision- We seem to hear through the glory rimmed cloud which intervenes, her sweet familiar voice saying as in other years-

   Hail, hail, all hail ye blood washed throng
   Sav'd by grace
   I come to join your rapturous song
   Sav'd by grace
   All, all is peace & joy divine
   And heaven & glory now are mine
   Oh hallelujah to the Lamb
   All is well-

May we with her one day assist to swell the chorus of Paradise-

         Most Affectionately

         Alfred Cookman

[Letter to Mrs. Lewis from Mrs. Peet]

Tuesday Sept. 26- I passed with Mrs. Wentworth in waiting upon and endeavoring to mitigate her pains. She was calm and manifested a sweetly subdued spirit. I inquired if she thought she should recover from this illness. She replied, "I think it doubtful", and continued, "I have had a great struggle in giving up my Father and Mother, the idea of not seeing them again in this world I could not dwell upon, but now it is otherwise. I have been enabled to resign them wholly and feel that it will be well. My babe too, I can give up. My Mother will take charge of her, and train her for God, this is pleasant to me." During the day she repeated several passages of scripture. Psalm 23, 2 & 4 verses. "He maketh me to lie down in green pastures, he leadeth me beside the still waters." The fourth verse she cited with deep fervor, as she did others. At one time when I was rubbing her limbs, she smiled and said, "I sometimes think when I see how poor I am- Can these bones be mine?"

The following night, Wed. 26, I watched with her. She was rather restless and suffered much pain. As the exertion of speaking seemed to produce nausea I avoided conversation. A little past midnight she asked if I would select a portion of scripture and read to her. A bible being near, I turned to the 46th Psalm. She lay perfectly quiet with one exception, when she exclaimed with emotion, "Oh how good every word of it." I read it rather slowly, but no sooner had I finished it than she requested me to read it again, which I did. After the second reading she said, "I have often derived comfort from that Psalm, but it never appeared so precious, as now". She shortly after fell into a slumber, upon waking she spoke of family, friends, of her sister, next younger than herself, and of her dear intimate friend, Miss Bell. I had before heard her allude to this young lady, and of her engagement to a son of one of our Missionaries, long in the field, (Dr. Goodell of Constantinople).

Thurs. morn. I left and did not see her again till the following Monday eve. Oct. 1, when I passed the night. She was wandering in her mind, though occasionally lucid intervals. I inquired, during one of those intervals, if she had received letters from her Father? "Oh yes", was her answer. I replied that I did not know but he was so full of business, he could not secure the time for writing. She then looked at me and smilingly said, "He is too full of his children not to write to them." I passed most of the day, Tuesday, with Mrs. Wentworth. During the morning she did not appear to suffer much pain, and exhibited great pa-

62

tience. As I stood over her bathing her head she remarked, "Since coming to China, I have not known health, scarcely seen a well day." I replied, "God will be glorified in your suffering." "Yes," said she, "it is all right."

Gentleness, patience, a readiness to be pleased, and gratitude for the least favor, were marked characteristics, during her whole sickness. Lovely and pleasant, while with us, and we deeply mourn her early, and sudden departure.

ERASTUS WENTWORTH

ERASTUS WENTWORTH

LETTERS

April 8th 1857 - June 15th 1858

Fuh Chau April 8, 1857

My dear Sir,

Your Jan. letter came yesterday. After detaining our Mar. mail in hand as long as possible we despatched it on the 31st, as a last chance, when lo: today turns up a forlorn hope. If our post boat can cut off the down steamer from Shanghai, this may accompany those already sent to the U.S. by this month's out-going mail. I enclose a Bill of Lading for a chest of tea shipped on the "Don Quixote". I send it's fellow to Mr. Terry. You had best write him about it. The ship is an elegant Clipper of 1400 tons & ought to be home in three months- say Apl- May- June- In July or August- the package should reach you if ever. I send also by the hand of a passenger, Capt. Wilson, to New York, to be forwarded by "Adams Express" a model of Anna's monument made of the same kind of stone- & of which all the monuments here are made- It is as many inches as the monument is feet & a pretty good representation of the original- The bottom stone is granite, though in the model it is all porphyry which gives the base a heavy look which the reality has not. Again the workman has exaggerated the mouldings of the shaft in the model & the whole lacks the simple grandeur of the thing as it appears on the spot. I hope it will reach you safely- But do not be over disappointed if it does not as it is only five or six lbs of black stone, & I can replace it hereafter if you desire.

"Fuh Chau beggars", Mr. Lewis inquires after. The streets are full of them. I have counted thirty of both sexes of all ages, in a ride of a mile & a half. They are blind, lame, halt, withered, old & exhibitors of every phase of disgusting deformity & disease to which our rotten humanity is subject. Begging is a profession. There is said to be a beggar king & the whole community under common laws, having common interests & possessing a common caste. Of their interior economy I know but little. I can tell only what I see daily. The beggars, besides being subject of some natural infirmity, loss of eyesight, stumps of hands, & stumps of feet, dress themselves in rags, filthy shreds of rush mattings, leave their hair shaggy, black their shrunk faces & withered arms, & look as squalid, filthy & wo-begone as possible. It is said that parents maim & blind their children to make them beggars- At any rate all the particularly filthy & disgusting abortions of nature & accident are brought up to the trade of poking about the streets asking alms- Here is a little girl- sitting on the cold stones of the bridge in winter or under the glaring rays of a fierce sun

67

in summer with the crown of an old straw hat turned up by her side- calling out in most piteous tones from early dawn to evening- "I'm blind- I'm blind". A few steps from there is a boy with a most terrific "scald head" prostrating himself at full length at the feet of the passers by, knocking his head against the stones & vociferating "Help- for the love of God". There is a man with two glassy transparencies stretched like drum parchments over eyeless sockets- two holes in the centre of his face where a nose ought to be & a lip-less mouth, level with his face or sucked into toothless jaws, led by another & sending a thrill of horror through all beholders. Some carry live snakes- some musical instruments- the women- squalid children led by the hand or slung to the mother's back- They are usually armed with a gong & whenever a customer enters a shop, one of them is sure to follow & raise such an infernal clatter that trading is impossible till she has been quieted with a cash. You ask why do the shopmen stand it? Why do they not turn them out at once? By law, each beggar in a given district is entitled to a "cash" a day from . . .

Fuh Chau April 25, 1857

Very Dear Friends-

The accompanying notes failed of reaching the last mail steamer & after being a week at the mouth of the river came back to my hand- I am too lazy to re-write & so forward them by the up-steamer to Shanghai with the usual motto of failure "better luck next time!" With this popular blessing I hope they will reach you safely- Time flies rapidly enough in some respects. In others it begs- I wait with impatience to learn of the safe arrival of my children in America- If they got home in season for the March mail I hope to hear from the . . . now six weeks ahead- If not- I cannot expect to learn of their welfare before July. O for telegraphs!

A week or ten days of summer sickness might finish my career without the enjoyment of the sad pleasure of knowing that my babes were safely lodged in homes five thousand leagues away- I have been in Fuh Chau almost two years. God only knows what the next two years may bring forth. At present there are in prospect even chances for remaining & for forcible expulsion from the country over its intestinal commotions or resistance to a foreign power- The country above us is over-run with banditti, cities plundered & burned- business at a stand & the entire population flying homeless from lawless plunderers- Fuh Chau is full of troops now, on their route to the scene of devastation & the viceroy himself starts in a few days for the scene of action. Hundreds of cowardly wretches in petticoats, with bows & arrows- bamboo shields- gingals & matchlocks, are stringing along the streets daily to the rendezvous. A hundred well armed foreigners would put ten thousand such to flight & I doubt not the more practiced rebels will rout them with ease- If you will look in Black's Atlas or any full map of China- find Fuh Chau & trace up the river Min you will find the next city up the river to Yenping- a few days sail in boats from here. Every place & all the country above this city is reported to be in the hands of the insurgents. They are in this province & considerably this side of the mountains that separate it from the next. If Yenping falls of which there is hourly expectation there is nothing to prevent their coming to Fuh Chau- They say their object is plunder & that they do not care to take the cities in which they find nothing but Mandarins & old clothes- They have heard that there are wealthy foreigners in Fuh Chau & they hope to come into easy possession of their treasure & opium.

69

Rumors always magnify as they spread like ripples in water so that we know not how much to believe- The merchants are putting their premises into a state of defence- Their treasure in boats, such up the country to buy teas have all returned- reporting fear of thieves & that there was nobody in the tea district to sell or deliver the teas. Half of this is shrewdly set down to the drive of the Canton men to create an alarm & thus raise the price of teas the coming year-

At the Pagoda Anchorage ten miles below are two armed opium ships & a British sloop of war sufficient to protect all the foreigners if once down there- At present we feel our apprehensions- It is time enough to provide for danger when it is near-

Kisses for Anna & love for all

E. Wentworth

My Dear Sir,

Your Dec. letter was read yesterday. I have as little confidence as you in physicians & trusted more to faithful nursing than to Dr. Welton in Anna's case. You wondered she was not ordered to Shanghai. After her confinement she was never able to go. Before her confinement she did not seem to need it & between that event & her death only about six weeks intervened. The first few weeks after accouchement it would have been impossible to remove her & after that she was too much reduced to think of it. With my present knowledge if I had the thing to do over again from the commencement- it seems to me I could prevent similar catastrophe- But alas! for our limited knowledge in this world- In shunning Scylla we fall into Charybdis. We avoid rocks & shoals only to founder in the open sea.

I am pleased to hear of Anna's improvement & that she is learning to think of me- My greatest pleasure in her situation is that she fills, in her little measure, the terrible chasm in your family circle produced by the death of her mother. Of course the loss is irreparable- but is this far compensable. I have felt my loneliness since my children left less than I expected to do- The first winter after Anna's death was terrible. I remember it with fearfulness now- Its long days & weary nights. Baby was then at Mrs. Maclay's. In the Spring she came home- just old enough to begin to be interesting & she brought instant sunlight. From that time till her departure, Jimmy & she & I were inseparable. She was bolstered up between us at the table- sprawling on the carpet in the study- hammering the piano in the parlor- or riding in our arms about the garden- or bestriding Leo- Jimmy's favorite great water Spaniel- & every day becoming more interesting- It was the cruelest thing I ever did in my life to send her to the nurse's cabin for the last time on board the Sancho Pansa- shouting "papa! papa!". The words ring in my ears still & then Jimmy's manly form standing in the gangway, waving farewells as our boat pulled slowly away from the vessel is an indelible picture upon my memory- Shall I ever see the darlings again. I fear not. Life is uncertain everywhere & doubly so in this treacherous climate- I am not wedded to life.

The long expected clothes came a short time ago- Terry never informs us what is coming & seldom tells us the name of the ship in which articles are coming. He likes to surprise us.

71

My health has been good this winter- Never better. The opening of Spring will be trying- More so than the heats of mid-summer. There are about three months in the year in which we simply vegetate. The throe of a single thought is sufficient to start perspiration & induce weariness. I never attempt to labor-This winter I have preached frequently- Our congregation is small but highly intelligent. The merchants are all well-bred & generally well-educated gentlemen- It is difficult to tell them anything they don't know & appeals to passion are out of the question before a scene of intellects as cool & calculating as those of the Judges of the Supreme bench- Maclay, Gibson & I preach Methodist fashion- with the usual modicum of want. The Presbyterians more swiftly read their essays- taking care not to set their manuscripts on fire by any inherent heat manifest or latent. We have baptized six or seven recently & others are inquiring-This is encouraging after laboring ten years- sacrificing four or more lives & expending a hundred thousand dollars- The new converts are quite zealous & exhort as long & as loud as their prototypes at home. One of them has been circuiting in the country, preaching- He has four interesting boys- the oldest sixteen or eighteen- who will all become Christians- of course- as in China-a man would never think of doing other than his father did before him. The American Board have about as many- but only two missionaries left- Six men to six hundred thousand Chinese in this city alone- Once here & acclimated- residence is very pleasant here. I am sure Anna would have enjoyed it. There is romance enough in the style of life & its surrounding circumstances to interest anyone- The scenery is beautiful- our houses are comfortable- society is increasing- Steam communication now connects us with the world once in two weeks & recent events in China make it certain that residence here will be more agreeable than ever- & certainly safer. The Indians are now nearly trampled into absolute submission- Canton is held by the throat- Pekin is menaced- & the whole empire may be considered under martial law from without. The Western nations will never back out-

We expect Mr. Read here before long. Had the Lord Bishop of Victoria here last Sabbath dressed in cambric & satin-to offset which I preached in the afternoon in the worst coat I could muster from my rusty wardrobe.

Truly yours

E. Wentworth

Fuh Chau June 15th 1858

My Dear Sir,

Either you are losing your regular habits of correspondence, or there is a "screw loose" in the mail communications somewhere between this & the dependencies of Great Britain vulgarly called the United States. As you are as methodical as clock work though you don't happen to have the misfortune to belong to the par excellence Methodists, I take it the mails are out of order, especially as no number of that very methodical paper the Christian Advocate & Journal has come to hand for two mails past. The poor Advocate has been coming here these ten years & never missed fire before except in a solitary instance. How frightened the poor thing will be to be found thus unwittingly a party to dereliction and delay. It will tremble for its membership in the church. Formerly whatever else was missing from John Bull's mail bags, I was sure of two Advocates & your monthly epistle. Even these have at last succumbed to that everlasting law of mutation which reigns throughout the universe.

I have no news to write- so little that I fancy it can be of as little interest to you to get my letters as to the rest of the family who have long since judiciously ceased to bore themselves & be bored by even semi-occasional communication with me in this far off land of Sinim. I heard from Charlty by way of James in March as Professor of Troy University- a great honor for one so young though not unmerited. It is fortunate that he did not stay West & that he did not apply for Dickinson- Troy is worth them both. Dr. Miller speaks in high terms of Charlty- says he is "well informed on every subject even to the minutia of politics."

Jim confided it to me as a great secret from Charlton- that he thought I would not babble because I was so far away, that Steph Darlington & Joe were engaged to be married. I suppose all the world knows the happy circumstance by this time. Mr. Sutter- now a teacher in the Mute Asylum at Hartford, Ct. and a candidate for the bar at some future time- speaks of a visit to you & little Anna- Says he saw only Mrs. Lewis & Charlton & spoke of the changes made by death & departures in your once joyous circle. All was now silence & quiet where once so much hilarity reigned. I fancy if he were to happen there at some time when the children were all at home he would find life enough to make up the echoes- though the autumn of life is necessarily more quiet than its boisterous spring.

73

The citizens of my native town Norwich, Ct. are preparing to celebrate a bi-centennial on the 5th & 6th September 1859. I hope grandpa Miner will have life & health to get there & other virtuous of Wyoming. I cannot be there- but have written them a letter. Poor families have gone up & rich ones down- I believe one of the richest men in the place at present- if still alive- is a Methodist tinker- that used to make pots & pans for the aristocracy. If the celebration had been in 1860- as had been talked for years- I should have made an effort to be there. As it is- I must give it up & with it the expectation of visiting home for some years to come if ever.

The board have sent out three ladies- but neither of them is to my taste. They will doubtless improve on acquaintance- but the memory of the departed is too strongly imprinted on my mind to be easily obliterated or supplanted. I freed myself to set about a second marriage as a duty. Its fulfillment brought unexpected pleasure- I have not the slightest expectation that the third would be equally fortunate. It is not in the nature of things that one man should have so much more than his share of the best that life affords. Perhaps I ought to content myself with the average & fulfill higher duties in the act. It is hard to set about a thing when you have no heart for it. The ladies sent out are good looking, well educated & well instructed housekeepers but have the misfortune to be measured by superior standards. I may conclude to give attention to the matter in the fall- but it is too hot to think of it at present- Perhaps the tenor of my life is such that I may not need another marriage. I could surely consent to it with great cheerfulness if such were the will of heaven- I am still building my house & have infinite daily trouble with ignorant Chinese mechanics. Their walls are one third mud, with just half burnt brick enough in it to keep it steady. Their lime is from oyster shells & only used in scanty sprinklings. Their boards are all sawn from small logs by hand and are peppered with knots of all sizes from peas & pigeon's eggs to the palm of your hand- Paint covers them up- but cannot obliterate the rough planing, the marks of which lie in your doors like furrows in a ploughed field. Floors are a series of hills and hollows where you are in danger of thumping your toe against the elevated ends of boards- & which shake under the tread like the guards of steamer under full head way-

I have just got a bell weighing 200 lbs for our church. We have had a ship bell hither to.

I like our new reinforcement very well- Dr. Durbin said for three years, "Where are the men?" & only found a man after a show of infinite trouble for China, & then turns round & finds ten for India in two years without the smallest difficulty in the world- . . . is not the only way in the world that should be indicted for humbug.

74

I am making great efforts now to get a press for Fuh Chau- You may not feel much interested in the mission work generally- but if this particular machine- as an effort to make the Chinese acquainted with English literature strikes you favorably & you are inclined to aid it- direct a donation to New York labeled expressly - "for a press for China".

Kiss baby for me & tell her papa is well-

Yours truly,

E. Wentworth

Joseph J. Lewis

ERASTUS WENTWORTH'S DIARY

to

ANNA'S PARENTS

January 16th 1856 - July 28th 1856

Saturday. Mar 1st 1856. Have been waiting - rather too impatiently for christmas - I fear - for the arrival of the February mail. None has come nor has any opportunity as yet presented itself of sending letters to Hongkong for the March mail. It matters not much as we have no letters to answer & no news to communicate. On Wednesday last we despatched our latest advices by the Fanny Forrester which will doubtless reach the United States in due course of time. We are gardening vigorously. The plot, including the house is one hundred & twenty by one hundred & sixty feet - beautifully laid out in squares, ovals, circles & terraced to accommodate the rise of ground. I have risen at six for three weeks past & inaugurated the day by vigorous exercise of the rake & hoe for an hour before breakfast beside running out at all the intervals of study to superintend the coolie in transplanting, cleaning & arranging for the coming season. I am having all the walks graveled. It is singular that nearly all its plants are shrubs very few are herbaceous. I can think of nothing that would have afforded dear Anna so much pleasure as the superintendence of this lovely spot. We took turns in it occasionally - particularly in summer moonlight evenings & cool mornings, the moon at one time breaking through the olive branches & at another the golden beams of the coming sun streaming through the foliage streaking the walks with brilliant pathways. Jimmy, "sister" & the kitten are frequent companions of my labor. "Baby" loves nothing better than a turn in the garden with the privilege of plucking now & then a harmless leaf & plunging it with due eagerness into her mouth - the infant's receptacle for everything new, whether silver, ivory or cats fur

Sunday. Mar 2nd. Bro Macbey preached at his own house to the assem-

Sample of Erastus' Diary
March 1st 1856

Fuh Chau Jan. 16th 1856

Last evening arrived our long, long expected mail bringing down dates from home as late as Sept 15th. They arrived in Hong Kong "Dec 2nd" according to Post Mark & consequently were not long coming up the coast- Sixty-eight days from the U.S. by steam and forty-four here by ship. There were eight envelopes & between twenty & thirty sheets & pieces amounting perhaps to fifty or more pages of closely written letters. I trembled as it was handed me by the servant & still more violently as I tore off wrapper after wrapper & recognized one well-known hand after another & laid the coveted treasure in a pile. The servant looked on in mute astonishment at the mass of communication before me -

And now where begin! Take up one at hazard--"Dear Anna" - Cannot read that! lamp too dim for suffused eyes! & the blood rushing from heart to brain blurs the sight with reeling shadows- To another & another & another "lie there! missions of love! lie there! ye are not for me." I have more than half wished in the selfishness of agony, they could quietly have found the depths of the ocean or the bottom of the Nile! Yet, the first excruciating thrust past, I have enjoyed line after line & page after page as if addressed solely to myself as I often do on other occasions- "how Anna would have enjoyed this or that".

It was not until after her death- so closely did her condition confine my attention & care, that I paid my first visit to Fuh Chau- three miles from here & clambered to the summit of the rugged hill inside the city wall crowned with the monastery, inhabited by the English missionaries, & grounds beautified for the residence of the officers of the British Consulate. High up from the monastery itself rises an altar crowned peak- reached by flight after flight of granite steps & over topped by an urn for incense carved out of a gigantic boulder- As I stood for the first time on this lofty eminence panting for breath & surveying in awed silence its sublime & commanding prospects I almost cursed myself, if that is not too harsh an expression, that I had not brought Anna hither to see & enjoy it before she died. There was a month after our arrival in which she might have been brought hither by coolies & it seemed to me that one ought not to go to Heaven - even without witnessing so glorious a panorama when the view was to be obtained at so little expense-

At the base of the hill to the North lay the city- so compactly built as to look like so many square miles of tiled roof, slightly inclined, ornamented everywhere with the carved, hornlike projections & elevations that form so striking a feature of Chinese architecture & intersected by streets & lanes so narrow as to look like mere lines at a distance. Two towering pagodas are the sole relief to the sombre expanse, unrelieved by chimnies, spires, & variations in altitude & color so striking in a city of the West. Around the whole undulates the wall with its parapets, buttresses, towers, gates & watch towers. Beyond, frown the mountains, smile the valleys. It is the centre of a glorious amphitheater. It is, or rather, isn't the basin of some magnificent lake, or inland sea, from which the water has escaped through earth-quake opened barriers, leaving only the serpentine Min, winding among the green islands & garden flats & reflecting the towering peaks whose bases it laves with its quiet waters on their way to the sea. Not less serpentine are the retreating masses of sombre roofs pouring along continuously from the South gate to the river- spreading themselves up & down either bank & climbing the hills on the opposite side, on the top of which gleam in the distance the clustering residences of the foreigners, with the broad cross of St. George floating over the English Consulate & the Stars & Stripes fluttering over the American & thus indicating the exact locality of our own beautiful Olive Orchard & its comfortable cottage.

I wish Anna could have seen it, & I wish she could see the missives of affection brought by every mail. But where the use of wishing? There I turn the weapon upon myself & feel again for the ten thousandth time the "iron" piercing my own soul. I ought to find consolation where she found it when she said, "I shall see them all ere long" & believe that she had had the privilege denied her while living, that of looking into the hearts of those what love her & drinking thence such sympathy as pen never put on record. But whither- have I wandered?-

As usual I despatched those epistles that were furthest from the heart first. Those addressed to me, those that dealt in news & indifferent matters & at length was dreamily aware of the contents of the whole pile & then went to bed to weep myself to sleep,- excited, restless, agitated & broken for the whole night. This morning I gave the dear pages a more careful perusal reading most of them aloud for Jimmy's benefit who will scarcely allow a word of their contents to escape him so eager & covetous for home information do time & isolation make us.

How must it be with our neighbors the Spanish Jesuits immuned in the parsonage of the Romish Church near our new chapel, who when they left Spain for Fuh Chau dropped all correspondence with relatives & friends & became as literally dead to former associates as if the coffin lid & earth had closed upon their faces.

Yet, into how many home scenes did these silent pages introduce us exiles. There were my sisters on a visit at home when they wrote & the Northern package contained letters to Anna & me from my father- Dr. Miller, my brother Noyes of Norwich- sisters Abby- Frances (Mrs. Miller)- Elizabeth (Mrs. Alexander) & Nancy, at home on a visit from Virginia. From the South- Mr. Lewis- several times over- Mrs. Lewis- the late sent letters not excepted- Lettie, fourteen or fifteen pages of highly interesting particulars- Willie & Allie, the venerable grandsire Miner, Carrie Thomas, McVeagh, Mrs. Keene & Andrew Longacre & Cassie Bell. I am glad my "Notes by the way" gave the pleasure they were intended to produce & while Anna, notwithstanding all my diffidence on the subject, always insisted they would produce- The dear girl heard nearly all, even of its late pages. It was dropped immediately after & I have not had the heart to truss up in bad penmanship scenes & occurrences in which it seems to me you will no longer have any interest. Life has become a dull monotony. If it has any enjoyment it is intimately associated with the never ending feeling how Anna would enjoy this. When I have had two or three of the missionaries to dine with me, or have dined at Mr. Maclay's, as on Christmas, or Mr. Baldwin's as on the week following New Years I have asked myself the same question. Above all I propose it day after day, as at the hour of twilight I drop in at the nursery to inquire of the bright & beautiful, radiant eyed "Anna Lewis" if she will come to papa "for a little while". She was five months old on the 12th- yet strange to say, though she has seen me almost daily, she is shy of me yet. She loves to sit on my knees, between my arms while I play on the melodeon when she will alternately look & wonder, & chuckle & jump, at the manifest risk of pitching forward upon the instrument & bruising her little chubby Lewis nose upon the keys. In a few days she is coming home to live with us. After a good deal of cogitation we have concluded to put her to house-keeping with her two nurses in our chambers. Her faithful Ling Choah is like a mother to her & the wet nurse E-yong Choah (in English "Mrs. Wood-House" & Mrs. "Sheep Fold"- or as Maclay bungles it, "E-you Choah" "Mrs. Oil Jar!") is equally careful & attentive. I think we shall like the change prodigiously.

81

January 26th-

Miss "Anna" and her nurses have been now several days domiciled with us. Their residence is the chamber reached by stairs from the verandah, and totally disconnected with the house. The women are never allowed inside unless bidden for a special purpose. Indeed no Chinaman has access in-doors but the table-boy, who is the responsible steward of the establishment inside. You could not trust yourself to claim your own eyes, if these thieving varlets were allowed to range unwatched through the house- It seems mean & degrading to keep suspicious oversight of those constantly about you but the Chinese do it themselves & expect nothing else from us & take advantage of any slackness to exercise their natural propensities for pilfering & wronging their employer.

Every morning "Anna" descends to the Library after getting dressed and spends an hour or two with "brother Jimmy" & "Papa" while her women breakfast, or as the phrase is here, "eat their rice." She is usually quite sedate on these visiting occasions having little to say and being exceedingly chary of her smiles. She likes the looks of our kitten- but the kitten cannot endure the sight of her & flies the room the moment the baby enters. I don't know how we shall introduce them to each other. Jimmy has the promise of a puppy, which we think will make a playfellow for her- Here she sits lashed into an armed rocking chair amusing herself & us till sleepiness or hunger call her upstairs again.

Ling Choah is as faithful & devoted as even Long-or, as you would call it Eē-Yong Cho-ah is a faithful nurse, but a termagantish woman. Her wages are extravagant now for one of her class but she renewed her demands to-day. The new application was founded on the fluctuations in the Fuh Chau money market, which is now undergoing the fourth or fifth grand upset since our arrival. When we came paper money was unpopular but the banks would not discount- so iron cash was scarce and copper cash out of circulation. Because we were foreigners we got about two thousand iron cash a week to pay chair coolies & were as careful of it as if it had been so much gold. At least I was- Anna-dear girl couldn't bear to handle the cumbrous stuff- because it begrimed her fingers & wondered why I was so particular about it. The tailors felt themselves to be a privileged class & stipulated for half paper & half iron cash for their weekly wages- In a few weeks the market was flooded with iron cash and the government banks passing over to the opposite extreme refused to take it in exchange for the bills & so iron cash became unpopular & the bills gained the ascendant. Latterly government has repudiated the iron cash altogether till within a week it has vanished from circulation altogether. Copper cash & bills are now the currency, the former being of course greatly the more valuable- as you may judge from the fact that sixty copper cash are worth one hundred cash in bills. I paid the nurse her weekly fifteen hundred cash to-day & she declined it- wanting me to pay the amount in copper cash. This would be giving her nearly four dollars a month & board whereas Ling Choah works for two & finds herself. I fear she and I will part company before I submit to any such "squeeze". My teacher tells me upon inquiry that the iron cash have not gone entirely out of circulation but have depreciated fifty per cent- paper as already seen has depreciated forty. All our dollars are "chopped"- that is stamped all over & are exchanged by weight- The Chinese weigh everything ever moved probably for the greater convenience of cheating. We burn pine at about $3. per cord- brought to the door in cut & split bundles- probably water soaked to increase its gravity. It would have saved all trouble in the wood chopping line if Anna's little cooking stove had been four inches longer-

January 27th-

For two Sundays we have attended service with the Missionaries of the American Board. Our effort to invite the Ch. of Eng. in an American enterprise has been a dead failure & has even resulted in our expulsion from the assemblies of the Church altogether. They can read prayers & that is all they desire- Preaching they do not value a brass farthing- And the devil cares as little for their prayers. We offered them the free use of our new chapel every other Sunday for English Service- Liturgy- Litany & all & bore ourselves to attend it- if they would give us an American service on the alternate days in which to pray that the Lord would grant Franklin Pierce "in health & wealth long to live" & strengthen him that he might vanquish & overcome all his enemies" particularly the handy bottle & that the loving Lord would "abate the pride, assuage the malice & confound the devices" of all the enemies of Uncle Sam. The American Church Episcopal has had the good sense to leave out all this antiquated nonsense which Dr. Welton puts on his surplice to repeat Sunday after Sunday with as much pride & pomp of solemn diction as graced the age when Episcopalism was hatched from Popery- I do not regret the change- I only wish the Americans had as much national pride & spirit about their religion as have the attachés of the Establishment. Brother Hartnell read us a sermon from a book last Sunday. To-day brother Peet read us one of his own. A very good production. Next Sunday I am to preach at Bro. Maclay's.

January 28th-

Paused, as I often do, in my evening's walk over Anna's grave. There has been no frost but the cold has deadened the grass as it does in the late fall with us. Yet the turf on her grave is green. Only one sod is dead and out of that are keeping numerous leaves beautifully & brightly green & contrasting pleasingly with deadness & winter desolation all around there. The hardy olives preserve the dark green lines of their heavy foliage & the pines like pines in all countries are darker still.

January 29th-

Gibson & I are talking building a substantial brick house on our vacant lot- double for the use of two families. O that the chief incentive to such an undertaking was still with us. It will be of little use to me I fear but I must labor for the good of those who come hereafter. The house I now occupy is pretty but wood & one of the first built by the Chinese after English models- Of course its architecture & structure are imperfect- Beside the builders had a mistaken idea of the climate and made it too summery- too low between joints (two feet).

I shall hate to leave the beautiful garden. Our view of the river & city is shut off since Consul Jones constructed his huge house directly in front of us. The new lot is one of the highest spots in the vicinity and commands extensive views of the river, city- suburbs & mountain scenery. A lovelier spot for building could not be found in Fuh Chau. The lot is spacious being 120 ft wide by 240 deep- purchased for $600, & would now command $3000 to $6000, such has been the rise of value in foreign property here within twelve months.

January 30th-

"Anna" & the cat are getting acquainted- Pussy will sit in Sister's lap in the big rocking chair & purr while baby pulls her hair with intense pleasure- Now & then baby gets her fingers in kitty's mouth who bites playfully- Whereat baby disengages her "paddy" with a rueful face & a quiet grunt of astonishment & displeasure.

January 31st-

The last day of the month has come & with it a bundle of papers from N.Y., most of which we have seen before. Mr. Spooner starts tomorrow for San Francisco- via Hong Kong- by whom I send a large packet of letters for the U.S. This bundle must go with the rest So farewell for the present.

84

March 1st 1856- Saturday

Have been waiting rather too impatiently for Christiones-
I fear for the arrival of the February mail. None has come nor
has any opportunity as yet presented itself of sending letters
to Hong Kong for the March mail. It matters not much as we
have no letters to answer & no news to communicate. On Wednesday
last we dispatched our latest advices by the Fanny Forrester
which will doubtless reach the United States in due course of
time. We are gardening vigorously. The plot, including the house
is one hundred & twenty by one hundred & sixty feet- beautifully
laid out in squares, ovals, circles & terraced to accommodate
the rise of ground. I have risen at six for three weeks past &
inaugurated the day by vigorous exercise of the rake & hoe for
an hour before breakfast, beside running out at all the intervals
of study to superintend the coolie in transplanting, clearing &
arranging for the coming season-I am having all the walks gravelled.
It is singular that nearly all its plants are shrubs, very few are
herbaceous. I can think of nothing that would have offered dear
Anna so much pleasure as the superintendence of this lovely spot.
We took turns in it occasionally- particularly in summer moonlight
evenings & cool mornings. The moon at one time breaking through
the olive branches & at another the golden beams of the coming
sun streaming through the foliage streaking the mists with brilliant
pathways.

Jimmy, "sister" & the kitten are frequent companions
of my labor- "Baby" loves nothing better than a turn in the garden
with the privilege of plucking now & then a harmless leaf & plunging
it with due eagerness into her mouth- the infant's receptacle
for everything new, whether silver, ivory, or cat's fur-

March 2nd- Sunday

Bro. Maclay preached at his own house to the assembled
American Missionaries- Mrs. Jones wife of Amer. Consul, Mr
Williams merchant, Brit. Consul- Medhurst- Vice Consul Hale
& a student interpreter present. Afterward I administered the
communion- It was a quiet & profitable time. At evening as Jimmy
& I were strolling along one of the cemetery paths young Mr.
Duus (pronounced deuce) overtook us & said our last chance for
mail carriage by way of Amory had expired for the month.

March 3rd- Monday

At 4 P.M. met the Missionaries at Bro. Gibson's for

monthly concert at the conclusion of which I baptised their babe "William Franklin"- the latter name having been apprehended after he heard of the death of his brother Frank at the Wesleyan University. Both names are from departed brothers- The living wear the names of the dead and soon to hand them to a later posterity. Mrs. G. was out to church yesterday for the first time since her confinement. She is decidedly better.

March 4th- Tuesday

Our mission to-day comes into possession of the house built by Russel & Co- a spacious building which we design for a girl's school, if any sister Wilkins will come out & take charge of it. Mrs. Maclay's three boys are school enough for her without the superintendence of Chinese girls. She proposed to take two or three of the half grown girls into her own family to teach domestic affairs, such as holding the baby & chasing after Rolly & Arty- The little-footed lard-haired beauties were too old to be domesticated in any such way & their withdrawal rendered the teacher's services useless & the school is suspended for the present.

March 5th- Wednesday

"Bang! bang! pop! pop!" by daylight- crackers firing in all directions like a 4th of July. It is the twenty-ninth day of the First month & sacred to some divinity. The Chinese number their months like Friends & have escaped the barbarism of disfiguring portions of God's time with the names of bad heathen princes & worse heathen divinities. They divide time like everything else- decimally, as far as possible- think the Sabbath a stupendous folly & observe no general abstinence from labor except New Years & its holidays which are most industriously improved by all classes in gambling. At 4 o'clock I attended missionary prayer meeting- Every afternoon we lock up the house & go out- Tonight when I returned I passed through the kitchen on my way to the dining room in the rear. The servants were at supper- Around a deal table on stools like carpenter's saw horses were huddled a swarthy group, just discernable in the twilight & grim & smoky dimness natural to the place- A stone bowl of chopped greens- boiled & seasoned with salt stood in the center of the table- leaves fried in lard & chopped fine- bowls of salted eels & other condiments surrounded it. Every sitter had his bowl of hot rice- boiled in little bamboo baskets poking it merrily into his mouth with chopsticks- & there sat, in the arms of her nurse "baby"- looking on most intently & illuminating the darkness- like a gem in a pile of charcoal- Poor little outcast- She is the only real missionary among us, for she is the only one that loves the hea- thens- I fear hers is not the wholly disinterested benevolence which some theologians account the height of christian perfection.

I rather imagine it is to be mixed up with the memory of the good milk on which she is thriving. She jumped & sprung to come to me & I took her in my arms into the brightly lighted library- where, surrounded by the comforts of civilization she seemed more at home than in the murky vestibule of ladies in which I found her.

March 6th- Thursday

Studied as usual diligently till dinner time at 2 o'clock & then went out to make application- "Where are you going?" asked a Chinese savant. "Into the fire"- said I- by making an e instead of an i in the pronunciation of a word like the one I wanted to use to say "yonder". The bystanders stared but wondered at my meaning till some one happily guessed at the word & wanted to set me right- They are as grave as Frenchmen where an English- man would split his sides with merriment. I was more successful with a knot of workmen among whom I paused, who began with "What is your coat made of?" "What did it cost?" & actually dis- sected & inventoried my apparel from outside coat to undershirt- hat to boots- watch- pocket knife & pencil. The last they wanted to beg, I told them they could buy one at the foreign store for five cents that would last them a year or two. A foreign pencil or pen is an awkward thing in the hands of a Chinaman who sticks it straight up in the air & awkwardly produces faint impressions upon paper.

The foreign community have been commenting for some days upon a sacrilegious outrage committed by the Chinese out of revenge doubtlessly. Two bodies- one of a boy twelve years old- another of a child- were torn from their graves in the night & exposed to dogs & vultures till nothing but the bones remained before they were removed. They bury only two or three feet deep & there were some poor wretches that had been placed perhaps too near the cemetery of some nabob whose relatives took this method of signifying their displeasure. It is a high handed offence- considering the wonderful respect the celestials have for the dead. In widening the roads winding in every direction over our romantic cemetery hills the Brit. vice consul was obliged to respect every grave & stone & tomb however humble. The Chinese will not scruple to sell a grave for a round price- but remove the remains carefully to some other locality-

In walking out tonight- I stumbled upon a child perfectly blotched with the scabs of recent small-pox- I gave it a wide berth you may be sure- The orientals do not understand & will not extensively practice vaccination- Innoculation is common- A mason with a terrible bruise on his leg asked of me, as they often do, a specific- I advised him to wash it & bathe it in oil- certainly harmless if not remedial- His limbs & water were certainly no intimate acquaintances.

March 7th- Friday

Stood an hour in the warm sun- with an umbrella however, to see the masons commence the foundation of our new chapel below the Maclay's house. It is "founded on a rock" & I hope "the gates of hell will not prevail against it." In two months we have cut down to a level a most unsightly pile of rocks upon a precipitous side hill fronting the river & city, so rugged, that the thickly settled portions around had never intruded upon their forbidding baldness. The natives could neither build upon them or sustain the expense of their removal- so we bought the lot for a song, about $150, & by expending a hundred in chiseling & dirt carrying, have produced a beautiful level to the wonder of the Chinese & the admiration of foreigners. By a long flight of hewn granite steps it opens upon the street & will be made accessible both from the level below & the hill above- Perhaps I can give you a rough idea of the location by what the geologists call a section outline of the district- starting from the river below Mr. Maclay's, & terminating at the top of the hill. See below.

March 8th- Saturday

Jimmy, boy-like, is disposed to amuse himself with "tricks upon travellers". Yesterday he put some dough-made lizzards on the walls- which looked so natural that I recommended him to catch them & send them in spirits to the Smithsonian Institute. Today he was teaching my teacher English & when I came in, the grave disciple of Confucious, proud to show his new acquisition cries out, "How do-you-do? you beggar!" A roar of laughter from Jimmy & Le Wock caused him to ask again "good?- no good?" He apologized crest-fallen while I rated the boys for their imposition upon the teacher
and second hand
impudence
to me.

Thus you see that dear Anna's resting place is only about a quarter of a mile from the river & twenty rods, or half rifle shot from my house in the immediate neighborhood of both consulates & the houses of Russel & Co- Wetman & Co- King & Co & but a little further removed from Mr. Maclay's-

March 9th- Sunday

Went to Mr. Peet's to church today. They live at the head of the island- As it is annually overflowed by the June floods, precisely like the bottom lands of the Missouri & Mississippi rivers, with their islands- the houses are raised a story- that is the foreign residences. I believe the Chinese take their chance with the fishes for a day or two at the height of the waters & it is said actually scrub out their houses on that occasion! It is a pity the visitation was not monthly instead of being annual- As it is they do not actually suffocate in piles of filth breast high, since the kindly waters once in a twelve month afford a general purgative.

Mr. Peet's family reside in the second story & have a beautiful up-river view from the West verandah- The parlor is neatly furnished, though, as it was one of the first houses built here by foreigners there is as liberal a display of posts & beams & wide doors as in a country built house in the interior of Pennsylvania. Female taste has covered these unsightly excrescences with beautiful Chinese wall paper & a new rush carpet-settees-sofas-rugs, rocking chairs, lounges & a foreign stove, with curtains to the doors & pictures upon the wall give the whole a home-like appearance. They have been sixteen years in the East. He is a portly man & she a woman of the build of Mrs. Lewis without her erect carriage. Mr. Peet preached, or rather read an essay on St. Paul. There were Mrs. Baldwin with two girls & a boy- Mrs. Doolittle with her little son- Mrs. Maclay with a brace of

boys & altogether quite a congregation. Mrs. Gibson was out though I had supposed her confined at home with diarrhea. The singing on these occasions is delightful.

March 10th- Monday

Deluged with Chinese workmen. A tailor on the verandah is making Jimmy shirts- A garden coolie is removing rubbish & transplanting shrubs- Two men at one corner of the house are making mud-brick- such I suppose, as the walls of Babylon were built of, by pounding, or rather ramming yellow, clayey, earth into a huge mould to raise up my garden wall next neighbor Jone's kitchen, to shut out the slops and impertinence of his servants- Two men at the opposite corner of the house are building a hen yard under Jimmy's direction- who has the Shanghai chicken fever this spring as badly as Professor Tiffany- Half a dozen are bringing gravel for the walks, which already present a fine appearance from the verandah of the house as well as from the verandahs of the adjoining houses- My teacher has not come & I am at liberty to superintend them all. This outdoor exercise does my health good. I go to bed tired & sleep soundly-

March 11th- Tuesday

This morning a sturdy countryman made his way into the yard with two basket loads of flower or rather shrub slips on his shoulders- He wanted a dollar for the lot- I offered him 500 cash- about 25 cents which he readily took and set out the plants along a vacant border- We have done a deal of transplanting & a coolie is engaged daily in turfing embankments, filling up & cutting down- The admiration manifested by darling Anna for bright flowers & waving leaves and the tall trees toward which she now and then fixes her upturned gaze as if she expected to greet the eyes of her sainted mother bearing maternal love upon her orphaned daughter through some one of their blue openings more than repays our trouble.

March 12th- Wednesday

Mrs. Maclay has detected her wet nurse thriving "a la Chinois"- While they were at church on Sabbath day she helped herself to thread- linen- & the like & last night rumaged the pockets of Mrs. Maclay while they slept & abstracted a bad dollar & a 2000 cash bill- nearby another dollar which they found secreted in her tobacco box- though she denied taking it. They decide not to send her away as they are all of the same color-

March 13th- Thursday

Flower man comes again. A few days ago he promised

to bring us everything we asked for. There was nothing I could get into Chinese that he had not. "Peonies?" "Yes"- "Pinks?" "Yes"- "Lilies?" "Yes"- "Bamboo plants"- "Yes of all heights from eight to thirty feet." "Will you bring in a lot tomorrow?" "O yes with pleasure." Tomorrow passed & he did not come- To-day he came again with precisely the shrubs he brought the other day & wanted as before a dollar or two for the lot- I offered him 400 cash-about twenty cents but he shouldered his load & went in pursuit of other customers. Mrs. Maclay gave him 200 cash for a single rose bush which she said bloomed all winter. We are deluged with rose bushes- I have transplanted twenty from about the house to the lower part of the garden to trail on & over the wall between us and Consul Jones. Flowers are like music- intrinsically beautiful-and yet like music they need old associations to render them spirit stirring. We are surrounded with magnificent blooms- white-red-purple- large and small peeping from the turf & bending from lofty boughs- but we are ignorant of their names & have no love-bouquet associations with them whatever. The rose is almost the only one that is familiar & we are crowding the embankment of the terraces with blue violets & primroses from the hills. I long for a snowball bush- a lilac tree- a few peonies- lilies & pinks & tulips such as we see at home- Just as we hail "Lang Syne" after an opera song, or Rory-O'More at the beat of a brilliant polka-

March 14th- Friday

Another package of dreaded but welcome letters from home- arrived in Hong Kong Jan. 30th & are answers to ours of July 20th which left Hong Kong in the August mail- Mr. & Mrs. Lewis- Mr. & Mrs. Cookman- Mrs. Elizabeth Pugh- the Misses Kelly & one of the Scrively's of Carlisle- The reading suspended my morning's work & Chinese took a holiday in favor of English Manuscript. My teacher wondered over them- compared the hand writings but could see no difference- All looked alike to him. They know each others writing as we do- but to me it is all alike. His brother came to-day- as did his son at New Years to see a foreign house. Admired the carpets-mirrors-portraits-daguerreo-types-melodeon-clock-astral lamps, piano, etc. It is only on such occasions that the now neglected instrument gets a peep at daylight & fresh air. They examined my sleeping room & admired my broad French bedstead & spring mattress-brushes for all services & convenient bathing establishment- All novelties to them.

Circumstances have precipitated it a little. A week ago or so Mrs. Gibson gave birth to a boy. She wished Ling Choah for a while as her own nurse understands not a word of English & is not instructed in English customs. This brought extra labor upon Mrs. Maclay- who has already had twelve wet nurses- heaven save the mark! to her "Charley" while Anna has managed with

91

two after we got to going & would probably be with the first if she had remained here, to this day. Two days ago, her wet nurse, Mrs. "Oil"- or "Sheep"-House fell out with Mrs. M's washerwoman, who procured her the situation for the consideration of 1000 cash about half a dollar, 300 of which she had paid & stood indebted for the remainder. The husbands of these "ladies" met on the street this week & after various threats & the usual amount of brawl, Mr. He- of the "Oil-Jar" paid over to Mr. He of the "Wash-Tub"- five hundred cash more- When the news of the street encounter reached the ears of the short pantaletted "daughters of China", they fell upon each other like Turks & Russians, & clawed & squalled like mad-cats, in defiance of the sacredness of the premises of a neutral- excepted by the "Treaty" & his credentials as a christian missionary- Mrs. "Sheep-Choah" was by no means as pacific as her name would indicate. She is a great stout two-fisted field woman & drew blood from the face & arms of her little antagonist.

Mrs. M. parted the Amazons- the one of whom vowed by Budh that she would not return to Mrs. M's. until the other was removed- I bring her here- to save her being sent further away. Gibson lost one valuable woman by straining a point of etiquette. He advised her to get longer pantalettes- She replied she was not going to wear long-legged trousers, like a man, to please anybody, & walked off.

Ling Choah has a vile husband, a wretch who would sell her for a matter of five & twenty dollars- If a foreigner wished to buy her, however, he would raise his price to a hundred. I would give $25 for her for Anna, notwithstanding the risk of the imputation of being a slave-holder. She is a slave now- working for $2 a month, & paying over full one half of it to a base lazy, thieving vagabond, whenever he can clutch her in the street- for I have kicked him off our premises when he came there with his beggarly insolence- He will even take her money from Le Wock, her nephew when he is out to buy provisions for her. During the week she spends at Mr. Gibson's she petitions to be set across to this river bank in a boat, instead of crossing the bridge from the island, fearing her husband may catch her and sell her without our knowledge! Now,- Kennet-Square,- what shall we do? Twenty five dollars would free her from intolerable oppression, but would make a christian missionary a legal slave holder. If he was a native & purchased the woman for a wife it would alter the case- He must assume absolute proprietorship from the hands of the husband or her ownership reverts to father or brothers, who sold her to the ragamuffin & would not scruple to see her again, at half price, as a piece of second hand furniture to any other scoundrel that might take a fancy to her.

She is a woman of education & refinement for one of

her class, & _proudly_ _attached_ to the rascal that abuses her. A few months ago he was arrested for stealing an article from one of Gibson's servants. Nothing could be proved & he was set free though all devoutly wished, both Chinese & Americans, that he might get flogging or imprisonment- Ling Choah was as much distressed as if he had been innocent & told Madame Peet that "if they were to be suspected of stealing, she could not live any longer with missionaries". I want her- & want her free from her husband & family- so that she may accompany Anna to America by & by without let or hindrance. But if I buy her- What of Mrs. Stowe's next Cabin & Key? There is a distinction which theologians & lawyers(?), moralists & reformers perpetually overlook - the difference between _equity_ and _justice_. We aspire after absolute _justice_, but absolute justice implies absolute knowledge & this resides with God alone. The highest attainable human justice is _making_ _things_ _as_ _right_ _as_ _possible_ with our limited knowledge of relations, this is no more than simple equity. The whole world is acquitted or condemned on circumstantial evidence & its judgement day history will convict courts of _justice_- facetiously so called of as many wrongs & rights. It is often said, "two wrongs do not make a right". This may be, but wrong may be offset against wrong to produce right, or perhaps omitting the moral element, which enters by human agency, evil may balance evil for the production of good. Virulent acids and destructive alkalies combine in harmless & useful salts. Shall I make a slave of a slave & better her condition? This is what the whites have been doing for a hundred years. The negroes were bondsmen at home to craft, cruelty & ignorance. Bondage to a second party has brought them along side of full liberty & themselves though slaves still into general betterment & comparative freedom- "Justice! justice! set them free- absolutely free & that instantly". Softly-Kennet Square- take things as they are & make them as right as possible. "Set them free" cries Kennet. What if they cut the throats of their masters? "Yes, justice demands blood for blood"- This is getting at the right through holes in the bodies of the masters- Without remuneration? "Yes- they have paid for themselves over & over again & there is no right of property in man"- Would the sudden impoverishment of thousands of your own color be getting at a right through a wrong? - If it divides the Union? "Yes, if it divides the Union." The Union as it is- one party suffers- divide & there are _three_ suffering parties & the miseries of the present sufferers unalleviated. There are two sides to the question. There is immense wrong- but take care court of equity, that the satisfaction of the many eventuate not in the production of wrongs of still greater magnitude. But all this is nothing to the purpose. Shall I buy Ling Choah?

Last week Mrs. Maclay spent several days with Mrs. Baldwin & took our little fairy along. Coming back, Madam Maclay's great weight combined with the addition of her boys to break the chair poles & down came the whole edition of white humanity in the middle of a Chinese street. Five years ago a lady would have been insulted in such a case. As it was the servants picked up the boys in their arms & trudged ahead while the crowds parted respectfully to allow her to cross the long bridge to the island in perfect safety on foot- Its unusualness attracts attention, for high-bred ladies and dignitaries seldom go on foot. I have never seen a Mandarin, even of the lowest degree, who was not in his chair, preceeded and followed by a retinue of attendants. If he is of very high degree, he is accompanied by soldiers, who look remarkably harmless in petticoats, & preceeded by a bully with a fierce look & harsh voice crying out to "make way". The crowds shirk to the sides of the narrow streets & suspend conversation & business till his mightiness has passed, when travel & commerce resume their wonted interminable flow.

January 26th-

The John Wade is "circulated" for Hong Kong and by her I made a hasty mail for the U.S.- letters to Mr. & Mrs. Lewis- one to the Board petitioning for the addition of a minister to our Mission forces, & another to General Conference asking for the visit of a bishop to Fuh Chau- If Bishop Scott should be appointed Charlton may get the position of "traveling companion" & pay his little niece a visit at the expense of the church & a few months of time.

March 15th- Saturday

Is a busy day- Things have to be put in readiness for the Sabbath by strict oversight of those who know no Sabbath only as it is taught them by christian example. Our missionary work begins-you see-right here by inculcating the necessity & sanctity of a day of rest. Foreigners employ hundreds of natives & so if they would all strictly observe the Sabbath it would soon get them in the habit of attending to this most important agent of religious training. At evening comes the wet nurse for cash. The tailor is to be paid off & the coolie.

March 16th- Sunday

At 1 o'clock P.M. I preached in Bro. Maclay's parlor to a small company about twenty in all, & spent the evening there talking over home matters upon which when the inspiration serves we delight to dwell.

March 17th- Monday

My expenses the last week were fourteen dollars- enormous for myself, Jimmy & babe. This morning I gave the cook five "chopped dollars"-in other words-Spanish dollars- so beaten over & indented with Chinese stamps ("chops") as utterly to efface everything like an inscription- Out of some of them some shrewd genius has picked a grain or two of silver & ingeniously filled up the hole with some metallic composition- in others some shrewd dealer has picked out the bare metal & showed the hole made by dishonesty some times quite through the dollar- Of course it is impossible to dispose of this deteriorated coin at par- So it goes by weight. In an hour- cookie returned from market bringing the dollars back saying he could get only 2650 cash apiece for them. Their rate of exchange of late has been 2700- I suspected his stew-pan-ship of a design to speculate & took the silver back rather unexpectedly to him as he had done the same thing to show his honesty several times before. In the afternoon I went to the banks & after the usual chaffering got 2690 as the average- saving a couple of cents on the dollar- Not much to be sure but a slight preventive of the dishonesties that plague us like mosquito bites every hour-

March 18th- Tuesday

For the record of the morning of this day- see the 2nd page of this sheet- An amusing scene occurred in the afternoon on our new church lot. We bought the ground of a family boasting illustrious ancestry & rags- living on the right as you face the river. To enlarge our entrance way from the street we bought a few feet from the family on the left who in removing their wall stipulated that we should furnish a gate into our flight of steps leading from the church to the street for their accommodation. To this we readily assented- the wall was built & the gate left invitingly open. The other family, however, remonstrated. The land was theirs. The right of way was exclusively theirs. The alley was a private family affair & these neighbors should not be allowed to use it. As we, however, being between two smudges declined to interfere- they determined on summary proceedings among themselves. The people on the right came over in full force a little after noon with bricks and mortar all prepared to build up the obnoxious gateway- & then of course ensued a brawl- I wish you could have seen it- It would have given you more insight into Chinese character in half an hour than you can gather from the books in a life-time. Such a noisy dispute I have seldom heard- first the young men began to cane each other at a high rate with hard words & defiant looks & gestures- then came the women- big feet and little feet- old and young with babies & without- first one party would scale the break in the wall & drive the tide of intruders back- then the other would gain the advantage & the rest would surge in the other direction. Now the outsiders- headed by an old gray headed "Mother in Israel" with a shrill voice & voluble tongue would make an escalade- effect a lodgement & allow the work of filling up to go on- Then

95

the insiders would press outward- force a sally & drive the foe backward in desperation. Fair hands with wrist encircled bracelets belonging to the owners of little feet & dreadfully dirty linen would force some unwilling servant into the very teeth of the battle & the bricks- already laid would be tossed out again- If it had been an Irish row the bricks would have made acquaintance with the heads of the belligerents-

It was a Chinese affair. Very noisy & very bloodless- torrents of eloquence & no blows. The insides at last said if the outsides would put the wall up they should set it on their own land & not on theirs. So after the steam had expended itself for an hour- they became calm & the outsiders in the course of the afternoon built the wall up- sticking out a foot or two from the plain surface of our entrance wall- as Dr. Collins would call it an "extraneous fungus"- & rather unsightly. So all parties are annoyed. We had furnished the gateway & were secretly glad that the others were going to shut it up.

Now, after the storm has subsided, it will be a pull upon our pockets to get the unsightly excrescence removed. In all these matters the Chinese have an eye to "cash". It is called in Canton English "Squeeze pidgeon"- in English a "squeeze business"- setting up a nuisance to foreigners who, they know, will buy its removal.

The masons at work walling the lot & laying the founda- tions of the church looked upon the scene with the imperturbable- ness peculiar to Chinese character seeming to regard it rather a matter of course- The wall around the lot is chiefly made by pounding earth- solid between the bricks of a stout frame work. The foundations of the church lie upon rock, all the way round- It is most substantial- the granite is first rate & the work has been looked after hour by hour by Bro. Maclay & myself- They have had little chance to cheat thus far-

March 18th- Tuesday [Morning]

Mr. Maclay comes in smiling at an early hour with his hands full of papers- Advocates- Reporters- Nationals & Co., to the latest possible dates. Almanac and diary for each missionary from the Rooms- Thoughtful-very- I had a Chinese bookbinder make pocket diaries out of home papers for James & myself- so now am double shotted- but Jimmy says "ah- why didn't brother Terry remember me?" It opens up a window in the Western world to get a batch of papers & periodicals three months old. We get a glimpse of men & things in action & as the chain of communica- tion is continuous- we come at last to view the entire panorama- though long after the view we get has passed before your vision & its events mainly obliterated from memory. After all what does it matter- All of life outside of the narrow circle of personal sense is historical to us- The history may be an hour old- a day old, a month- a year- a century- The scenes here enacted, narrated- & imagination sets the Puppets upon the stage again in the attitudes they occupied but a single moment, as often as we choose to the remotest time. Like the booming of distant cannon which are half loaded again before the report reaches <u>our</u> ears, & certainly as interesting to us as though we were but a foot from the muzzle of the pieces.

I am often surprised at the extent & accuracy of the information of missionaries respecting home affairs. They get a few secular & a few religious journals, circulate them, & what with the interest created by monthly mails, & the cutting off of all the sea third lights that distract & disturb the vision of the actual looker on open homing scenes- the narrative makes a vastly more vivid impression than do the events of the Dailies upon the minds of those who read them.

The merchants take a great variety of Journals- English & American & Jimmy brings home loads of London & New York & Boston papers. The most important item brought by the river to-day is the rumor of Peace. I hope it will be concluded. It will save the British clergy from the wickedness of repeating that awful "anathema"- "abate their pride- assuage their malice & confound their devices"- which has been hurled at the poor Russians for over a time.

March 19th- Wednesday

The Steamer Antelope goes forward to Shanghai today. Mr. Spooner, head of the house of Russel & Co. of this part goes in her. He has been out of health for a long time. Jimmy has a fine lot of chickens & a new dog, brother of the one that was stolen. I worked an hour before breakfast this morning with a heavy Chinese hoe & blistered my hands over again. I thought they had become blister proof as I have worked for a week or two without gloves-

After breakfast & prayers comes a new deluge of Chinamen- They all go in droves- These are painters & have a new & perplexing job on hand-painting a sign for our retail store "Richards & Co." They neither know the letters or which end up to set them so he has referred them to me as a kind of jack-of-all-trades to show them how- We get on well with the job- the Chinese are expert & solid workmen when they know how-

Symonds, Richard & agent, has sent up a peck of Irish potatoes- worth here $5. to the 100 lbs, to brace up our stomachs for the work. Just as we were sitting down to dinner our ears are invaded with piercing female shrieks from the direction of

the cemetery- Is anybody being murdered? Jimmy and Le Wock
unlock the gate & run out to see-

A woman & little boy are trying in concert which shall
bawl the loudest. What is the cause of the misery? They were
walking quietly to tow- or more properly she was stumping along-
like a hen with frozen toes, when a full grown boy steps quietly
up behind & jerks out of her hair one of these gold or silver gilt
long-crane-neck hair pins, worth about a dollar, & made off with
it. The helpless thing, thus plundered in open daylight by a boy,
could do nothing but scream & this she did as long as she was
within hearing while she slowly staggered homeward to relate
her woeful disaster! Jimmy said the burden of her complaint was,
"I'm a poor lone widow & the villain stole my hair pin".

Baby & I took a turn in the garden at sunset. The weather
is delightful- quite warm through the day but delicious when the
afternoon breeze comes careening up the valley from the sea-
Places along the Atlantic sea-board are not more regularly visited
with afternoon sea-breeze than is Fuh Chau during all the warm
weather. Baby loves to pluck leaves from the shrubs- to gaze
up into the blue openings through the foliage of the olives & to
clutch at bright flowers whose petals she is not allowed to despoil.
She must have a wagon soon- The Maclays have one, pretty, but
entirely too bulky- looks like a Pittsburgh wagon of olden times
for four Pennsylvania horses. It is not too stout for two or three
great roistering boys.

All winter sister has slept with her nurse. Her woman
thinks she will soon need a separate establishment. She has a
beautiful cane open work crib with mosquitoe curtains & today
Ling Choah set the tailor to making a mattress for it out of dear
Anna's old ship bathing dress- to be filled with soft pliant shavings
of bamboo- softer than straw & more elastic than cotton- similar,
in fact, to hair. He has made baby several over-robes from her
mother's wrappers- selected by the ladies.

Jimmy is speculating on a bamboo-jumper. The best
baby jumpers in the world are Chinese nurses. They have nothing
else to do & tend their charge from morning till night with solicitude & apparent affection.

March 20th- Thursday

The weather is getting uncommonly warm like June &
at noontide- like July at home. Can I stand it outdoors without
an umbrella. Out every now & then to superintend the unknown-
the wall of the church- the builders of a wall between my garden
& Mr. Consul Jones' kitchen, the garden coolie- carpenters &
tailor- hands full of these dirty unreliables.

Our church foundation lies on a rock. We have not allowed a stone to be laid that was not chock down upon the granite of the precipice beneath. Once or twice they have got a smart fit & laid a yard or two of wall before we inspected its foundation. We have invariably made them satisfy us that it was on the rock. This afternoon we found a rod of wall that had sprung into existence in magic haste- looked suspicious- ordered a man to bring a pick & remove a stone or two- found there six inches of dirt beneath- made them throw everything out of the trench- clear out every particle of dirt & begin again. The Chinese do these things with astonishing coolness- It is amusing to see Gibson- who is on the building committee of the chapel at Long Fou- kick down yards of brick wall- not laid up to suit him.

March 21st- Friday

Sun on the equator. One would think here it was vertical. Residents here say such heat is unusual in March- Like the negroes- the Chinese labor all day in a broiling sun without hat or protection for their heads & bodies. They begin to fling off their clothing again & labor nearly naked.

To-day I set the tailor to make Miss Anna another mattress similar to the one he made yesterday & gave him the contents of one of her mothers corpulent hair pillows to stuff it with. He succeeded well & she is now comfortably bedded. I fancy she is getting less plump & solid of late- begin to feel anxious about her. Hot weather is coming & she will need all her strength to stand it.

March 22nd- Saturday

Baby's nurse is teasing for increase of wages. I am more than half disposed to think she does not earn what she receives. The Maclays think Anna does not get nourishment enough & that that is the cause of her not appearing so solid in muscle as she was a month or two ago- I shall change at once if anything of that sort is the case- She is becoming wonderfully attached to me- cries after me & comes to me with pleasure from anybody's arms- I think she is too gentle & good for earth, have scarcely any hopes of keeping her- She starts at the sound of Jimmy's voice & expects a general hurrah when he enters- He cannot take care of her any length of time. He is too rough and excessive in his caresses-

Visited Anna's grave with the Maclays at sunset- The cool breeze flowed directly up the valley as it always does at this lovely spot which commands an enchanting view down the river.

99

Today a man brought some mature lily roots to sell-
What to do with them in a dry garden- in a loose granitic soil
was a question- Chinese ingenuity settled. Two large earthen
jars- big as a great iron soap boiler at home- were procured for
half a dollar, stationed in turfed plots on corresponding sides
of the garden- filled with mud & water & the roots immersed
to grow at their leisure- I wish I were able to have a piece or
two of garden statuary- a fish pool & jet d'eau. I think I will
have a swing on a large scale betwixt a couple of olives.

At 7 o'clock in the evening a note made its appearance
from the kitchen, delivered two hours before, inviting us to tea
with Mr. & Mrs. Gibson. It was too late to go there, and useless
to berate the servants for neglecting to deliver it sooner. Jimmy
& I are amusing ourselves evenings with the Pickwick papers.
Retire at nine invariably & rise at six-

March 23rd- Sunday

Last night was rather warm and a few mosquitoes gave
us the prelude of the concert that will commence a month hence
in good earnest for the season. In one of her late letters Mrs.
Lewis feelingly deprecates the annoyance of these pests of the
universal world. I call them universal because I have lost sleep
by them in Connecticut- New York- Maryland- Delaware- Virginia-
Pennsylvania- Illinois- Iowa & Missouri as well as in China. The
Western steamboats & hotels are all furnished with mosquito curtains of necessity. To Anna they were a novelty- to me second
nature. I was amused at the dear girl when she had the first one
of which she superintended the making, left open at the sides
to resemble bed curtains at home. I think we did not sleep three
nights under it before the tailor was ordered to sew it up from
top to bottom. I have slept under it all winter- because the semi-
dormant tennants lodge about the room, & when a fire is kindled
collect sufficient energy & momentum to make a dive at the
head of the nearest sleeper whose rest runs the risk of disturbance
in consequence. Badly as I dislike mosquitoes I feel that their
presence is more than compensated here by the absence of flies.
The mosquito is a bungling night marauder- cowardly & easily
shut away by bed hangings- The fly is busy- alert- impudent &
most troublesome on those days when you have the smallest supply
of electrical energy in the nervous system to repel his impetuous
assaults.

Today heard Mr. Doolittle preach at his home. He is
a stout built man & his wife is a stout built woman of excellent
taste- as every part of her neatly furnished house shows- Stopped
at Br. Gibsons on the island as we came back & staid to dinner.

March 24th- Monday

It rains. Set my tailor to making a straw hat for summer-
Neat heavy straw braids- "whole flats" can be purchased for half
a dollar- ripped up & sewed over. Mrs. Maclay has a shoemaker
in training for the growing wants of her little domestic circle-
Demand always arouses the question of supply & the man has
colored Chinese leather so neatly that it resembles the American-
A cabinet maker proposed to varnish it & theirs. We shall have
the regular varnished leather shoes so fashionable at home-

Made the stone masons throw out a rod of wall they
had built & buried in advance of our inspection.

Mrs. Maclay sends us several bottles of spring Beer-
compounded of hops & ginger. This reminds us of your two bricks
of hops which must come out & serve for beers.

March 25th- Tuesday

Jimmy goes to the British Consulate and returns early
with a package of letters. Opened as usual with fear & trembling.
The news of baby's birth has got home & occasions grateful joy,
but oh what tidings follow fast upon the train of this pleasurable
announcement. Anna's trouble with her breasts- diarrhea- nausea-
utter want of appetite- wasting- debility- early death! what tidings!
How intimate pleasure & pain. Three months- five months of
painful suspense- "Safe at Singapore"- hearts rebound- Another
month of suspense- "at Hong Kong"- Pleasure indeed- Another-
"Fuh Chau at last". Delight in America equal to our own as we
stood on firm land greeted by friends & welcomed to our long
looked for home. Two months more of suspense & you feel as
we felt- the Rubicon is past- safely- easily- happily- For a few
weeks hope flutters, & then follows the night of despair. Its shadow
has brooded upon your spirits- Its gloom mantles each like a pall.
Not an object is distinctly visible to the downward or level gaze-
Look upward & the entire firmament is studded with the brilliant
scintilations from the far-off- out of celestial day. Deeper darkness
awaits us. The mold of the sub-soil world will gather upon our
own organs of vision- Gloom- dankk- rayless- lightless- unphospho-
rescent will assert for a time its inexorable dominion- Yet sky
& grave shall end and the glory of the former shall flood the
deepest recesses of the latter without a barrier. The light of
the God-world will vanquish the gloom of the man-world & the
life of eternity thrill the motionless bosom of every subject of
the empire of Terror! Religion alone robs death of its sting &
the grave of its victory! Intelligence of a chance to send to Hong
Kong in season for the April mails. Too tired to write to-night.

101

March 27th- Thursday

Rise at 5 1/2 & busy myself till nine with letters for the closing mail. Busy with workmen till noon. Dine at Mr. Gibson's with the Maclays- Soup- Fresh Fish- Duck- sweet potatoes- Irish potatoes- yams- tongue- fresh pork- celery- fresh peas- hot rolls- mince pie- custards- pumpkin pie- fried cakes- oranges- English walnuts & the first ripened native fruit of the season- about the size & flavor of pine apples. No lack of good cheer.

March 28th- Friday

The tailor has made two nice straw summer hats by ripping up a whole flat braid worn by the Canton barbers. We have trimmed up the trees so that we can see a large portion of the suburbs over the Consul's kitchens- now hidden by a high wall from annoying our premises. We are planning a huge garden swing- a bamboo chair- suspended by poles from a transverse pole lodged in the crotches of the trees above- Le Wock is our purchaser.

March 29th- Saturday

It has rained all night- & thundered for twelve to twenty hours steadily- though at a distance. It is the first of the season- How superior is a natural shower to all artificial watering- It brings the shoots right out of our transplanted rose-bushes, & a leaf has struggled to the surface of one of the huge flower pots containing our water lilies. The turfed embankments have assumed a lovely green and all nature rejoices in the heightening of its living. Birds & flowers delight the senses on every hand. A house is going up on the West side of us- Wetmore & Co- thus we are surrounded by foreign residences. The builders make as much noise as the architects of Babel. Cutting away the five old olives- a grand pity- leveling the earth & bringing on timber & materials.

March 30th- Sunday

Babel resumes its uproar this cloudy morning in the lot next us- It will go on uninterruptedly for six months unless stopped at once- I stand it till 10 o'clock & then address a note to the Messrs. Wetmore & Co. begging them to stop the hubbub upon the Christian Sabbath. They comply instantly- send a Canton man to drive the noisy coolies off the ground & send a note of courteous apology for the annoyance occasioned. It is the theory of the East India Merchants to interfere as little as possible with the practices of the heathen in their contracts with them. They know nothing of the Sabbath & think its observance unnatural- absurd & a great waste of time which ought to be devoted to the honest acquisition of daily bread- Outside of Jewry & Puritanism- the Sabbath is laxly kept it must be confessed- Greeks- Romans- Churchmen- Friends- & outsiders at large see no particular reason for hallowing one day in seven- & being extra religious one day in the week by way of compensation for extra irreligion during the remaining six. The Bible commands it & experience proves its benefit. Nothing can be more monotonous than the never-ending routine of labor pursued by the Chinese. New years are their only general holidays.

At 1 o'clock brother Gibson preaches to the assembled missionaries. A good discourse on "Thy Kingdom come". He is the youngest minister & missionary among us, possesses a fine figure, fine voice, good rhetorical powers, ambition to excel & bids fair to become a good preacher if his life is spared. His wife looks like a walking shadow, yet she nurses her babe, rides out daily & gets out to church & other meetings regularly. Jimmy & I spent the evening at Bro. Maclay's as is our wont. I love to blend the chords of their sweet melodeon- the last earthly music to which dear Anna listened. It stood against the wall of the parlor next the head of the bed in her sick chamber & the very evening of her death- after permanent delirium had set in- while the ladies were attending to some of her female wants- I played her favorite, "Jesus Lover of my Soul" with the Eolian softness of chord of which she was so fond always & particularly during her last sickness. I asked her if she heard it- "Oh yes" she replied- "it was so sweet & soothing."

The evening is raining- We return at 8 o'clock & make preparations for bed-

March 31st

Just as we were returning last night- a great hubbub arose among the servants at Consul Jones. One was heard calling to another, "run for Mrs. Maclay!" "Quick! quick!" One said she was "dying"- I was alarmed- but as the confusion abated soon, I gave myself no further concern & went to sleep. It appears she had over-eaten cake of some rich kind & was sick as consequence. Beyond necessary vomiting & its accompanying spasms I do not think she suffered much. The Chinese are as great cowards in sickness as in War- hate the sight of blood & dread to see one vomit.

This is the last day of the month & our regular mission meeting. It was held at my home to-day- There is something pleasant in squaring accounts with the world month by month. Our salary is drawn quarterly in advance- that is- when we have any money. At present building two churches & buying new building lots & a house for a female school has put us upon short allowance

103

as we do not choose to go in debt by borrowing here- It is a year since the Board send funds & 10,000 dollars <u>ought</u> to be on their way here at this moment. It is the misfortune of the Book Coven like all other great establishments to think that no other concern needs funds but themselves & to forget that in addition to the consumption of the "ready" here, it takes three or four months to forward a new instalment when due- So that its payment ought to be <u>fore</u>stalled rather than to come lugging in the rear- We are fortunate enough to have capital credit with the merchants to whom we can apply in emergency-

We open our monthly sittings with prayer & then present our bills for mission payment- Teacher $6. Watchman $3. schools, native boys- (mine are Le Wock & his brother, 2 or 3 dollars), house repairs, chapel building- in short all our pecuniary affairs. Then we propose plans for mission action, building churches, chapels, schools, dwellings, printing & circulating books, & applying to the Board at home for reinforcements of various kinds.

After we adjourned Mr. Maclay & I went to Long T'an- I have walked all winter but now that warm weather has come- betake myself to Sedan again. The motion is exhilarating- easy as a canal boat- more resembling perhaps the walk of a horse- I felt a mournful pleasure in occupying the cushions upon which dear Anna reclined so many beautiful hours last summer in her daily rambles about the hills-

April 1st- Tuesday

Doubtless by way of April fool our teachers bring out from the city this morning the report that the rebels are out in full force in the province West of us and that they have taken its capital & eight or ten of its chief cities. The authorities here have drafted a thousand or two men to send to the scene of action but flatter themselves that the difficulty of the mountain roads and the poverty of the Province will keep the brigades at a distance from Fuh Chau. I should not be surprised if they make a descent upon us. We shall be three miles from the principal scene of action, the beleaguered city, and can see the flash of cannon- & listen to the roar of musketry at a safe distance from the balls of either. A few marines from an English man of war will suffice to guard the foreign settlement. A single field piece stationed at the end of the long bridge would command it against an army of Chinamen & in one of the stone hongs of the foreign merchants, ten men could make a stand against ten thousand valiant subjects of Hang Hung- (Hang-a as in father- Hung-u as oo)- Trade will be interrupted- prices will be high- & missionary labor precarious- A Chinese soldier with a woman's face and woman's dress- I will not provoke Kennet Square by saying his woman's heart- his flint matchlock & his bows & arrows- is not a very formidable looking warrior- In gas and bravado he is equal to a Western politician-

104

The great theme of the day was a wedding. One of the heads of an English house married the daughter of the wife of the Interpreter of the British Consulate. Dr. Welton officiated upon the occasion which was strictly private- A beautiful silk flag thirty feet presented by the happy bridegroom in honor of the occasion floated from the lofty British flagstaff & the American Consul hoisted his Sunday flag in due politeness. A cargo of ladies could find husbands among the bachelor merchants of China- greatly to the advantage of their society & morals-

April 2nd- Wednesday

Called chair coolies and rode to Long T'an betimes. Noted the time of crossing the long bridge. It took three minutes & we met three hundred persons. At this rate one hundred per minute- six thousand would cross in one direction per hour or twelve thousand in both. From six in the morning to nine at night the stream is uninterrupted so that daily in fifteen hours probably not less than 100,000 persons cross this crowded causeway daily.

The masons have begun the front gable of the chapel with red brick. They are laid in mud- Two or three feet of wall have grown since my last visit. I ordered the brick laid two inches from the face of the water table & the pilasters to be recessed or rather projected two inches. With their accustomed accuracy the bunglers have made each an inch and a half. Luckily there are but two inches in the Chinese foot & it is as long into half an inch as ours.

Mrs. Clay & Gibson come to my house for weekly meeting after which we descend to the garden to look at the improvements and try the new bamboo swing. It is pronounced capital & then we take a turn upon the hills for exercise.

April 3rd- Thursday

It has rained all night. The teacher reports the falling of one of the immense stone sills on which the stone flagging of the long bridge rests and that a poor market man stepping upon one of the unsupported stones before light fell with it through into the rushing tide beneath leaving his baskets and shoulder pole lying on the brink of the aperture.

April 4th- Friday

Rain all last night- Thunder in the morning. Mr. Comstock, merchant, sends us a fine quarter of mutton from a portion of which the cook prepares a rich soup for dinner. Rains all day & teacher does not come. Improve the leisure in writing letters to be forwarded from "Africa" to Shanghai & thence to U.S. Call at Mr. Gibson's at evening.

April 5th- Saturday

Roused in the night by a flash of lightning & tremendous clap of thunder all in a breath. It waked everybody in the neighborhood I think, as it was a universal topic of conversation with Chinese & English. The tailor told Jimmy the Devil threw the bolt & it boded no good when it thundered at such a rate. A huge pine tree in the cemetery some rods to the West of us was found to have been rived from base to summit by the explosion-

Jimmy spends the forenoon with Consul Medhurst who has undertaken to give him lessons in Arithmetic & penmanship, two essential branches of education.

This morning at an early hour- heard our kitten mewing at a moving rate at the gate. He disappeared last Tuesday & we had given him up as hopelessly stolen & either adopted into the family of some beggar or mandarin, converted into soup or fricassee or hung by the neck on some tree in the cemetery to gratify some departed lover of the feline species. Whether he went away or was carried off, he was delighted to get back & baby pulled his hair & tail & ears with extra energy to make up for intermission.

Commenced to improve the avenue between my front wall & the cemetery- filling up the irregularities- smoothing excrescences & turfing the embankment- Shall set out a row of trees along the front for the benefit of future generations. The whole population has been visiting the hills for a day or two to burn incense & cast to the dead- Every grave is heaped with fresh earth & covered with mementoes of affection. I told a fellow who stopped by me as I was leaning against a turf pyramid as high as a marble monument at home- that his load of good things- he had two huge baskets full of provisions sufficient for a pic-nic for a dozen- Could do the dead no good, "they neither cared to eat nor drink". He said it was true "but he did it for the looks of the thing. It was "beautiful" thus to honor the dead & I could not dispute him.

April 6th- Sunday

Church at the Hartwells. Always pleasant to meet the entire company of friends with their rosy cheeked little ones once a week. Returning from the American Consul, engaged in the very laudable business of beating the coolies off Wetmore's lot where they had persisted in working & making the Sabbath hideous by their vociferous garrulity notwithstanding orders to the contrary.

Went to brother Maclay's Synagogue in the afternoon to listen to his instructions,- to me mainly unintelligible- to such

106

of the street passengers as choose to drop in for community inter-est. Let open your door & the crowd flows in at once-hats on-if they are fortunate enough to own any- saunter up to the closed altar- lean over the rails- make remarks about the speaker, nod assent to his words- wonder that he speaks the dialect so well-interrupt him to inquire what his coat cost- whether the war is still going on between the English & Russians- how far America is away- how long he has been in the country-

If the speaker declines answering these secular questions-They inquire if Jesus belongs to the tribe of idols. Some old fellow starts up with his load of market baskets- says it is getting late & he must go, & cries out "good night" to the preacher' who says "here if you must go- take a 'Jesus book' along with you-" Others think they must go & beg to be served with books also & finally with a general rush for books & then for the door with many "Thank yous" & many "goodbyes" the house is emptied in the middle of the discourse- but as quickly replenished by new comers to whom the speaker may finish out, or begin again at pleasure-

Went to Mr. Gibsons after meeting who has been confined to the house by a bad cold. His wife was out at church but he has been under treatment & looks like a man with head or tooth-ache. A little sacred music on his gentle melodeon had a soothing effect. While we were enjoying this between two and eight o'clock, the coolie brought in a letter- always a sight to thrill the blood here- It is from America.

Coolie and lantern are put in requisition notwithstanding the silvery outline of the moon's first crescent for the month & five minutes walk through streets crowded with passers hurrying homeward & up the silent alleys to the hill brought me home fluttered with expectation. A glance through the glass doors showed Jimmy pouring over fresh papers on the Library table. "Are there letters?" said I- "Yes- four- but none from Mr. Lewis' family!" The tale was told- Eloquent silence! Anna's forty correspondents are overwhelmed with astonishment and grief. Voiceless heart! voiceless house! voiceless grave! voiceless home: at last-How can I restrain tears! I weep again in sympathy with those who wept the fountains of grief to arid scorching dryness- three months ago! Bishop Waugh, Dr. Durbin- Dr. Peck send letters of touching friendship- Would they could repair the loss! My father has heard that "Anna is very ill" & writes with pained concern. The news of our common loss must have reached before his letter got off from New York. Stunning news! overwhelming affliction! mysterious Providence! Temporal results widely devastating- eternal, who can estimate! But for the belief in a superintending God, who could endure such a stroke? Apathetic indifference- palsying sorrow-or fruitless imprecation would be our only lot. Anna's caution when the frightful fact of her apprehended dissolution began to stare us in the face has been of infinite service to me all winter. "Look at it in the light of religion & not of speculation & philosophy-" I was disposed to speculate upon the propriety of this & that in our history- to reflect here & censure there- herself- myself- physicians- friends- circumstances- all. Like Aeneas, [Editor's note. The author was Maimonides.] when he lost his beloved companion- "Quem non incusari amens hominumque Deorsumque". Dear-dying Anna would listen for a moment to none of this. She said- she & I & our friends had at every step done what we conceived to be duty according to the best of our knowledge & ability & the results were to be left with God. "Tho he slay me yet will I trust him." He gives- he takes- Who shall gainsay.

April 7th- Monday

Forenoon with teacher- Afternoon call coolies to go to the church at Lang T'an. The rascals come but will not go short of a fourth beyond their usual price. Dismiss them & employ myself in superintending the turfing & beautifying the bank along the avenue opposite my front wall- a spot where Anna spent many evening hours last summer either in a rocking chair or reclining upon some Chinaman's grave.

April 8th- Tuesday

The milk woman comes with her bill for the month. Will you be interested in the detail of all our domestic affairs? Alas is not the only charm of life in China gone already- Is it not irksome to toil through pages no longer illuminated by the presence of one whose welfare was a talisman of interest in whatever had the slightest connexion with her. Mrs. Lewis inquired in one of her recent letters if we could get good milk? that Mrs. Woods said they got only the milk of buffalo cows at Shanghai. So I heard about Fuh Chau- & my imagination set up- in some corner the image of a buffalo cow & gave it the hump & shaggy head- short horns & fiery flying tail of a buffalo of one of our own prairies. Fancy & fact usually diverge.

The animals that pasture all over the broad expanse of unfenced hill & dale about us are regular cows- about the size of home cows- with a slight rise over the foreshoulders- short horns lying backward- no surplus of hair- small bags & gentle dispositions. The cowherd is usually a child who leads the animal by a rope to the best pasturage. Our milk woman keeps seven of these animals & supplies a number of families with milk as pure & wholesome as you would get in New York or Philadelphia- I except the country. Before the coming of the whites- the natives raised the animals for food & agricultural labor- The sale of milk is a new branch of industry- Mrs. Maclay makes all her butter from her daily supply of milk & so do others. It costs us about ten cents a day or $3. per month for an ample supply. Jimmy drinks it at meals instead of tea or coffee & the cook uses the common amount in bread- cakes & pies. The Chinese never use it at all.

April 9th- Wednesday

Wakened at four o'clock in the morning by a regular typhoon of about one hours duration. Such sudden & temporary gales are rare in America.

At nine o'clock Jimmy & I got into our Sedans to go to the city. The coolies started off at a brisk pace shouting to the throngs of people in the narrow street "get out of the way"- "keep your own side"- "look out for the chair"- Accidents are unavoidable in such a crowd. Bump! goes the chair against a fruit stall- & pyramids of oranges- apples- pears & cuttings of sugar cane go rolling about in sweet confusion. Its keeper hurls a volley of oaths after the carriers who by this time have plumped the end of a chair pole into some pedestrian's eye, or nearly taken off the arm of the customer of a rice shop- or upset some country-man with his great basket of fowls as he was stooping forward to select for a buyer a choice specimen. Here they splash the buckets of a waterwoman or crush the boxes of a flowerman & nearly run down some urchin who ventures to trip across the road in advance of the dashing coolies, as boys at home experiment in speed with horses & vehicles. Now they crush some frail basket of market ware, crowd past a chair coming in the opposite direction, narrowly escape the brittle merchandise of glass pedlar, get entangled with the poles of a wood carrier & overturn a cake boy & strew the stone flagged pavement with his confections. At certain points the street is so choked that passage is hardly possible-If a chair in advance turns into a side street its poles reach quite across the narrow avenue & block all passage till it is out of the way. It is impossible to enumerate the articles you meet in transit in a five minute journey through a Chinese thoroughfare. Every thing is suspended from human shoulders- Huge ship timbers-house timbers- cables- stones- iron- immense trots of indigo-large strings of iron & copper cash- furniture of every description & thousands of lighter articles.

In five minutes we had descended the hill, threaded the narrow street running parallel with the South side of the river-passed through the court of the Ningpo temple with its imposing display of Chinese architecture- reached the Short Bridge, jostled its Indian file of passengers & pushed into the thickest of the dense crowds hauling all manner of meats & vegetables for morning marketing. Anon we are across the island and urging our way across the Long Bridge with its rows of shops on one side & its throngs on the other. At its further extremity we descend a throng-ed flight of steps, flanked with cook shops- barbers shops and

public offices & are pell mell with rushing tides of swarthy humanity. Coolies of all descriptions crowding- hustling- jostling- shouting-
scolding- swearing as if noise and blasphemy were essential to
locomotion- or would aid in unraveling the net of inextricable
confusion- made by thousands of anxious pedestrians hurrying to
the business of the morning.

Through this melee- without jostling & overturning more
than a dozen footmen- with less momentum than a heavy chair
propelled by two or three coolies under naked leadways, we journey
along- ordinary crowds- now crossing the ridge of a hill by ascending
steps on one side & descending on the other- now crossing a canal
bridge in the same manner- we come in forty minutes to our
new chapel at Long T'an. There we pause to look at the progress
of the workmen. The brick gable front is rapidly going up & commands the involuntary wonder of the thousands that pass hourly
from morning till night along this miniature Broadway of heathendom.

Resume our chairs and in a minute more are passing
through a huge eating establishment- which roofs in the road
& spreads far out on either side & embracing half a block in extent.
Here- in every direction- are waiters- cooks- rows of tables-
customers eating at the little side tables & stalls- bright rows
of brass pipes stand upon some of the tables for the indiscriminate
use of all frequenters of the establishment- Its bill of fare is
as extensive as the capabilities of the Fuh Chau market & its
motto is "meals at all hours". As the thoroughfare passes right
through the centre of it- heat & wet must cause numbers to become
involuntary guests to say nothing of the demands of nature &
its convenience for travellers to & from the city.

Three quarters of a mile through dismal vistas of courts,
shops- turning shops- blacksmith shops- brasiers shops & a variety
of other noisy trades each congregated in its own individual locality
& we reach another general press & uproar at the gate of the
city. There you pass under a broad archway like a railroad tunnel
thirty feet through with huge gates covered with plates of iron
about midway opened at six in the morning & shut at about the
same hour at evening- Under the archway are all sorts of tradesmen
& the press of chairs- coolies- porters- pedestrians- men, women
& children- clean & dirty- well dressed & ragged- peaceable &
impudent- quiet & brawling- at either end- is certainly worthy
of the most crowded thoroughfare in London.

Fairly within the city, our road turns off from the great
central artery of trade & travel & skirts along the Southern wall
to the West. On our left rises the parapeted wall- like the inside
of the Western fort- It is low inside, accessible by flights of steps-
& broad enough on top for a buggy drive- Outside it is thirty

feet high & surrounded by native rice flats & canals which might serve the purpose of a moat- Watchtowers rise at little distances from each other in which lie a few rusty-surmounted canons & a few idle soldiers lounge looking as much like ragged mulattoes out of business as the gallant defenders of the interests of his Imperial Majesty. On our right rises a huge hill & along its Congrit's base- between that and the wall runs a single street- the houses of which are of the most disconsolate description- Women are peeping from the doors & ragged children tramping without in no hazard of being trampled by horses. The dwellings have one room open [to] the street and two or three back of it in a line- with dirt floors & pigs & chickens common tennants with the inhabitants. Handicrafts of various descriptions are prosecuted by the inmates.

The silence of this isolated quarter contrasts strikingly with the ceaseless roar from which we have just emerged. It grows more & more rural as we advance, houses cease to appear & the domain of temples begins- The silence deepens. Our right is flanked with old temple walls- some in partial ruin- covered with grotesque paintings & barbaric sculpture & overhung with the foliage from trunks which are the growth of centuries. It is impossible to feel, in this sequestered & romantic belt of ever green shrubs & flowers- with towering precipices up which climb temples- high at our right, that we are within cannon shot of the noisiest bustle of a city as large as New York. The coolies pause at length in a quiet nook of this lovely retreat- turn short to the right through folding gates & set us down in a banya shaded court- with here & there a fugitive inmate flitting about in pursuance of the domestic affairs of the morning. Our way lies up the steep ascent first to the left & then to the right- winding over natural & artificial steps- till on looking back we are on a level with the city wall- then high above it- & finally at the resting place of a temple- half way up the mountain side, which has been remodeled into a dwelling- the former residence of the Interpreter of the British Consulate- now occupied by a couple of students attached to the Interpretership. A tailor is working at one end of the verandah & two carpenters are making a rocking chair at the other. Mr. Gregory- student interpreter- formerly of University College London, receives us with great cordiality & after brief repose we sally forth to take a more leisurely survey of the Woo- Se- Tang- or Black Stone Hill.

Our first clamber was to the deserted temple or monastery at its South Western extremity, fitted up formerly for the residence of the British Consul at the port of Fuh Chau- It is several stories & a curious combination of dwelling & temple. Gilded gods still occupy their niches & some listened to the revelry of dinner parties & consular fêtes instead of the booming drum & bell & morning & evening chant of priests- now silent & deserted again- the doors swing on rusty hinges & lizards play about the moldy walls- A beautiful breeze was pouring along the decaying verandah & through the papered parlors & silent dining room.

Yet the landscape is as lovely as the eyes of beauty that once sparkled with delight from neglected halls- deserted first by heathenites & then by a later civilization. The view stretches down the valley & river for miles- blue mountains fade into the blue sky at the South & roll in serpentine ridges along the entire Western horizon- girthing the entire valley with their azure peaks- Koo Shan rises in the East & lofty landmark for the traveller in any direction over the tide flats that lie at our feet. These flats spread away from the city walls to the river glittering along the base of the mountains- supplying numerous canals & flooding with artificial irrigation the rice flats- cut up into all manner of geometrical figures & covered with wheat & rice under vigorous cultivation.

To the left recedes the winding line of houses & trees that marks the passage of the great road from the South gate to the bridge & river- Conspicuous above all other objects a mile away is our new church at Long T'an- out-topping the low roofs of the Chinese & beautifully embowered in the trees & shrubbery. On the highest floor of this temple we get a view of the city & North Watch tower with the mountains beyond- Grotesque sculpture & screen work- shell work windows & rock work fountains show the taste & labor of the priests & their adherents in former times-

Jimmy is exceedingly anxious to find a loose piece of carving to bring away as a memento of his visit. Despoiling old places is a species of vandalism for which I have no favor. I would not suffice him to mutilate the sound screen work & he did not succeed in finding any loose fragments- to his mind.

From thence we clambered by winding ways through richly wooded grounds to the summit of the Woo- Se- Shan or Black Rock Mount. I have described the view from this commanding elevation in a former letter. It has lost none of its sublimity- There the mountain stands as it has stood for ages with the altar crowned summit & temples nestling among the embowered precipices of its sides- surrounded the wall of the city- One side the rural retreat of gods & holy men & the other side overlooking the square miles of crops of which it is the giant guardian-

We descended its eastern slope to the temple inhabited by the church missionaries, Dr. Welton & Mesrs. Fernley & Macaw. The Dr. was immuned in his rooms- fitted up- in about the centre of a long suite of temple apartments- looking down upon the city on the North & far out upon the river valley toward the South.

112

His entry verandah made show of a formidable row of boots & shoes & slippers for all weathers indoors & out & at the right a broad dispensary displayed its assortments of gallipots & labeled drawers for the cure of all comers. We passed through his dining room to an inner room on the right- a sort of library- beyond which was his sleeping apartment. He was suffering from the recent extraction of teeth but as conversable as usual & as usual most French-ly polite. The Dr's manner always appears to me as though he was born and reared under some great man's nose & that he had an inborn reverence for nobles & kings- the Church of England & Book of Common Prayer.

Descending from the lonely retreat of Dr. Welton whose only family is a servant or two, a litter of black puppies & a fountain of gold fish in the front court of his bachelor apartments we reached by devious ways the back entrance of the temple rooms of Rev. Mr. Macaw. We surprised him at dinner- tiffin he called it. An Englishman seems to think it vulgar to breakfast before ten or twelve o'clock & dine before six to nine at night- Mr. Macaw's orphan boy "Johnny Straham"- "Jack" his mother used to call him- is getting along well with his Chinese nurse.

From thence we passed through the main temple with its court arranged with a stage for a theatre in front of the great idol whose wooden ears tingle night & morning with the telling of matins & vespers & mighty chanting accompanied by the roll of a monster drum- then a side temple- the shrine of some goddess- the sides of which were lined with woman balancing babies in their arms in all the postures possible- Where heathen Hannah's come to offer up their petitions. From this hall of little footed clay & wooden beauties- a wooden door opened directly into the Western range of two file apartments occupied by Mr. bachelor Fernley. He has a dining room- sitting & sleeping rooms- all sufficient in space and convenience, if not in civilized elegance for the accommodation of the nicer student. After a brief call we returned to tiffin with Mr. Gregory- At 11 o'clock resumed our chairs & reached home in about an hour- highly gratified with our day's visit- Baby was glad to see us after our unusual absence-

April 10th- Thursday

Engaged all day teaching two carpenters how to make the ornamented work of the frieze and cornice of the church at Long T'an- Go to Long T'an in the afternoon-

April 11th- Friday

Got a pretty flight of stone steps six in number laid up the first bank of the cemetery in the path leading to our own graveyard.

April 12th- Saturday

Walked to Long T'an betimes. The jobber had but few men at work, as the workmen are all on a strike for higher wages- Poor souls- they work now for 250 cash when foreign dollars are worth 2500 to 3000 & they ask for 300- or one tenth of a dollar- ten cents a day per man!- Twenty of the poor wretches cost us $2.00 a day- the wages of a first rate workman at home- & they find themselves- set up a brick furnace on the ground- provide a few camp & tea kettles- a deal table or two- chop-sticks- bowls & daily rice, fish & greens & they are as well furnished as a crew of sailors on a voyage- I set five or six men at work, under my own superintendence on the mouldings & finish above the doorway. The poor ignorant contractor, according to the best of his knowledge & ability had laid out to build the whole solid of two inch plank with little moulding ploughed in their outer edges! I threw his benevolent designs all aside & set them to construct a hollow box faced with mouldings outside- I suppose it is always done in Christendom, yet I never remember paying any attention to their construction but once & that was to the furnishings of an old house of the first class in Norwich where my father lived a few years when he first went to housekeeping.

A fall wind showered the dead leaves of autumn like snow & among them fell a bird's nest which I grasped as a prize & hid while I should be away to school in a hole rotted by time in the threshold of this antique & imposing doorway- When I re- turned- the wind had generously deposited a three dollar bill in the nest- but shattered the crazy doorway so much that carpenters men were sent for to repair it- I remember how inquisitively I looked inside of those mysterious boxes out of which wasps & bats had flown since my earliest recollection- Yet I hardly think my box device cornice at Long T'an is equal to them.

April 13th- Sunday

At nine o'clock this morning witnessed the solemn cere- mony of the baptism of the first native convert in Fuh Chau. A teacher of Rev. J. Doolittle- who has been soliciting instruction in Christianity as admission to the church for the last six months- Nearly all the missionaries were present with their teachers- & about a hundred Chinese, half of whom were adults & the rest youths of the schools- Several native women were present- Mr. Peet prayed & read the scriptures in Chinese- gave out a hymn which all joined in singing to Old Hundred- Mr. Baldwin preached on the nature of baptism & the sacrament- Mr. Doolittle adminis- tered the rite of baptism & Mr. Hartwell the Sacrament all in Chinese. This is the first fruits- exactly eight years since brother Maclay landed in Fuh Chau. The laborers have had the language to learn- the Bible to translate & the prejudice of the people

114

to overcome. Five years ago Msrs. Peet & Doolittle were <u>stoned</u> <u>off</u> the very spot where this seal of conversion to Christianity now took place. He is a man of education & intelligence- a public school teacher & of late a fluent expounder of the truths of the religion he has embraced. In the afternoon Mr. Maclay preached in his own parlor.

Mon-Tue-Wed-Thurs-Fri-Sat- Have been every day this week to the chapel at Long T'an. Starting regularly every morning at 8 o'clock in a Sedan chair & returning at 5 or 6 in the afternoon- At noon the houseboy has brought me tiffin & spread it out on a board under the carpenter's shed & a crowd has uniformly gathered to see what & how I ate. The boy brought tea-milk-sugar & table articles from home & <u>bought</u> boiling water! at a neighboring restaurant, a regular "Taylor's Saloon" half a block beyond the church toward the city. I have superintended the construction & putting up of Doric entablatures to doorway- cupola & church front- piece by piece. An immense labor- sufficiently perplexing & fatiguing yet inducing sound sleep at night. It will look remarkably fine when finished.

April 20th- Sunday

Mr. Peet preaches at his own house- Rain with lightning & thunder keeps us at home during the after part of the day-

April 21st- Monday

It rains so as effectively to prevent work out-doors on the chapel at Long T'an-

April 22nd- Tuesday

Spend the day sitting on my haunches in the shelter of a bamboo fence looking up to the carpenters at work on the ornamented part of the facade of our church. I directed everything from the ground not choosing to risk my neck thirty feet from the ground on their crazy scaffoldings. It is impossible to give any adequate idea of the multitudes of people who daily pass the, to them, astonishing fabric. Every eye is bent eagerly upward as soon as its owner comes in sight of the prodigious pile that has caused so much noise & talk among the people & so much apprehension among the authorities. It would be a very harmless affair in West Chester being 38 by 72 feet & only two thirds of that space in the audience room.

The Mandarins have other sources of uneasiness at present- The rebels have subdued the next province & are hovering in clouds upon the confines of this. . .Rumor exaggerates their forces & anticipates their movements. Sometimes they are coming from

Amoy- sometimes are about to evoke a descent through the defiles of the mountains- sometimes not coming at all, on account of the poverty & insignificance of the province- or its great abundance of natural laziness. Troops of soldiers with coolies bearing their baggage on bamboo poles were struggling toward the city all day. They were as curious as the citizens to see the foreigners & their works-

April 23rd- Wednesday

At home all day- Rev. Mr. Reeve- Church of England missionary from Shanghai on a visit here for his health dined with me & Jimmy to-day, after which we took a long stroll till nearly dark upon the hills.

April 24th- Thursday

Spent in study- Visited Long T'an in the afternoon-

April 25th- Friday

Wrote letters to send to the U.S. via Armory by an over- land runner despatched by Russel & Co. this PM at 4 o'clock- It is curious to be obliged to send off our letters twenty days before the mail steamer starts from China & yet we must do so or lose the chance of sending. In the winter this is precarious enough, in summer, during the tea-season we frequently have one or two chances after the case seems past hope. Mrs. Hartwell & Mrs. Maclay spent an hour here this forenoon- Sister was pleased with Mrs. H's little girl- for whose amusement the neglected piano was thrown open & drummed a little.

April 26th- Saturday

It has rained steadily all night. Cold water must have had a bad effect upon the tempers of the workmen on Wetmore's lot-next us- as they were brawling lustily till midnight. Perhaps liquor had more to do with it. The Chinese use it extensively. Five in ten- one told me the other day- use opium. A smoker lives, or rather drags out a miserable existence, next door to our church at Long T'an.

My teacher is telling me that our front is beautiful & wants to know if we do not intend to cover it with flowers- ser- pents- dragons & tigers in variegated colors like a Chinese temple, & is disappointed when I tell him the wood work is to be painted simple white & the brick work merely redded uniformly & lined with white. It occupies the ground that formerly supported six Chinese stores & dwellings. Foreign building is very monopolizing- English & Americans have claimed lot to lot until they have com-

passed the whole hill- not used for sepulture- & are hardly restrained from setting their residences over the bone-patches of
past generations. Indeed a spirited dispute is going on now about
a piece of ground- perhaps as large as your home lot- lying between
the wall of the British Consulate & a time honored banion shaded
temple to the East- It is claimed by different parties & probably
owned by the dead- yet the foreigners have bought it for a billiard
room! The Chinese- like the American Indians- have been crowded
off the foreign quarter & yet we are not content. An old fellow
lives at the Maclay's back gate- the last of an odorous line- whose
hut stands right where we want a road to our new church- & Americans like me have bribed the cupidity of the owners of the soil
to oust the superannuated pagan & sell the land from under him,
that foreigners may have more convenient access to our church.
We want to rout about a dozen families to make a road from
the river street back to the hill- They will retire for a price.

April 27th- Sunday

At 1 o'clock Rev. Mr. Reeve- church missionary at Shang-
hai- who had agreed to preach in my place to-day- at Bro. Maclay's
called to say that he had had a fever for a day or two & wanted
to know if a substitute would answer. Mr. Fernley, one of our
English missionaries preached in his stead. He is a good, pious,
learned man, a graduate of Cambridge, a correct reader of prayers,
but by no means a favourite preacher among his own people.
This was his first appearance before the Americans. He read the
first chapter of Solomon's Songs & spiritualized that doubtful
ballad for the edification of those present- Mr. Consul Medhurst
proposed to appoint a committee of ladies to wait on Mr. Fernley
and ask him to preach on other topics than love- kisses- & matri-
mony in future.

Sister enjoyed the afternoon with Jimmy & me in the
parlor- a new world to her which has been desolate all winter-
but begins to be thrown open now that warm weather is approach-
ing- She is a great observer & admirer of flowers in dresses-
carpets- bouquets & they always attract her attention. I show
her daily her mother's portrait, which she instantly recognizes
& is fond of looking at, but whether attracted by the face or
the frame I am unable to determine. She is fond of the melodeon,
but is getting so fond of helping by putting her own hands on
the keys and reaching for the music book, that I can no longer
play with her in my lap as formerly.

April 28th- Monday

The workmen are laying down the stone steps leading
from the street parallel with the river to our new church, the
foundation of which is now entirely complete & waiting for the

super structure. There will be one hundred in continuous flight, which I should fear would be almost repulsive to church goers as the "hill of difficulty" but for the fact that rising & descending stair ways & inclined planes is our daily business in this elevated neighborhood. Coolies will climb them with sedans & their occupants with great alacrity. In China all hills are passed by steps because of the absence of wheeled vehicles.

April 29th- Tuesday

The "Chrysolite" is reported as on the way for Hong Kong with this month's mail- To-day Bros. Maclay & Gibson with families go down the river on a health excursion. Mrs. Gibson needs it sadly. She is thin as a shadow & has an obstinate diarrhea. She persists in nursing her babe & in attending to various household duties though both are trending upon the little strength she has. They have fitted up a large tea-chop- whose hull- except room for the lookout on small decks at the bow & stern- is all in one room- ten feet high & thirty or forty feet long- floored for the occasion with loose boards & covered with matting & carpeting. A whole boat load of conveniences- beds- chairs- tables- everything mindful for comfort & luxury, was put on board the tea-chop- Curtains divide it into three rooms- Mr. Maclay's family sleep in one apartment, Mr. Gibson's in another & the third is the sitting, dining & reception room. The sides are from six to ten feet high to gangways & roof so that there is no especial danger of "Robby & Arty's" getting overboard, though I doubt if such lofty piles of plank will dispel all apprehensions of their being drowned.

"Don't meddle with that gun, Billy" said a careful mother & Co. "There is no danger- Mama- it has no lock on it."- "Never mind- it _may go off_- even if there is no lock." Guns are frightful things to anxious nurses even if they are without lock, stock, or barrel-

Anna's vaccination is taking finely. What a mercy in Providence to have bestowed on the little orphan such uninterrupted health during the first nine months of her existence. Dr. Welton calls in the afternoon, thinks Anna's vaccination is taking "Finely! finely!" & wishes to have Mr. Macaw bring his babe to take the matter from Sister's arm tomorrow- Is distressed that the stupid Chinese show so much reluctance to adopt & practice vaccination when annually exposed to the ravages of so fatal a malady as small pox-

Baby & I took a walk on the hills at sun down- I often admire our situation, as retired as if our dwelling was in the centre of Wyoming Valley. A large garden surrounded by high walls- sufficient area of itself for abundant recreation opens to the South by a gate upon broad acres of hill & vale dotted with forest patches over which the breezes of evening careen as freely as upon the unhedged prairies & yet five minutes walk- the opposite direction plunges you into the noisy labyrinths of city life- crowded to suffocation & reeking with filth, profanity, commercial chicanery, wealth & poverty, & every species of folly peculiar to those doubtful blessings to humanity dominated cities. With distant hearing of the everlasting war of this Babel we are as quiet as if upon the banks of the sylvan Susquehanna & entertain our little charge with daily visits to a coop full of cackling chickens & with the gambots of a cat & puppy.

It is growing warm rapidly. Last year, May was one of the most oppressive months to residents of the season. After our arrival in June the weather was continuously hot- except a few rainy days, but not suffocating as it sometimes is at home. The mosquitoes which have enjoyed a vacation of several months, begin their concert afresh. We are provided with the mosquito-whips- made of some material resembling horse-hair- with the gentle waving of which we keep the thirsty musicians at a distance. All of us have curtains to our beds closely drawn & mosquito-whips inside with which to defend ourselves against any straggling intruder-

Mr. Reeve is leaving to return to Shanghai & by him I write inviting Mr. Freeman, our fellow passenger on the Star- to make us a visit. I hear his health is poor in China- Shanghai is a sickly place. It is low & flat & is subject to fever & ague. Fuh Chau, excepting the tendency to diarrhea, common to all warm climates, is far more healthy. They are favored with ice- we scarcely know frost.

April 30th- Wednesday

Rose at 5 in the morning after a nights sound sleep, a rare visitant to my loneliness. It is pay-day. The Watchman did not fail to remind me of it by asking before breakfast for his three dollars month of beating a bamboo rattle about the house to scare away thieves & keep me awake. The teacher receives his six dollars & begs leave of absence tomorrow to attend the wedding of a sister. Their usual excuse for the loss of a day now & then is the death of some relative. He has buried all his during the year & has taken to wedding what are left to satisfy me that his day at home is legitimately employed. Poor "Little Brother" our table boy (that is his name in Chinese) feels badly- He allowed a beggar to come to the kitchen & steal the keys of the outside gates. We got an artisan to make new ones- big enough for a State Prison- & I made him pay for them the tall sum of 280 copper cash- 1500 of which make a dollar! It grieved him sorely that I "cut his cash"- but he must be more careful.

119

Sister's wet nurse begged to run home with her dollar- meanwhile the young lady sat propped by a pile of pillows & amused herself for an hour upon the front verandah.

Mr. Macaw brought "Johnny" in the afternoon. He screamed lustily while his father scarified his arm with a needle & took vaccine matter from baby's arm & inserted it in his. No wonder- it is the fourth time he has been thus tortured. Anna's lip quivered as if she would like to join him out of pure sympathy.

Mr. Gibson is house-cleaning during his sick wife's absence. He tea'd with us to-night- We were delighted after it- with the sound of a violin, an actual fiddle & tambourine serenading the American Consul, played by some scraper from H.B.M. Ship of War Race Horse- They were merrier when they left- playing Yankee Doodle with all their might. It was refreshing to hear once more the vibrations of catgut-

I don't know but I must "clean house". My boy sweeps daily & the coolie washes weekly- yet I doubt not dirt is quietly reposing in many a corner from which a lady housekeeper would rout it.

May 1st-

Retrospective. One year ago we were about in the centre of our delightful stay at Singapore- dear Anna's last continuous quaff of the cup of terrestrial pleasure- Transient sips only were afterwards allowed in the midst of the long twilight of suffering through which she passed into the upper brightness. Seven months ago I was watching without sense of weariness her latest pulsations & drinking with coveting heart all the loving expressions peculiar to cherished affection on the eve of being surrendered forever. " 'Tis past, 'tis past! & I think on it now- with quivering lip & throbbing brow."

Baby rolled about the parlor floor to Jimmy's infinite amusement- though an uninterested spectator would have been puzzled to tell what he was laughing at.

About 9 o'clock comes the contractor for our new church with a tale of robbery. He had a "shanty" half a mile up the river in rather a lonely nook- where he bought timber by the raft as it floated down the stream & wrought it into posts, beams & boards for his jobs among the foreigners. Two nights ago a mob of boat- men-opium smugglers beset his establishment- beat off a dozen workmen- lodging there- & carried off a dozen axes- two dozen saws- several pit saws- bedding- clothing- rice- cash & Co- to the amount of a hundred thousand cash- Some fifty or sixty dollars- a great loss where two dollars a month is good wages for a workman. I went with him to the Consul who promised to appeal to the authorities, in his behalf.

Visited Long T'an after dinner, the whole front of which is done all but painting. Found Gibson on my return up to the elbows in house cleaning- whitewashing- relaying carpets & putting everything into summer dress. Brought him home with me to tea.

Consul Medhurst has invited Jimmy to take a trip up the Koo- Shan- a towering mountain to the East- overlooking Fuh Chau in one direction & the ocean in the other- the celebrated locality of a Budhist Monastery.

About this hour- here 8 o'clock at night- with you 8 A.M. the elect elders of Methodism are assembling for the quadrennial Grand Council at Indianapolis- It will be August before we hear of their doings. With us Congress is still hanging in the air without a speaker, though we hope the coming of the "Chrysolite" will place one in the chair & redeem the President's message from ignominious slumber among the documents of the Secretary's table.

May 2nd- Friday

It would amuse you, the negligent manner, something after the style of college chums, in which Jimmy & I conduct our housekeeping. I rise at 5- he at 7 or 8. Breakfast is ready by 7 & the table boy is pacing nervously to the sleeping room door & inquiring if "Cheemee" is "cownge" or "Key- lee" asleep or risen. I give Jimmy a call & he says apologetically, "pa, why didn't you call me when you got up?" After a hasty toilette we repair to the breakfast room. He is almost always behind the "grace". Sits down & takes up his chop-sticks- bethinks him of his dog & rises to attend to master Loo's morning wants. At dinner he is equally tardy & goes out between soup & solids or between meats & desserts to look after the dog or cat or to berate the cook for something under-done or over-done or for a stray hair in a favorite dish.

It rains all day. A ship arrives from Shanghai bringing a letter from Mr. Freeman saying that he cannot visit us immediately. His health is tolerable but he thinks he is gradually acclimating- I think the coming summer will give us all a pull.

May 3rd- Saturday

It has rained hard all night- Mr. Gibson started at 10 o'clock in pursuit of his family- met the pic-nic party two miles down the river with a boat leaking atop like the roof of a tent at camp meeting- Mrs. G. has had rather a siege for an invalid, with her own boy & Mrs. M's three, two of whom are at an age to be full of all manner of mischief & perpetually doing things for which they <u>know</u> they will be whipped- like older sinners transgressing for the love of it with eyes wide open to the consequences- The G's appear to have pretty much <u>furnished</u> the expedition & returned with battered tables, & silver the worse for a week's <u>tear</u>, not to say <u>wear</u>. Her health was improved by the trip. They went quite down to the mouth of the river & out to sea- where they caught a few hours draught of the breeze fresh from the surface of the ocean. Madame M's fear of pirates shortened the stay somewhat. While there, the "Mansy" came in from Hong Kong, commanded by Capt. Fletcher who, two years ago lost the tea clipper Oriental at the mouth of the Min with a full cargo of teas. She stands, it is supposed, on the bottom, with sails set & half upright, yet entirely below the surface, topmasts & all. You can imagine the depth of the strait in which she was swallowed so completely.

May 4th- Sunday

Church at Mrs. Baldwins. In returning it was amusing to see six or seven sedan chairs in a row, Indian file, passing rapidly through the narrow Chinese streets, containing the women & children, objects of great curiosity with the gaping crowds that parted right & left to let the train of chairs pass. Seen in a line they reminded me of miniature cars.

Sister paid us two long visits to-day. She does not keep the Sabbath very strictly. This morning she was petulant- evidently out of sorts. I was afraid she had got a little cold & was sick. She was brighter & better humored this afternoon- sat an hour in a champaign basket, the library repository of waste papers, & played with rattles & other things, throwing them upon the floor for the pleasure of hearing them fall & troubling brother Jimmy to pick them up for her- She likes the melodeon, but is getting too fond of playing herself to be a help to the performer- if she is sitting on his lap.

Jimmy & I sing hymns for an hour to-night, & in connexion with supper, enjoyed a glass of home-brewed beer- ginger root & hops- of our cook's making. The English are great advocates of stimulants in hot climates, & accuse the Americans of living on "Hops". If they do eschew "Hops" they certainly love to <u>swill</u> ale. It is astonishing how much of this compound they consume in India in a year-

May 5th- Monday

In the midst of clouds of mosquitoes I commence at a quarter before 9 & bedtime to note the occurrences of the

122

day. A whip keeps these miscreants at a respectful distance. An hour ago I had occasion to refer to a volume of bound Miscellany & lighted upon the name "Enoch Lewis" on one of the little pages of the tracts of which it was composed. How the pamphlet came there I do not now recollect- It has remained unread in the volume for years. This evening I read it through without stopping, greatly admiring the vigor of "grandpa Lewis" style & the strength he displays in argument. I found many points of agreement & several of discrepancy between my own opinions & those of the Friends.

(Torn Page) - Our monthly missionary prayer meeting was held this P.M. at Mr. Maclay's. It is an-------putation upon his eloquence or my hearty dinner that I fell quite asleep in the midst his exhibit of the persecutions missionaries were-------eafter to be subjected to in Fuh Chau. Visited the Capt. & Lady- Fletcher -------the Maury staying at Russel & Co's. They were bargaining with China-------for lacquered ware. It is pretty but expensive-

My teacher told me of a bank robbery- $5000 by some Canton men- of whom the Mandarins had apprehended one or two who would probably pay the forfeit with their heads.

Anna is well to-day but fretful. I have great solicitude about her health as the hot season approaches- It is of no use- The way is to commit her to the care of God & be resigned whether she lives or dies. Can I? Trial would soon determine- I am selfish enough to hope God will spare me another affliction. Johnny Macaw's vaccination from Anna's arm is taking finely- The weather is delightful- Good night-

May 6th- Tuesday

A beautiful morning. I take advantage of its earliest coolness to sketch a little on the hills so as to be free from the curious Chinese who annoy one exceedingly examining his paper & pencil & praising his work-

The carpenters are raising the frame of the Chong Song Chapel to-day. The posts- a la Chinoise are to be embedded in a brick wall faced outside with handsome red bricks- The Chinese are rapidly learning to gratify the taste of foreigners in every particular in building. Every house erected is a new achievement. We have nearly completed one church & the workmen bring all their experience to bear upon this- so that we expect to make it twice as good as the other & that is one of the best built edifices in Fuh Chau-

To-day noon a beheadal takes place of a Canton burglar or two- which we hope will stop the thieving which is getting rather common of late.

(Torn page) - The leaves of the olive trees in the garden which have been green all winter now begin to fade & fall, illustrating the line "leaves have their <u>time</u> to fall".
It keeps the coolie busy raking them out of the paths-
You will think the poverty of the poor met---
extreme when I tell you that he saves them all & carries th---
to his mother to cook their rice with. Poor Mrs. Gibson see---
to be the victim of disease & misfortune. Yesterday the ba----
poles by which her sedan rested upon the shoulders of the co----
gave way & precipitated her & her babe to the pavement---
the midst of a crowded Chinese street. The concussion stopp---
her breath for a moment & caused serious fears of internal injury. This is the fourth time a similar accident has happened to her chair. None of us has had similar luck- Mr. Maclay says he has not got a fall in seven years- She is better to-day.

Mrs. Peet is a mere shadow & ought to return to the States without delay. She has been in the East sixteen years. Her three daughters need the expansion of civilized life. They talk Chinese like natives, but all their ideas of Christendom are in miniature. If they could spend a few years in America & then return as missionaries their services would be invaluable as interpreters & laborers among native females- beside- that Chinese life is second nature to them & not something which it would be the labor of years to acquire.

Capt. & Mrs. Fletcher called on us at evening. He is an amateur musician- Plays some on the Piano & more on the melodeon- Is a fine singer- with a rich full voice. I told Mrs. F. she ought to take him from the sea & put him to the Opera- He is impatient of the restraints of scientific cultivation.

May 7th- Wednesday

Carpenters still raising the church. The sun is beating hot. Singular how these Chinamen will endure its almost vertical rays upon their shaven sculls.

Spent part of the day assisting Jimmy to provide roosts & boxes to lay in for his chickens. His big Shanghai rooster has been dying of consumption some time & to-day was so near giving up the ghost that we told the coolie to take him away.

After our regular weekly meeting Mr. & Mrs. Maclay & "Robby & Arty" staid to tea. Four of us had our hands full to look after them. Mrs. M. watched the front verandah to see that they did not break their necks over <u>it</u>. Mr. M. watched the verandah above & the well for fear they would go to (   ) before their time & Jimmy & I guarded all the loose & breakable articles about the house generally. Their table habits have yet to be formed-

124

They help themselves without asking, bite the article & spit it back on the general plate if it is not to their liking. They are pretty, happy children but need to be "trained in the way they should go". Everybody can see fault in everybody's household management but their own- Had a pretty thunder shower in the evening.

May 8th- Thursday

Hot but pleasant- Ling Choah has gone home which gives us an extra amount of baby's company to-day. It is always welcome but not always profitable for study, if she insists upon being held in the arms- Often she will sit an hour- lashed into a chair, or in the waste paper basket- or propped with pillows & will some times roll contentedly upon the carpet.

A smart thunder shower in the afternoon drove the coolie up from the garden- so I set him to taking up the matting of the front verandah by way of house cleaning- At sunset, with heavy thunder clouds veiling the West- through whose rifts- sunbeams laid those diverging pathways of brightness that painters so much delight to copy, Mr. & Mrs. Gibson, Jimmy & myself took a boat ride up the river. The scenery is beautiful- the breeze was refreshing- the hum of semi-civilization & the delights of nature conspired to render it balmily exhilarating. We tea'd with them & had the first strawberries of the season.

May 9th- Friday

(Torn page) - Cucumbers at dinner- Chinese strawberries for dessert- monstrous things with a sort of stone in the center yet flavoured exactly like the home berry, juicy &, with the ordinary accompaniment cream & sugar- delicious. I ate one- We have to be careful of fruit- My favorite pies- crab apple & pumpkin- have passed the season & give place to a sort of "June Apple" & custards-

Ling Choah still absent & Miss Anna has spent most of the day below- She has not yet quite acquired the art of self support- but pillows break her falls & her brother's drawers are exhaustless storehouses of toys. He likes to roll & tumble upon the floor with her- She likes him as she does his-----
best- at a little distance. They are rougher playfellows than she-----
The Maclays came at sunset to take an airing on the hills one of the
---drawing the lake- a monstrous boy of ten months- in a cave-------
A thunder shower drove us all to the shelter of my verandah. -------
did not relish the wagon much. She grows fonder of me daily. -------
come to me from any one- even the wet nurse- Set the coolie to-
over the well-mouth to save apprehensions- Of accident there was v-
danger- Caution in excess is a troublesome bump. Maternal instincts
rebel against tree climbing as powerfully as the hen's, whose
young duck brood takes to the water.

It is getting warmer- Punkah's are in requisition- & Bros. Maclay & Gibson appeared to-day in white- I have not yet shed my winter dress- excepting to diminish the thickness of under flannels & the quantity of bed clothes at night-

Was this evening looking over the music books Anna brought with her to Fuh Chau- Saving a few standard extracts or rather extracts from the standard operas & a few favorite songs they are principally made up of variations by Prof. Grobe, which I suppose would have been hardly worth the buying but for the names of school fellows to whom they were dedicated. Yet I intend some day to get the volumes all back to the U.S., knowing that the girls will value them because of their original ownership. I shall keep those sheets from which dear Anna & I used to play last summer- the flute & melodeon- If Sister lives I want her to have as many things as possible that were her mother's. I can hardly believe that she is to know that mother only from pictures- mementoes & descriptions- darling orphan! It is ever so!

May 10th- Saturday

The shower of last evening drove myriads of mosquitoes into the house for shelter- I wrote with one hand & flourished the whip with the other until the bed curtains shut out intruders and gave me a few cubic feet of space as free from the annoyance as though there was not a mosquito in creation. Their hum is like the soothing murmur of a locomotive breathing a moment upon the track at a station house. It puts me to sleep & shortly after the innumerable tribes retire also, & when I wake with the first cock crowing between four & five in the morning they are quietly sleeping upon the walls, windows & curtains awaiting the light of my rising when the roar of pinions rises to a pitch of fury equal to the appetites of blood-thirsty millions for a sip at the life-fountains of my meagre humanity- At sunrise they shirk to the walls for the day-

Your mosquito is a voluptuous insect- like his brethren of the carnivora generally- He cannot endure the light & is very sensitive to cold- shuns rain, & sleeps during the hours of darkness- gets into warm corners- nestles in your clothes basket & water jar & bath tub for an equable & genial temperature. Man is a continent to a mosquito- His veins rivers of good liquor- & I doubt not he wonders that we grudge the globule that so slightly impoverishes us yet gluts him to bursting- Give him a fair insertion of his suction pump & he troubles you for the last time- It is as fatal to mosquito to glut himself with blood as to the bee to have its sting in an enemy's skin. But my epic is Southeyish & my theme Wordsworthian- Enough of mosquitoes-

126

Jimmy fell this morning with baby in his arms striking the back of her head- defended by a wadded silk hood, upon the gravel walk- She screamed lustily- he was as "pale as a cloth" & we were all pretty much frightened. We were glad to find all more scared than hurt. Yesterday a heavy girder fell some fifteen or twenty feet from the roof frame of our new church, hitting a couple of celestials in its way earthward- They were slightly hurt. Thunder every evening regularly- Man reported killed by lightning last night.

May 11th- Sunday

Rain all day. Yesterday removed the stove from our sleeping room & to-day had to kindle fires for comfort in the library & nursery. I expounded the 13th 1st Corinthians at Mr. Maclays to nearly our usual congregation- Baby has been our company most of the day-

May 12th- Monday

The whole of the Min is inundated- The landscape, at our evening walk, far as the eye can reach was one interminable lake, quite to the base of the mountains, out of which rose innumerable islands, lines of trees, villages, solitary houses, elevated on high posts, or built on rafts of logs, purposely constructed to rise & fall with the floods, and all the receding shores lined with boats, whose semi-circular bamboo roofs shelter thousands of a population, as amphibious as ducks, born on the water, reared on the water, & expending all the energies of life & crowding all its hopes & fears into the narrow compass of the deck of a San-Pan six feet wide by sixteen or twenty in length. The rush of the tumbling floods through the arches of the bridge of a thousand ages is worthy of comparison with the rapids of Niagara. The waters were level with the base of Mr. Gibson's house wall at the head of the island & now and then careened (saucily) in at his gate. At very high floods, his yard & basement floors are all covered. Our carpenter reports no water in the lot of the Long T'an Chapel though we built the Church itself on a foundation of stone six feet above ground to escape the annual drowning experience by all the lower levels between the river & the South gate of the city. My teacher could not get here from the city & I spent the day with the workmen on the Chong Song Chapel.

May 13th- Tuesday

Last night just as we had retired & were composing ourselves to rest at 9 o'clock, very orthodox bedtime- the servants came for the keys to let in a knocker at the outer gate- He is the bearer of a letter. It is from Mr. & Mrs. Lewis- (Feb. 11th) Was directed "care of Russel & Co." & has outstripped its fellows of this month's mails- Wrapped in bed clothes- Jimmy & I sit down on the floor to read it by a night lamp. Could not get to sleep for hours afterwards. Made up for the loss by dosing in the middle of the day.

Went to Long T'an & found myself in the outskirts of an innumerable multitude assembled a few rods beyond to witness the decapitation of five Canton men for bank robbery. I seemed carried back to the days of the guillotine.

May 14th- Wednesday

Seized at breakfast with a violent fit of palpitation of the heart- Felt for a short time like fainting & dying. Mr. & Mrs. Maclay came in about nine. Told them what to do with my children & effects in case of my being cut off without opportunity to confer with friends- My mother's family die suddenly- my father's lingeringly- Which shall I copy?- Time will reveal-

Went in the afternoon to dine with Capt. Gilles Fletcher at Consul Jones! Sat down at 4. Pea soup- first course- Turbot- second- Roast Beef, roast goose- boiled mutton- chicken pie- third- Strawberry pudding, bread pudding- currant pie or pudding- fourth- pea-pa's (a sort of June apple-delicious)- Arbutus (a sort of giant strawberry)- pumalo (a huge orange)- English Walnuts- dates & peanuts- fifth- Coffee- sixth- crackers & cheese- seventh- Wine & English beer all through for those that like them & cordial to sweeten the breath of the ladies after returning to the parlor. It takes two hours to get through an East India dinner & when you reflect that the time of our fashionables- like that of your own, is mainly consumed in dressings, breakfasts, dinners, games, novels & bed- you may conceive the worth of this butterfly style-existence.

The merchants are very busy during the shipping season from June to late fall, & I should think, a good deal idle the rest of the time. Dogs, horses & guns, pleasure boats, light books & lighter amusements are abundant-

May 15th- Thursday

Have a carpenter commence the model of the entablature of the Chapel at Chong-Song- I sit outdoors- sometimes with baby on one knee & a treatise on architecture on the other- dealing out to him feet & inches.

The servants are cleaning the house. Make another alter-ation in rooms. Put the library & study in the centre of the house- so as to be readily accessible to the servants from all directions- & transfer the parlor furniture to the North room which is a few feet longer than the other. Jimmy & I sleep in the South West corner room with a nice bathroom adjoining. Water is indispensable in this climate.

May 16th- Friday

Everything in the house topsy-turvy- White-washers & ( ) in every room. How it would rejoice a Miss Ophelia & how it bores a man. I let the servants take their own gait & keep in full retreat from the advancing pile of lumber & rubbish. By sun down the new parlor is fitted & I loll awhile in it- soothed by the evening serenade of a few millions of mosquitoes. Mr. Peet's personal teacher & a friend of his look in, in the afternoon & Jimmy arrives then with the Piano-melodeon-flute & C.- Call in the evening on Mr. Neilson of the firm King & Co. & spend an agreeable hour in conversation.

May 17th- Saturday

Roused from deep sleep about 4 o'clock this morning by the shout of the watchman "thieves! thieves!"- The servants got up and rattled about- Jimmy looked at the watch- I lay still- knowing that discovery was equivalent to defeat- that the house was securely locked & nothing of value outside of the well-shuttered verandahs. This morning it appeared that the burglars had dug a hole through the mud & stone wall beside the cemetery gate- nearly large enough for free ingress, & egress when they were discovered- This is a presumption upon our peace principles- We neither keep dogs or fire arms- It suggests to me a reason why Quakerism supports no foreign missionaries. It can only subsist in the midst of a well administered government. Peach principles flourish most luxuriantly behind batteries of cannon. You will point me to Penn establishing his republic in the midst of savages- Savages indeed, but not endowed with the ill-restrained cupidity of the half civilized Chinese-

At noon a box comes from Hong Kong- Eagerly opened- Shoes for Jimmy! two pairs! grand! but who from? Don't know but suspect young Marshall of Vandalia- No bill with them. I fear he is generous beyond his means. He is a lovely youth & his lovely helpless sister was a great favorite with Anna. The box is followed by letters. Bookworms- Lutton- Kidder- Charlty & others. Advocates full of news & to the mission a thousand pounds sterling to build churches with. At tea Jimmy was absent, so Le Wock- bolstered "Sis" up in an armchair & she sat like a lady biting a "Whee pah" (doughnut) all supper time-

May 18th- Sunday

Read the Bible & Christian Advocates which most Meth-

129

odists think a part of the inspired writings- until church time when notwithstanding a slight rain we repaired to the Hartwells. Sunday C- Meets our scattered forces- exchange "how-dooze-do's" & posts us up upon the general condition of health & mission prospects.

May 19th- Monday

Carpenter comes to make the model for the capital of an Ionic column. O what study- what contrivance to supply the lack of models- tools- experience in a place where such things were never seen or heard of before. He brings a professional flower cutter with him & the two require my undivided attention for the day.

May 20th- Tuesday

Mr. Clark- of the house of Russel & Co calls to say "good-bye"- He goes to Shanghai via Hong Kong & takes with him down the coast our letters for the June mail.

Sat in the back yard all day directing the carpenter and carver how to proceed with their models. The carpenter is a tall youth- impetuous & ingenious- but a coarse workman. His ambition is for quantity rather than quality- which in ornamental designs is destructive of the end. Our greatest lack is that of suitable timber. Broad planks are manufactured as they are wanted by pinning together narrow ones with bamboo pegs. In cutting flowers on the surface the tools of the carver got among the wooden pins of the carpenter- by the destruction of which the board came in two again. The carver a modest youth of twenty one with beautiful eyes has been married a few months to a damsel of fifteen or sixteen. He told me how much she cost but I did not note the price. They wanted to know how much we paid for wives in America & said "good-good"- when I told them money was no element in Western contracts. That either might have money & the other not- or both might have it or not- mattered not- if the parties liked each other the money was a secondary consideration. The carpenter said that five men in ten were wife-less- through inability to buy- I asked them about infanticide. They said a man liked one or two daughters- but generally all beyond the third were thrown into the river. I asked them about polygamy. It is tolerably common but has its limits. If a man's first wife has no boys- the great object of desire & especial nurture among the Chinese he takes a second with the consent of the first & even a third but never more. If unsuccessful in the third trial- he gives up in despair- They in turn questioned about our customs. I told them no man took a second wife until after the decease of the first. They asked if he could take one beyond a third- I told them it was not common- yet sometimes happened

130

& instanced that old Bluebeard of the New Jersey Conference who has buried five wives & promises to outlive the sixth. Both workmen dropped their tools & very sensibly exclaimed "high-yah-h-h!!" the Fuh Chau note of profound astonishment or doubtful credulity.

I neglected to say that little "sister" was the occasion of this dialogue who came out occasionally to pull the clean shavings & struggle after the tools upon the benches of the artisans- At evening Jimmy had her dressed & Ling Choah carried her to the Brit. Consulate to call on the babe of a Mrs. Smith, wife of one of the house of Drut & Co. I regret to say that the behavior of Miss was reported as not what might have been expected from the pains taken with her bringing up. She was afraid of every one & screamed lustily when the little stranger laid its hands upon her- This frightened the other little girl into screeching & produced a powerful if not very edifying duet to the ears of the representation of British Majesty. She must be taken abroad oftener.

At evening we called on the gentlemen of the house of Wetmore. There was quite a gathering of young men- six or eight- They put aside cards upon our entrance- & substituted cigars- conversation & tea. Several were English & the relative greatness of England & America- a frequent theme- was catholicly discussed- We staid half an hour & returned when <u>Sattee</u> our houseboy, came in, shut all the blinds on the front verandah- shut & bolted all the doors- shook out the mosquito nets- set the night lamp into place- brought in the silver- & said "all right" when we bolted <u>him</u> out for the night.

May 21st- Wednesday

A warm day- Went to Long T'an in the morning. The masons are making mottled work coloring the brick front. Ordered a halt & imparted fresh instructions- The Chinese- like savages and children are immensely fond of the gaudy- It is hard to instruct them to our severe notions of simplicity in taste. The capitals of Ionic columns grow in my back yard- We shall spoil timber enough for ( ) set in learning how-

At evening, after our usual meeting took a long & circu-itous walk on the hills. The sunset was calm & beautiful- the air bracing & the breeze balmy- Groups of foreigners in white- usually surmounted with black dress coats- dotted the eminences in one place conversing about the news of the day- in another shooting at a mark- here & there a lady in a palanquin & a few infants in the arms of nurses- Chinese were streaming along all the paths leading from the town- wending their way homeward after the toils of the day- now & then pausing to witness the skill of foreigners with rifle, or to admire a foreign lady or child or to inquire familiarly of the well-known missionary if he is taking his "pleasure walk" & telling to "walk happily". To these we added our mission caravan- Mrs. Maclay & Mrs. Gibson in chairs- Mr. Gibson in white- even to hat & umbrella- Mr. Maclay with a relic of winter in the shape of a black coat- & my aged limbs enveloped in black & flannels as if in January. Mrs. Gibson took Anna in her arms, who graciously surrendered her scruples on the score of walks of familiarity in favor of the easy motion of the open chair & the pleasure of a ride. We went to the foreign cemetery & thence fetched a compass of a mile or more around the hill skirted with gardens which form a broad belt between the grave-sown hills and the extensive prairie rice-flats, now beautifully green as far as the eye can reach- Sis was fast asleep before she got home. Passing a village- a woman gave her a flower & said she was "ching-chong" - "very pretty".

May 22nd- Thursday

By the aid of my teacher- translated a file of Chinese Title Deeds to a small lot of ground recently annexed by Wetmore & Co. to their Tea King- The oldest transfer was in 1793 & the latest this Spring. It had changed hands twice since.

After a hot morning, regaled, in the afternoon, with a thunder shower & smart wind from the West. Still engaged on Capital of Ionic column. Three men at work & very little perceptible progress except in the way of spoiling timber.

Sister dined with us. She eschews spoons & chopsticks, helps herself with her hands to boiled rice which I pile on the corner of the table- About half of it finds its way to her mouth- the rest adheres to her cheeks- forehead- ears & hair or rains down her dress to the floor. She behaves very well- except spatting the table during "grace" & taking occasional "slices" at the castors with my napkin ring. Her affection for me is getting decidedly troublesome- She will not remain in the arms of any one else a minute when I am in sight without tearing to come to me & screams violently when I return her to the arms of her nurse. She is fond of the antics of "Leo" who pimps & barks & licks her hands & face at which she averts her head, makes up wry faces & snuffs most comically-

May 23rd- Friday

Morning sultry- afternoon showery with heavy thunder. Mr. & Mrs. Baldwin surprised us with a call while we were at dinner. They were engaged to dine with the Maclays. My carpenters to-day constructed a hollow drum a foot & a half in diameter- to represent the upper end of one of our church columns. They

132

are ingenious in their own way when they understand what you want.

The heat rendered sister fretful- Through the aid of Ling Choah she shed a flannel skirt or two & felt more comfortable I doubt not. She is learning rapidly & is proportionally eager to go everywhere- see all that is going on & to handle everything. Gave her her first lesson in obedience to-day- by forbidding her to put papers in her mouth. The waste-paper basket of the study is a favorite play-house & her great amusement is tearing up the loose fragments- Now & then a handful goes into her mouth & then she is choking with the effort to swallow it. She must learn not to indulge a trick so hazardous & in prospect the leaves of books will suffer when she gets a few months older.

At evening James & I called on Consul Medhurst. There were present- the Captain of H.B.M. Sloop of War Racehorse- & Mr. & Mrs. Smith of the house of Drut & Co. Mrs. J. plays well on the piano & sings sweetly. He sings Letty's favorite- Genoa Air. It was touching- reminded me of West Chester- the ocean-moonlight nights- guitar & Anna-

May 24th- Saturday

A beautiful day- Showers have moderated the weather- The granite for the bases of our columns has come & I spent part of the morning in instructing workmen to hew them into shape. Every stone had its man chiselling away with all his might-

Jimmy is building a new chicken-coop on a larger scale- His speculations in Shanghai's & Fuh Chau's will break me up & I shall have purpose to sell out or make an assignment & come home-

In the afternoon I had a visit from a picture painter living near the Long T'an Chapel- He brought me some blue paint in powder & a picture of some Taouist demon- sitting on the ground & blowing bats out of a huge bottle with smoke & fire after the manner of the genni of the Arabian nights. I gave him in return half a dozen wood cuts from the Sabbath School Advocate which I tore out of the cover of Le Wock's writing book, & which he deposited very carefully in his wallet with as many thanks & as much pleasure as if they had been engravings of merit. I laughed to myself at the way his ignorance imposed upon him- He said Chinamen could not paint like that & he would copy them on a large scale to exhibit in his shop-windows- I would say- if he had any- The glass of civilization is a great impediment to seeing & knowing all your neighbors are about- transparent as it is. Chinese shops are conveniently near & the partitions obligingly thin & above all the people accommodatingly communicative.

133

A Chinaman is the most transparent creature in the world- with no opake spots- his doings except his cheating- Called Mr. Maclay & the head carpenter to see the head of the column in order to bargain for the construction of the eight wanted for the chapel. He proposed sixteen dollars apiece- by which he meant eight. A Chinaman always asks twice what he expects to get & if you demur- says "which you give?"

May 25th- Sunday

A lovely morning. The sky is veiled with clouds, the mountains with mist & the intervening landscape with azure vapors- It is cool- yet scarce a leaf stirs & the air has that peculiar density which makes it a good conductor of sound- I sit in the middle of the house with doors & blinds wide open South & North & the sounds of animate & inanimate nature flow in upon my senses with the soothing effect of distant music or a murmuring waterfall. Fowls are cackling- birds chirping- chickens peeping- morning doves cooing- crows cawing- magpies chatting- Servants bells ring in the neighboring houses- crickets chirp in the garden- the merry laugh of children comes in the air, the roaring of the river rushing through the arches of the bridge with the falling tide & the like, barely perceptible hum of business from the crowded thoroughfares along its banks- compared with which our elevation is as Sunday among the days of the week or heaven above the terrestrial orb- Birds innumerable twitter among the leafy boughs & ever & anon a carrier pigeon whirs overhead on his mission of friendship or commerce with a beautiful sound like whizzing of angelic pinions- a sound utterly indescribable yet successfully imitated by the Chinese in their beautiful bird kites with which the skies are clouded in September & October. It is a delightful concert in harmony with the feelings- in harmony with the day.

Sister does not enjoy it. She is restless with prickly heat & the occasional bite of the numerous insects with which the season abounds. She is a nervous thing & by her sovereign attachment to me seems to indicate that she is getting old enough to appreciate her greater loss. During morning prayers she lay sprawling & kicking upon the carpet of the dining room- tolerably quiet during the exercises. At nine the servants went to service at Mr. Maclay's school house- At 10 they returned & knocking at the outer gate- there was no one ready to open it as the nurses- left in charge- were both upstairs- so I stepped down & shot back the bolt & was not a little surprised at the array of white surplices before me & ran my eye over the group before I could be satisfied that they all belonged on my lot- There was the Watchman- Cook- Coolie- Table boy- Le Wock- Chung work & Mumma- which with the women & teacher make ten as our regular force besides the troops that report to us as carpenters- tailors- masons &C.

134

Mr. Maclay preached at one. The Brit. Consul with one of his interpreters- Wife of the Amer. Consul & wife of Capt. Fletcher were added to the usual mission band- making quite a respectable congregation. Went to Mr. Maclay's chapel after a fine dinner at which Miss Anna assisted in doing the honors-

There was a theatrical representative at the Ningpo temple within a stone's throw of the chapel which caused an unusual rush to hear the "red haired dollar boy" & receive his books. As the books were passed around there was a perfect shower of hands ready to receive them.

Gibson and I took a walk "among the tombs" for meditation & physical exercise- A mile out of town at a point just reached by an overshadowing peninsula of lofty pines- with young banians to the right & left of our position & a grand old banian overshadowing a village temple some little distance in front of us- & beyond that through openings among the trees- the green rice glades- the silvery river- the azure mountains- all- like ourselves fanned by the evening breeze- We sat down in one of the monster sepulchres to enjoy the scene. The peasantry returning from labor in their fields- in marketing in the town- immediately began to gather about us. A very ragged urchin attracted our attention & we asked him why he wore such vile apparel- He said he had no money- his father was dead & he had no money. We said why not work and get money. He had no employment, another had put in as spokesman & said if we would give him money he would get better clothes- We told him we did not like to enourage beggars- Carriers of these terrible tubs of "night soil" stopped like others- but we shouted to them to carry their odious & odorous vessels to the leaward- They obeyed like children- set them down in formidable array a few rods off & then returned to wonder at & talk with the "dollar boys". Gibson told one little chap his trousers were too short- whereupon all the little boys pulled up their tattered jerkins & pulled down their blue and gray grasscloth apologies for pantaloons- to show that though they were apparently a mere circlet of thin texture about the highest part of the thighs- they would by stretching and smoothing out the wrinkles & folds, reach within an inch or two of the knees especially in little chaps not more than three but high on the average. One poor little shepherd had no breeches on at all and showed that he was sensible of his nudity by keeping behind the other lads & vainly trying to make his ragged jacket a few inches longer by tugging with great hazzard of breakage at its lower rim.

May 26th- Monday

Baby suffers tho in a single thin slip with a narrow strip of flannel next her waist- We live an outdoor life mainly in this climate at this season. The shade & breeze are constantly courted. Jimmy finished his coop & I my column.

At noon I visited the church now roofed & floored & waiting the erection of the brick walls. The workmen were lolling in various manner- the stone-cutters were perched upon the board platform which they use for a bed in their rude shanty- playing at cards on the church floor- one fellow was leaned back against a post reading- another lay on a plank asleep- a third was tailoring on his own account- another sharpening a new axe for some out-sider- & a group instantly gathered about me to see my watch & discuss the virtues of the lead pencil. I asked the lazy beggars why they did not resume their work- They said they were taking their "nooning". I inquired how much "nooning" they took. They said three hours, or if they took one- just for dinner- they received a hundred cash a day more- How many hours a day do you work then? From 8 to 12 & from 3 to 6- about six or eight hours & the best part of the day- the morning- lost. No wonder they work for ten cents a day. At evening walked upon the hills. On one of the highest points to the West of my house- overlooking all the foreign residences- the river- suburbs- city & extensive views in the opposite directions- met- without previous concert- three sedan chairs. Mrs. Maclay with her husband & three boys were there- poor sick Mrs. Peet, worn out with the missionary labors of sixteen years- was there with her husband & three girls- the wife of Capt. Fletcher of the Maury- with Jimmy for a gallant-was there- & myself with baby in my arms completed the group-On an opposite knoll- quarter of a mile away, in front of the English Consulate was gathered a group of merchants & ship cap-tains & along the far reaching paths of the cemetery solitary horsemen usually enveloped in a perfect whirlwind of foreign dogs were galloping along in quest of amusement in this more solitary mode of exercise. A coming shower drove a portion of the party to the shelter of my house- An hour after they had gone- Mr. Comstock- merchant- burst into my parlor all on a sudden- while I was fingering the melodeon- with a party of Cap-tains. Captain Fletcher sang for an hour to the melodeon & piano-to the admiration of all present- He has everything at command-Sacred songs- sentimental songs- sailors songs- negro ditties and all. He is a natural musician- They drank some home brewed beer-which my cook had concocted of hops & ginger- & left.

The mosquito net of sister's crib is good but she gets bitten when the nurse takes her up in the night. To obviate this-put up the curtain over the large bedstead for sister & the wet nurse & give Ling Choah- Mrs. Farley's net to spread for herself over a settee bed.

May 28th- Wednesday

Started down the river yesterday morning in a boat with Capt. Fletcher to visit his ship. It is always exhilarating to get upon the water. Our run down to the Pagoda was accomplished in two hours & there we were in the presence of a fleet of ships riding quietly at anchor waiting the coming down of the first teas of the season. The Maury, Ringleader-Wild Duck-John Wade, America- The Chrysolite & Lord of the Isles- English. They will all load as quickly as possible when there will be a grand scamper for London & he who arrives first will bear an enviable palm. It will give Fuh Chau uncommon advantage over the other ports that the earliest teas will always be shipped from here. The Chrysolite is one of the faster sailers in the world & the Lord of the Isles- a beautiful iron hull- will not be much behind her. The Maury is a pretty little vessel about the size of the Storm. Cabin not much larger & yet she brought out to Shanghai eleven passengers- nearly all missionaries. The wife of the Capt. has sailed with him these seven years. Judge of their feelings two years ago when in the dangerous pass at the mouth of the Min- they hastily landed on a rock projecting from the shore upon which the splendid Oriental- a Clipper of 1500 tons- settled to the bottom before their eyes- engulfing the second cargo of teas ever taken from the warehouses of Fuh Chau-

It rained a good deal while we were on board so that we were confined under the awnings of the quarter deck. At night we retired once more, after nearly a year's respite- to the narrow berths of confined state rooms. It awakened many interesting reminiscences to be once more in a little "cuddy" with not room to stand straight- just length enough to bestow six feet of humanity lengthwise & two to roll over in width-wise. I seemed to fear being pitched against the lamp- into the wash basin- out of the berth- against the side anywhere by some unlucky roll or lurch of the vessel- riding on the uncertain wave. She was securely harbored & lay as quiet as a sleeping infant. Not so her ill starred visitors. The night was hot- rooms close- & mosquitoes furious. There were no mosquito nettings & escape from the thickening battalions was impossible. The only mode was to lie awake with some loose garment in your hand flourishing it about your head to repel their onsets. I was awake all night- A brief doze between three & four was the only time I was unconscious during the whole of the tossing hours of darkness. The Captain fared no better while he divided the night betwixt his state room & the quarter deck. Jimmy was nearly raving. After fighting the vandals till two in the morning he arose & dressed & walked the deck till daylight- We had doleful experiences to relate at the breakfast table. Dr. Leicester dined with us. He & the American Consul are at odds- The Dr. is said to be in debt to some Chinaman- who complains to the American Consul of its non-payment- Mr. Consul summons Dr. L. to appear & show cause why he does not fulfil his engagement. The Dr., with a little of that independence which characterizes the Americans world over, delays or declines to come. Whereupon Mr. Consul deputises one to arrest him & bring him before him by force- which after some knockings down-a great display of knives- revolvers- swords & bayonets & a great deal of swearing on both sides was finally accomplished. His trial is to come off this week & until that he is attending on his patients upon his parole of honour. He is an adventurer & has recently been a hundred & fifty miles up the Min- probably further than any foreigner has ever been before- The third mate on the Maury is a Stonington boy & the first mate a Philadelphian.

We left for our return about 2 p.m. & soon found ourselves in company with a fleet of native boats & the boats of foreigners. Within hail of us were four boats belonging to two firms which had on board a hundred & fifty thousand dollars in specie for the purchase of teas. In a day or two it will be scudding up into the tea district-

Baby was glad to see us on our return. She was quartered at Mrs. Maclay's nursery during our temporary absence. I read on the Maury "Norma Leslie" "Shady Side" & "Which-right or left". Shady Side is shady enough & after one or two settlements of the puritan incumbent gets tiresome. Right or left is a tragedy of power & perhaps an overstrained justice upon the reigning religion of fashionable life-

May 29th- Thursday

A rainy, yet sultry day- I slept as well as studied. It is a day of preparation & event. Mrs. Consul Jones gives a large dinner party & the hum of conversation is distinctly audible across my garden intervening. I hope it will eventuate in better feeling than the party of the Brit. Consul on the queen's birth-day. A question of procedure in seats arose & the Interpreter- whose wife claimed the seat of honor at the Consul's right- "gallantly" awarded by him to the lady of the American Consul- drew off his family forces in disgust without waiting to toast the buxom representative of divinity & the might of the people of the British throne. Fashion & folly are inseparable.

May 30th- Friday

The Watchman sends up word to the breakfast table that this is pay day- with a gentle intimation that $3. for keeping me awake with his miserable bamboo sticks will be acceptable. The Chinese sensibly measure everything decimally. Their weeks, if they have any, are periods of ten days & their months of thirty. I remind Mr. Kang-Kang that Western months are of variable lengths & that his cash is not due till tomorrow. Sister has a trifle of cold- the first she has ever had. I tremble at the slightest quiver of a leaf pertaining to my beautiful bud.

It is a hot day- the first of the season. Foreigners have

to keep still through the middle of such a day- The evening is seductively cool & pleasant- I avoid drafts as I would North-Westers. Their insidious coolness is more to be dreaded- Yet Anna used to court them last season with impunity-

Dr. Leicester had his trial before the embodiment of American Democracy today- I hear that the umpires fined him $100. for contempt of court in not appearing before the Consul when first summoned-

May 31st- Saturday

The last night was exceedingly oppressive. Though sleepy I could not sleep & a fit of nervous palpitation lent its sickening effects to the distresses of the night. Rose at 5 this morning. It is the pay day & mission meeting day for the month. The servants receive their silver with modest nonchalance- but spend the next hour ringing the dollars- guessing at their weight & speculating over them like a boy over a holiday dollar.

In mission meeting all our affairs are wound up for the month- Our masons are a great trouble- It is almost impossible to make them build walls straight- To them, our little churches are perfect "Trinity's" & the work superior to any they are ever called on to do here. Yet it lacks a grain or two of artistic perfection & that lack we are laboring to supply- Gibson kicks over their bungling fortresses of brick & mortar without ceremony if they are not built to suit him- We find here the attendant curse of building contracts- the world over- extras- for every change & addition- The carpenter already has a round sum for doing the wood work of the church- but will now have to be paid extra for building columns & cornice- a job which had been included with the contract of the masons but which they are unable to perform. I have all along wanted granite columns single shaft of which are readily procured of the desired length- but their weight- five thousand pounds apiece- deters the workmen- who manage everything by hand- from offering to bring them to so elevated a spot as our church is located on.

At evening make my first essay in white for the season- We changed our dinner hour also- It is too hot to eat in the middle of the day- So we tiffin at 12- & dine at 4- The experiment worked well for the first time.

Our hopeful merchants & foreign officials instituted this evening a "brandy & soda-water" club, subscribing over a hundred dollars for the purposes of public drinking. While the prohibiting system is urging its way in their states at home- they are repudiating the doctrine in daily practice. This illustrated the fact that man is always as bad as the circumstances about

139

him will allow. Virtue is as often the result of external pressure as of the attraction of internal principle. Out of sight of his fellows man will indulge every passion without license- To the East India fashionables license would be perfect- but for "these damned missionaries"-

June 1st- Sunday

Morning hot- June is inaugurated in a blaze- I donned whites- all but frock & boots- The naked servants wonder how I can endure woollens in such weather- The service is at Mr. Peet's & the audience- it would be a misnomer to call such a handful a "congregation"- is in summer array & white dresses & thin gauzes flutter in the breeze that plays freely through a room two whole sides of which are wide open to light & air- The sleepy few listen with exemplary patience to father Peet's third or fourth homily on "thy will be done". It is great proof of piety to listen well to prosy essays in hot weather. A stranger youth was present- In dress & mien American- At 4 I visited the Chinese Chapel- while brother Maclay was discoursing on idols- a gong was heard rattling furiously past the door- followed by a devil or two & four or six gigantic figures in procession- It was in honor of the god who has in charge the dysentery & other complaints peculiar to this season. If their gods tips had tumbled fruit stands- with their arbutus- cucumbers- squashes- peas- beans- & peaches- into the river or laid an embargo on public glutting- the prayers & offerings of the day might prove efficacious.

June 2nd- Monday

Visited at noon by one of the curiosity pedlars- Never intend to buy- He spreads them out that we may look- Dont rush us to purchase unless we wish- "This is pretty"- "That is pretty"- It would take a fortune to buy all the beautiful houses of Fuh Chau & the inimitable carved work of Ningpo. Two dollars & a half gone for a couple of pieces- For what! "It will be so nice to send to friends in America!"

Monthly Mission concert this p.m. at my house- Mail has arrived- letters & papers of March- How pleasant- Mr. & Mrs. Gibson stay to a dinner prepared for young Mr. Sargeant of Salem, Mass.- passenger on board the Ringleader- but who did not come. Five hundred dollars take him via the Horn to California- Shanghai- Fuh Chau- Hong Kong & via Good Hope- to London & home- Round the world!

June 3rd- Tuesday

Today the bricklayers commence the wall of the chapel on this side of the river. I was over at 8 o'clock- They had not begun- Over again at nine & they had initiated the performance with two men instead of the twenty promised & at a point- exactly where we did not care about their working at present- I called Mr. Maclay & together we drove a dozen or more from various piddling jobs to the central interest- showed them where & how to set to work & then I watched them all day. In the afternoon the perspiration rolled from <u>me</u> in streams- with the mere effort of looking on. You may judge of the intensity of the heat when such an iceberg as I am begins to run to water. The naked natives enjoy it- provided they have plenty of rice at meals- a few bowls of steaming hot tea to refresh themselves during the day & three hours sleep while the rays of the sun are fiercest. It is the hardest thing imaginable to make them build anything straight, level or rectangular. Any approximation to exactness satisfies their rude tastes & they wonder at our scrupulous care in lines & angles, "Pang-pang" (a as in father) & "Tick-tick"- "Level" & "straight" are in our mouths from morning till night & even then walls & doorways will emulate the Hogarth's "line of grace & beauty"! They are improving under instruction. The Chinese- you know- are by no means slow to catch & adapt an idea- Our greatest difficulty is with their perverse attachment to preconceived notions of their own. A Chinaman is as obsequious as a money lending Jew or a Court parasite- yet as obstinate as an ass. He will fawn- ingly say "Yes-yes-yes" to your directions at the same time that he is doing & probably in his own mind- intending to do- exactly as <u>he</u> thinks it should be done. Our sole remedy is watchfulness & preemptoriness. Leave them to themselves & they would cover our christian temples with horns & dragons- build the sides leaning & prop them with unsightly posts from without.

To-day our retail store has been sold out at auction under attachment for the debts of the firm recently "smashed up" at Shanghai! It will be carried on by the young American who has been clerk in it for a year. It is a great convenience though every article is at California prices.

June 4th- Wednesday

Had a bad night. Hot & rainy- could not sleep. Overtaxed myself yesterday- commencing the brick laying- Went to bed tired & sleepy- but tossed restlessly half the night. Spent the morning in overseeing the workmen.

Mrs. Smith- recently arrived from Shanghai- is sick- Mr. Maclay was sent for to converse with her in connection with her religious experience- day before yesterday- To-day Mrs. M. went to sit with & attend upon her. There are so few ladies here that they have to perform their kind offices for each other- which at home are so apt to be <u>over</u> done by one's own cousins & aunts & neighbors-

141

The middle of the day was hot- but- as yesterday- about five the heavens gathered blackness in the West & by seven- after a great deal of marshalling of heavy masses of clouds- a great deal of distant thunder & lightning- from the coming storm- it reaches us & bursts with all fury in wind- lightning & pouring torrents- It is about the season of the year corresponding to our rainy voyage for Hong Kong- The river is covered with noisy "drag- on boats," long canoes holding thirty to fifty men with paddles which they ply furiously in keeping time with a drum & the bow- flying madly in all directions in pursuit of some virtuous maiden who thousands of years since drowned herself in despair because he was not able to reform the corruptions of government.

This evening- at last Jimmy practiced an hour- "Fischer's Horn Pipe" by rote- on the piano. He is impatient of scientific labor & though- a good deal of a rote man- will never- I begin to fear accomplish anything which requires application.

June 5th- Thursday

Bricklaying & dragon boats.

June 6th- Friday

The church walls go up rapidly betwixt bricks & mud- Lime mortar is not used. The Chinese substitute the more readily prepared soil at their feet. A mortar bed is conveniently made wherever they happen to light- The courses between the bricks are not the thinnest imaginable, but the walls rise rapidly & mud saves bricks to the contractors. I spend the whole day among the workmen- mangling Chinese as they mangle their work.

Racing on the river goes on furiously to-day. Jimmy spends the day on the island to see it close at hand. Sister dines with me. She dislikes sweet & flavoured things- Prefers tender meats-

June 7th- Saturday

Dreamed last night of being in a crowded vehicle with Mr. & Mrs. Lewis & others apparently nearing West Chester- It was dark & the road heavy- Rising a steep hill- I gave the reins to Anna & floundered upon foot. The horse- a large fiery animal pulled furiously for awhile but finally gave up & floundered & flounced till assistance came. We reached home shortly after- when Mr. Lewis said he had never known the horse act so before- It seemed as though I was to go further- but Anna pressed me to stay all night with one of those sweet winning smiles so charac- teristic of her- I had consulted & was yielding myself the full satisfaction & enjoyment in her society when the agreeable vision fleeted away.

142

This is the 5th day, 5th mo. 6th yr. (ye quakers) of the reign of Hang Hung & the anniversary of the festival of the dragon boats celebrated on all the waters of this great empire. The rowers have been exercising these four or five days- & the river has presented the most animated appearance- Passage boats- house boats- junks- rafts & all kinds of river craft were moored conveniently so as to allow free avenue in every direction for the sporting boats- while they were so disposed to allow those on board to see and enjoy to the full extent the exercise of strength & skill put forth by the holiday rowers. The banks were lined with spectators & upon the roofs of the houses rising out of a multitude of courts might be seen gaily dressed women enjoying at a distance pleasures which their confined situation would not allow them to participate more nearly. At noon the workmen upon the chapel- itself situated high up the hill receding from the South bank of the river- mounted piles of brick & timber to have a better view of the exciting spectacle watched by shouting thousands below.

The dragon boat is a sort of shallow- airy canoe- sixty feet long & barely wide enough for two persons abreast. The Chinese commonly row standing with long oars and sculls- in the dragon boat sit thirty pairs of rowers- each with a short paddle in his hand- the strokes of which are regulated by the strokes upon a huge drum in the centre of the boat & the waving of a flag in the bow

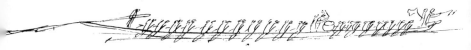

When one of these airy pleasure sheltops is approaching or receding from you- the numerous paddles plied on either side with regular & vigorous motion resemble the legs of a crawling centipede- The racing constitutes the chief zest of the pastime- When two get along side headed in the same direction they fairly fly through the water & the foam & spray rebounds from their numerous paddles as from the wheels of a steamer.

June 8th- Sunday

A year ago today we were essaying to leave the harbor of Hong Kong- What an eventful year! It- added to the six months previous seem as long to me as any ten- of my previous life so rapidly did events of the utmost moment succeed each other- like the thickening incidents of a plot approaching a stirring close-

Young Mr. Sargeant of Salem, Mass. has been staying with us for a day or two. He is a modest youth- well informed & agreeable company- It is refreshing to have a visit now & then from a white man.

June 9th- Monday

Wall building at the church all day. The unknown need constant watching- Here is a corner crooked & there a side two inches too short, windows & doorways out of proportion or askew. Everything in Chinese building is as awry as a Chinaman's optic organs. Mud takes the place of brick & is used unspairingly by as much as it is cheaper than either lime or brick- In some places we have detected seams of mud between the bricks near an inch thick! It is provoking to find a rod of well laid wall so out of proportion as to be obliged to order it taken down & re-laid once- twice- thrice before it slopes itself to the square according to Western ideas of rectangularity-

June 10th- Tuesday

Stirring betimes, this beautiful morning- After a hasty breakfast- embark at seven o'clock on board a spacious coolie boat to go down the river for the day. The craft is large-fitted either for sails or oars- with a square house or cabin in the centre- accommodated with a carpeted floor- cushioned seats & venetian blinds- capable of containing eight or nine persons- The rowers are ten lusty Chinamen who wield their oars standing & row to a wild chant or antiphonal melody- consisting of a few simple notes in the minor- One leads the solo & the rest join the chorus- with energy proportioned to the zest of the occasion.

Jimmy & I with our table boy went on board at the foot of the street leading from our house alongside the office of the British Consulate where, about twelve months ago we first debarked in Fuh Chau. By our order the boatman dropped down to the head of the Island & knocked at Mr. Gibson's watergate- whence after the usual delay in preparing women & babies- issued Mr. & Mrs. Gibson- with nurse & baby to join the expedition. I was sorry I had not brought sister along. The tide was setting down strongly & it- aided by the oars of the boatmen- soon shot us under the arches of the bridge & urged us for half a mile through the mazes of boats & junks & lorchas that throng the shipping ground for small craft for a long distance below the island. The watchful jealousy of the government alone- & not the want of water- prevents large ships from coming up to town- As it is, the anchorage for foreign ships & clippers is kept at a respectful distance from the walls of the Capital city of the province- Several miles below the town- an artificial barrier of sunken stones- prevents all access except through one narrow channel, the stoppage of which- at short notice, effectually bars the progress of any vessel of dangerous size, city-bound-

Our trip was delightful- The wind aided the oars & in two hours after enjoying the infinite variety of mountain, valley

144

& river scenery- we were nearing the anchorage- where were scattered about- six or eight large ships with a number of small craft- floating the flags of various nations- Two opium receiving ships & the British man of war lie here constantly- The smoke of the little steamer "Pluto"- engaged in towing out tea ships & running from port to port reminds us of the lands of steam- & sets our Chinese to wondering how a craft can go backward & forward at pleasure without wind or any visible means of propulsion-

We first climbed up the lofty sides of the Ringleader- a Boston ship- loading with early teas for London- Mrs. Peet & family are enjoying its hospitality for a week & receive us with pleasure- After admiring its princely accommodations for passengers- we went on board the "Golden Racer" from New York whose cabin was no way inferior to that of the "Ringleader". Thence we called on an English ship "John Taylor"- whose cabin exhibited substantial comforts- rather than showy ornaments- Her steward- an old Englishman- is a virtuoso in music & entertained us with several agreeable airs on a superb silver mounted flute- for which he wished to find a market & whose recommendation was having belonged to some distinguished player in London- I was reminded of Paganini's effort to sell a violin- It was not the violin on which he had achieved his triumphs & the British cat gut scrapers were shrewd enough to know that Paganini's fiddle required a Paganini! A good musician may bring ravishing strains out of a poor instrument & a superb instrument in the hands of a tyro is of small advantage. I often think of the sublime chords & movements yet slumbering undiscovered among the mines of the piano & wonder what angelic genius will fennel out their hiding places.

We returned on board the Ringleader at noon. The Captains of two English ships- with the wife of one of them called. Dinner appeared immediately on their departure- for which I was finely prepared by an early breakfast & the exercise of the forenoon- in clambering ships sides & rambling over their cabins & decks- Soup- duck- Irish & sweet potatoes- with genuine Yankee apple sauce (sass) & a dish of baked beans- by a New England cook- made it a princely meal. By the time it was well over- wind & tide were setting strongly upstream- & after two hours agreeable conversation in our little cabin we were landed at our own doors-

Before the mast- on the Ringleader- is Robert Adams- a youth of 15- son of Dr. Nathaniel Adams of "South Side" celebrity. He called on us at evening in company with Rev. Mr. Hartwell- where he is staying.

June 11th- Wednesday

Dear Anna's birthday- a rallying point for a thousand tender recollections on both hemispheres.

June 12th- Thursday

Baby is- let me count- how many months old to-day. August- September- October- November- December- January- February- March- April- May- Ten months & Madam Maclay exclaims "how she is improving". She already appears like a human being & begins to exert sway among her fellow mortals. Her table tastes are peculiar & decidedly carnivorous. She declines all excessively sweet things & such as are flavoured with essences. In their stead she prefers soups- meats- the gravy & softer parts of butter & milk toast- eats bread & likes nothing so well as the drumstick of a fowl. Bolstered in a chair at my right hand she signifies her pleasure or displeasure at whatever is passing- throws bread under the table to the cat- or sends my napkin ring spinning over the table or across the room- Yesterday the table boy was removing my finger glass before she had washed- according to daily custom. She forbade him most preemptorily.

June 13th- Friday

Jimmy drops down the river to the anchorage in company with one of our merchants. The masons on the church "strike" for the afternoon, because Gibson struck one of their number for swearing at him because he kicked down some badly built wall.

At evening take a sail with Maclays. In forenoon go to Long T'an to look at the finished Chapel- It is pretty & wonderful considering the builders- Foreigners speak of it with surprise & pleasure. Its angles are by no means right & its corners vary from perpendicularity- Yet if one takes the advice of the old head man to Gibson when he called to squint along the face of a wall- not to "look at it in piece-meal but take it all in at a glance"- it is a superb affair- I presume it is one of the best built foreign churches in China-

June 14th- Saturday

One year ago to-day we were at the mouth of the Min. It is raining as it was then & will doubtless keep up a wet anniversary- Masons' strike continues. Sister eats soup with us at dinner- Jimmy has the "chicken-coop" fever badly-

June 15th- Sunday

Rain- Mrs. Peet- the "nursing mother" of the missions was brought home from the "Ringleader" last night in apparently dying condition. She had been recruiting on the vessel- for a week- Yesterday morning her husband was awakened by her struggles for breath, just about light. He roused the Captain & both thought Mrs. Peet dying. Dr. Pritchard of the Brit. ship of war Racehorse was immediately summoned- who pronounced it congestion of the brain- a sort of apoplectic attack. Word was immediately sent up to town when Mr. Hartwell procured a spacious merchant's boat & brought the afflicted family with the insensible patient to their own home. Dr. Welton spent the night with them & did not encourage them to expect her life from hour to hour. To-day she is revived & wonders how she came to be in her own house-

It rains so severely that no one goes to church. Mrs. Gibson- perhaps affected by the news of Mrs. Peet's illness had a violent recurrence of diarrhea last night. She thinks she must make a health trip to Shanghai.

June 16th- Monday

Terrible rain- pouring all night- About 9 o'clock last evening- the flood undermined a portion of the wall of our neighbor to the West- Wetmore & Co. which fell with a terrible crash- alarming the whole neighborhood-

Mrs. Maclay watched with Mrs. Peet- who said it was the first time in all her sicknesses during sixteen years residence in the East that she had had a watcher-

June 17th- Tuesday

The sky is trying to clear up- An inside jam to one of the windows of our church- partly built up of native bricks- was washed down by the rain of Sunday. Steamer Confucious arrives from Shanghai. Rev. Dr. Bridgman- the oldest missionary except Dr. Medhurst- came a passenger. At night the full moon struggles up among the broken cloud masses of the East while sharp lightnings & protracted thunders in the opposite heavens indicated that the weather was still far from settled.

June 18th- Wednesday

One year since we landed in Fuh Chau- Commemorated by a violent rain. How full of vicissitudes! The little community of Fuh Chau has changed half its population in the time. The new cemetery just being laid out as we arrived has half a dozen graves. Yet life thrives upon death. There are six interesting little specimens of humanity who have entered upon light & life since our coming- all healthy and well.

June 19th- Thursday

Rain & flood-

June 20th- Friday

Rain- rain & flood- all communication with the island is cut off. The yards of the foreign houses on the island are all under water & the residents confined within.

June 21st- Saturday

Intelligence brought this morning of the death of Mrs. Doolittle- She was confined last Sabbath night & has finished her course in five days from that event- She leaves a husband & boy, two or three years old to mourn her loss-

June 22nd- Sunday

The day appointed for Mrs. Doolittle's funeral- Rain & the height of the flood in the river prevent- Mail comes- Letters from Mr. & Mrs. Lewis dated Dec. 23rd & Jan. 14th which appear to have gone astray at Hong Kong as they bear the Post Mark of that port April & May & the stamp "returned for postage"- From which I infer that it traveled back somewhere on a collecting tour. An English steamer comes into port- & anchors along side of the Confucious just at the foot of the island- She is tender to a British ship of the line which lies at the mouth of the river-

June 23rd- Monday

Funeral of Mrs. Doolittle attended by many of the American community at 1 o'clock- Mr. Hartwell & Dr. Bridgman conducted the services. The bier was followed by a long procession of Sedan Chairs- native & foreigner- Tears.

June 24th- Tuesday

Steamer Confucious does not leave till to-morrow- The weather has cleared off, beautiful & bracing- Afternoon a terrific shower- a perfect cloud burst for half an hour. Hill at evening covered with foreigners- officers of the British Ships of war- consular dignitaries, merchants- passengers from various ships- ladies in sedans & all attended by dogs & Chinese too numerous for calculation. The scene was quite lively & exhilarating-

June 25th- Wednesday

Dismissed my cook this morning. He refused to take in a few articles from the shower yesterday- he causes it was "Not his business"- though every other Chinaman was absent from the premises at the moment- I paid him his three dollars for the month & cut him adrift- In ten minutes he took his departure with all his worldly effects in a little bundle. Convenient poverty.

June 26th- Thursday

Teacher appears to-day for the first time since the floods. The Fuh Chau floods- I mean- not Noah's- Says he has been sleeping in his second story for the week past. The city lies low as well as the suburbs except abrupt hills & gives its inhabitants an annual chance to play amphibia.

June 27th- Friday

Hardly anything occurs to break the monotony of existence. A fire on the Island this week- one night- swept off a hundred houses & left a clear space of an acre or two. It would be agreeable if foreigners could buy it & never allow it to grow up to dingy shanties again.

My teacher & coolie are engaged to-day in wiping my books which have accumulated mould from the long rain.

Discovered my trunk with a few cast off articles of my own & Anna's in it perfectly alive with white ants a few days since- Scalded them out of their lodgings & rot- though every article was riddled & the wool itself converted into honey comb.

June 28th- Saturday

Uncomfortably warm in morning with cooling showers in the afternoon. Baby insists on her usual evening walk on the hills- points to the gate & begs & teases, greatly to the amusement of her nurses & cannot be made to understand by English- Chinese or dumb show that it rains & she cannot be indulged.

In the evening Jimmy & I call on Mrs. Consul Jones- She has invited all Fuh Chau to dinner on the coming 4th. Fifty-seven invitations. She said the missionaries are reckoned among the "relatives" partly from their own known aversions to oriental jollifications- partly from their being cumbered with babies without which they never stir out of the house, & partly for personal reasons- the nature of which you can conjecture from your acquaintance with passengers in general- Two have declined. The wife of the Interpreter of H.B.M. Consulate & daughter, the ladies so deeply affronted on the queen's birthday in the affair of the seat of honor. The wrong will be amply avenged on the Republic by slighting so notable an occasion as the "Glorious Fourth". Mrs. Jones entertained us with her journey across the Isthmus on a mule before the days of rail-road.

June 29th- Sunday

Another contest with heathenism this morning. The workmen on Wetmore's lot next us commenced in full band to work this morning as usual- leaving our ears no rest from their din even upon the Sabbath. I sent for the head man- told him it was Sunday & begged them to desist- He acquiesced- but many of his workmen demurred & raised such an outrageous din that Consul Jones threw open his blinds and discharged a pistol in that direction which quelled the noise & scattered the rioters- The Chinese have a wonderful fear of foreign arms. I was in the city one day when a crowd collected as usual curious to see my umbrella & asking if it contained a dagger like a sword cane. I took hold of the ivory head & made a motion to draw it out when the whole crowd stept back as instinctively as if I had flashed an actual sword in their faces.

June 30th- Monday

"Chee-ing" is the first word that salutes my ear this morning. The Chinese are good time keepers & "cash" is an omnipresent idea- if not- an omnipresent reality. The watchman gets his cheeing & rejoices in the chink of silver more than I do in the thumping of his nightly bamboo rattle- The old wet nurse cannot wail- but comes in to the house to dun for cheeing. Finally all are "cheeing"-ed around & sent on their way rejoicing till the conclusion of another month.

In mission meeting to-day we resolve to authorize Bro. Gibson to build a house on one of our vacant lots at an expense not exceeding $2500. Our first mission houses were erected here in much trembling- mere bungalows at $500. a piece. Dr. Wiley built a brick house as he was leaving at a cost of $1500- five premises on the island- The British Interpreter's house built this winter cost $6000- American- Consul's $2000- Wetmore & Co. $4500- now building Dent & Co- $10,000- Gilman & Co- I should think $10,000- It has a stone colonnade the whole length of a long verandah- indeed running all around the house- Russel & Co. are preparing to build a handsome house. I hope to replace mine within two years if I live- If not it will be work for some body else-

A thunder shower cools the air at evening- the third in succession- at the same hour in the evening. To-day came a cask of vinegar- a cask of meal & a box of Boston crackers from N.Y. All right except the crackers of which half had been stolen by the sailors- we judge- on the voyage- There were but 3 lbs- & the freight on them from Hong Kong was $2.00-

July 1st- Tuesday

Yesterday we received a box per Mandarin with the whole of three pounds of crackers in it- to-day a barrel of meal & a cask of vinegar both of which came directed to "Gibson" who expected in lieu thereof a barrel of flour & a barrel of butter- The mission also received a large safe for the deposit of papers & funds. The little one I brought was a great comfort to dear Anna from the sense of security it afforded among people who are habitual pilferers- though I used to laugh at her for locking the safe & keeping her key of it in an open drawer- At one time I recollect going to it & after making desperate efforts to turn the key found it had not been locked at all. However, it stood in her apartment, draped like a toilette- none of the Chinese ever saw us open it & I doubt if they knew what it was till after her departure when my Chinese boy took oversight of my personal matters.

July 2nd- Wednesday

A box of National Magazines- Ladies Repositories Quarter- lies- newspapers & Conference Minutes came to-day- Such an occasion is always a treat. We lay aside everything to read the held over dal- monthly or quarterly effusions of the fortunate scribblers who have found their way into print. My article on Singapore in the National Magazine (Dec) is printed quite correctly. It says we rode after "mule ponies" instead of male ponies- which does evident injustice to the shaggy- fiery little vagabonds of the pure equine species that flow with us at exhilarating speed- over the hills & smooth roads of that lovely island- It was our only taste of real India life & I have never been able since to conceive how the garden of Eden could have been located outside of the tropics. Batavia- the old Dutch city on Java- one corner of which we touched on our voyage- is said to be the loveliest place to reside in of all the East- Yet in former years it was a perfect charnel house to foreigners- Since the fall, every Eden- except the upper Paradise is cursed with the flaming sword- Burning fevers & noxious pestilenses are hand & glove with luxurious cli- mates-

July 3rd- Thursday

While I was at the church this afternoon between 3 & 4- a couple of the workmen brought news of a riot in progress between the Canton & Fuh Chau men. They are common & I paid little attention to it. Between 5 & 6- standing at my upper gate- the American Consul passed on his homeward way with a posse of sailors from the British Man of War & I learned that Americans had been mixed in the disturbance & that one man- clerk with Augustine Head & Co. had been seriously wounded. The firm had built a new house & were moving into it their furni- ture & household stuff- A quarrel arose between their Canton men & the people of the ward to which they were moving. While they were beating the boy- Mr. Comstock- head of the house in Fuh Chau attempted to rescue him- but was roughly handled by the mob & obliged to go in quest of assistance- Mr. Cunningham next arrived and probably attempted to disperse the crowd & rescue the boy by discharging his revolver- as two Fuh Chau men were afterward discovered with serious shot wounds- Mr. Vaughn- the third man of the house arrived immediately after & by the vigorous use of a sword cane succeeded in dragging poor Cunningham out of the crowd who were beating him as he lay bleeding & covered with bruises. He was found to have received a severe wound to the side with a sword or spear- The surgeon of the Race Horse & three other doctors are in attendance & his life is despaired of-

July 4th- Friday

Rose at 6 to attend the funeral of the mate of an English ship. Mr. Maclay read the English burial service at the grave- Went thence to Comstock's- Cunningham died at 2 this morning of his wounds. It was a ghastly sight- the body of a young man three & twenty years old covered with bruises & lifeless- I thought as I looked upon it of the declaration of the Savior "they that take the sword shall perish by the sword"- A post-mortem examina- tion showed that some sharp instrument had punctured the side- passed through the liver & gall & entered the stomach- severing an artery or so in its passage- He suffered great pain & bled profusely but died quietly at last from loss of blood & exhaustion.

Mrs. Consul Jones' preparations for the celebration of the "glorious fourth" were brought to a stand & we poor missionaries who were not included in the expected "route" had to help consume a portion of the extensive preparations for the ostentatious occa- sion- Our share was a fat duck- a pigeon pie- pastry & cakes- Her dining room was gorgeously ornamented with flags & the verandahs illuminated like day with all manner of Chinese & foreign lanterns & astrals fantastic & elegant- All this note of preparation died away in gloom & sadness-

At six o'clock on the evening of the 4th- the entire foreign population repaired to the house of the deceased- the coffin- covered with the American flag was borne on the shoulders of British sailors from the Man of War & followed by a procession of sixty or eighty English & Americans- Consuls- Merchants-British officers- ship Captains & missionaries- Hundreds of the Chinese witnessed the imposing ceremonial & a mandarin of rank brought up the rear of the procession on its way to the foreign cemetery. Mr. Maclay conducted the services by extempore remarks & extempore prayers after our American manner. The British Vice Consul, in charge, issued a circular proffering protection to the foreign community but cautioning them against outraging the native mind in its present state of excitement & hostility-

July 5th- Saturday

Accompanied a young gentleman from Boston- passenger on the Mandarin- to the city to-day. Visited the English missionaries in their monastery home & went thence to the curiosity shops-where Mr. Gray made his selections of bronzes- roof work & the like & I cheapened the exorbitant charges of the shopmen from twenty or thirty dollars to eight & he came away with a respectable assortment of wares-

July 6th- Sunday

The rumor that Bro. Maclay was to preach a funeral discourse brought out a number of merchants to church to-day, a somewhat unusual occurrence with us- After service Mr. Doolittle administered the communion-

Letters from America to-day from the rooms & elsewhere- I received one from young Swively & no other.

We had an unprecedented misfortune with our dinner today- The soup was good- the bread, sent us from Mrs. Jones was spoiled- The boy brought a loaf of our own- It was spoiled- The meat came up- Madame Jones pigeon-pie- My olfactions revolted the moment it was set before notwithstanding the boy's assurance that it was perfectly good- The Chinese sense of smell is not the most delicate in the world. The pigeon-pie went to the dog & we dined on vegetables. Pumpkin pie followed- that also was sour- The weather is hot- there are but two of us & things spoil in advance of our light consumption. The cook was ordered to make less & more frequently.

July 7th- Monday

This evening called at the house of the British interpreter. The residence is new- spacious- tastefully & somewhat expensively furnished. A grand piano is one of the attractions of the parlor- We sat down to a cosy tea in the back drawing room- Mr. Gingell is small- slightly built- with large Italian eyes- glossy black hair curling in ringlets & moustache- & looking more like a Frenchman than Englishman. He is elegant in manners & delightful in conversation- if we except a few shades of a certain asperity frequently accompanying a bilious temperament. His lady small also- tolerably stoutly built- punctiliously dressy & polite, talkative & agreeable- They ride out every evening- She in an open sedan chair & he on horseback usually in the centre of a whirlwind of dogs, of every size & species- a favorite affection or affectation of the British gentry.

July 8th- Tuesday

Spent the evening at the American consul's- my days are devoted entirely to the new church- Mr. & Mrs. Gingell were present & at eight o'clock we sat down in the dining room with a punkah dispensing typhoons over our heads to aid in demolishing the sad fragments of a feast prepared but not enjoyed- The servants ran off with immense quantities of the articles collected for the occasion- as matter of course-

July 9th- Wednesday

Day at church- Evening at one or two merchants, conversing on the exciting topic that has thinned their little circle-

July 10th- Thursday

Mr. & Mrs. Maclay & family go down the river to spend a few of their "baking days" on board the Samuel Russel for change. The United States Commissioner Dr. Parker arrives in the ship of war Levant- very opportune & somewhat unexpectedly- though the Consul had sent a dispatch over land to Amoy- to expedite his coming. The doctor is getting to look rather venerable- bald & grey- with shaggy brows over hanging deep set eyes. His manner is blandness itself.

July 11th- Friday

Call at evening on Mr. Comstock- merchant- with whom Capt. Perit & lady of the Mandarin are staying. They are residents of Wilmington, Del. & Mrs. P. kindly offered to take Anna home with her. She is not ready for the voyage- Is not weaned yet & has no clothing prepared.

July 12th- Saturday

Consul Medhurst returns from Shanghai- The Capt. of the Levant invites me to preach on board tomorrow-

July 13th- Sunday

Breakfast at 6- Start at 7 in company with the Capt. of the Man of War & the Consul for the pagoda anchorage- In three hours we were on ship board- At 11 the men were assembled for divine service- to whom I preached a brief exhortation- We dined with the Capt. at 2 & returned to town by 6. Jimmy carried his hands full of Christian Advocates which were eagerly sought by the crew- The Antelope- steamer came while we were there having a-tow a yacht belonging to Mr. Cunningham of the house of Russel & Co- a beautiful little schooner built in the United States & sent out- Three steamers are in port & the fourth ex- pected- The Confucious- Amer. now owned by the Chinese- the Coromandel British- which brought Consul Medhurst- & the Antelope America- which brought Bishop Boone of the Protestant Episcopal Mission at Shanghai. Jimmy received a coop of Shanghai fowls & I got cheering letters from friends- among others- one from my old friend Freeman- fellow voyageur upon the bark Storm.

July 14th- Monday

Spent the day in ministering to the wants of Bishop Boone. He took a room by invitation at Bro. Maclay's & they are away. The voyage has damaged his system, & the first thing to do was to get him to bed- then to administer castor oil- then to get the servants to prepare rice gruel- then to get lemon water- then to leave him to recruit by sleep- at 5 o'clock to fetch him to our house to dine- then to get him back- get him lights- get him water- get him dover's powders- & lemon syrup & sugar to take them in- then to get him to bed for the night & leave the house which we had scarcely accomplished when Bro. Maclay & Mrs. Maclay & "Robby" & "Arty" & "Charley" & Charley's nurse arrived from their moonlight trip up the river & took the house & the sickness & slumbers of the bishop in charge for the night-

July 15th- Tuesday

Bishop much better. Better than I am- My rest was broken up last night. Mrs. Consul Jones gave a dinner party to 30 or 40 in honor of the U.S. Commissioner Dr. Parker. I was falling into my first sleep about 9 1/2 or 10- when a crash like the falling of a house roused me, broad awake- It was the stamping & cheering & table thumping ratification of a speech or a toast & by no means the last one- Cheers interspersed with laughter- loud jokes & songs lasted till midnight & after. It must be quite a change for the Reverent Commissioner from Watt's Hymns & the home principles of Total Abstinence- to the wine & brandy table of thirty years back & such ditties as "Away down upon de Swaney ribber- far, far, away" & sung in nefarious with all the company in chorus- wailing "All de world am sad & dreary- wheresoe'er

155

I roam- O darkies how my heart grows weary far from de ole folks at home"! This appeared to be the especial favorite as it was sung scores of times in the course of the evening.

I spent the day at the church- If church going were a test of piety I might feel encouraged as I spend all my time among the bricks & mortar of our rising sanctuary. I nearly lost my temper in the morning. The Chinese build the walls- face the sides & fill in the interstices with mud & fragments & even dirt- for cheapness & because in their wide low structures- strength is no object. But when we come to raise a wall 30 or 40 feet it is necessary to have it solid & we contract with them for solid wall- but the rascals stow away in it all the trash they can while our backs are turned. I went to the church this morning & found a couple of wicker hods full of mere dirt & fragments ready to be passed up to the workmen upon the scaffolds- I quietly emptied them out & told the men to pass up solid bricks instead. Where upon one of the attendants fell upon another with a great show of abuse & threatening- saying- how is it that you continue to give the bricklayers dirt & pieces when you know the Teacher has often told you to use only good bricks- Would you believe that half an hour later I detected this same embodiment of honesty in endeavour to pass up his hod laden with the same kind of trash- or would you think me to blame when I tell you I caught it up & emptied the contents all over his naked waitership- Half an hour later- when my back was turned they passed a hod full of the stuff up- I suspected it- followed it up the ladder- & with it pelted the attendants below till they got out of the range of my shot- This time I raised a grand row & threatened to thresh the whole of them- tear their wall down & do a great many other things in the grand style if they did not desist- They built solid wall for the rest of the day- Spent the evening very pleasantly with Bishop Boone. Assisted him to buy a few "curios" of a travelling pedlar (traveling peddler- if you prefer it)- He got a nice hand full for five dollars- for which the man demanded at least fifteen upon first setting out- It is only by learning what these fellows will actually sell for that we learn the value of their articles.

July 16th- Wednesday

Mission meeting at Bro. Gibsons- Resolve to ask appropriation of $2500 to build Gibson a house next winter.

July 17th- Thursday

In a morning call at Messrs Russel & Co. I present our church subscription & get $120., to which Dr. Parker adds $10. in the evening making our total $1088- of which $50. is from Consul Jones the only one not cashed-

156

July 18th- Friday

News comes that Mrs. Peet died at 10 last night- after
alternating for four weeks between fear and hope- A few days
ago she was well enough to go out to the parlor & dining room.

I go to the city with Bishop Boone- four coolies each-
quite mandarin-ist- but the bishop is heavy & it will take six
of the eight to carry him up the hill on which Dr. Welton resides-
The number did not prevent them from dropping one end of his
chair in the middle of the street- an experiment I have never
had tried on me yet- Our first landing after an hours riding through
the thronged lanes of the suburbs & city was at the "curio" shops-
a medley of old copper vases- urns- plates &C. inlaid with silver-
very much sought for by foreigners & commanding of course very
high prices- The bishop had left his purse behind- cheapened many
things- but bought nothing- We staid to dine with Mr. Macaw
& I returned home to attend the funeral of Mrs. Peet- a mournful
pageant- at 6-

July 19th- Saturday

Bishop Boone leaves for Shanghai in the Haley-

July 20th- Sunday

A hot morning- Too dispiriting to preach- so to save-
strength & avoid excitement- I read a sermon which I composed
a great many years ago- on "the fashion of this world passeth
away"-

Mrs. Gibson has a violent recurrence of the diarrhea.
Went down at evening & found her better but extremely weak-
She will look after her own household- persists in nursing her
babe- & loads herself with useless cases- if she would only think
them such- We took a boat back & found the river breeze grateful
after a hot day. Took tea, or rather a cup of hot milk & water
at Mr. Maclay's afterward.

July 21st- Monday

Excessively hot-

July 22nd- Tuesday

Hot & stifling- Got a Chinese mat between me & the
mattress last night & slept quite cool.

July 23rd- Wednesday

Heat increasing- The Levant leaves- all the bustle of parties for blue coats- anchor buttons & epaulettes will cease with the departure of these two dozen officials- over two hundred of the brave "defenders of our country" from the results of troubles of our own making- Fuh Chau is not battered level with the ground because a rash youth was killed by running upon the spears of an excited mob & our illustrious Consul will froth like a pot of his own ale for the next six months- The authorities have given full assurance that they will protect the lives & property of foreigners pursuing their lawful avocations & they will do so as far as their means extend- The chief good which I hope may result from it will be to teach foreigners that even the yielding- pacific Fuh Chau men will not stand everything- & perhaps induce our government to station a naval force at this port to protect us in case of a civil outbreak in which case protection would be worth something-

July 24th- Thursday

Cloudy- hazy- strength of heat a little broken- James & I go to the city with a couple of American Captains- Accompanied them all through the curiosity bazaars- They bought twenty dollars worth of articles- bronzes- soap-stone ware- wooden boats-gods & the like of which there appears to be an inexhaustible quantity- Saw Dr. Welton a moment in his temple quarters. He looks thin indeed- has had dysentery & been to the mountains-looks as though he might soon follow Mrs. Peet- on whom he attended till the last & who was one of the most devoted patients & friends he had.

July 25th- Friday

Cool refreshing rain to-day. The sun is a month on his retrograde journey to the equator it will not be so hot again. Went out to show the cook how to make an indian hasty pudding. Alas- what could one do with some meal- baked by exposure to many climes.

July 26th- Saturday

Our rain continues- It is cool as September & quite as invigorating- Barrel of butter arrived for Mr. Gibson. It is fresh & good tasted compared with what we brought out. He sent up a jar of it in payment for one he had of us a year ago. I overhauled our barrel- Found three stone jars of butter in the bottom of it- covered with brine & straw in good condition. The fourth had lost part of its contents- We have consumed four jars of about 12 lbs each in the year or about a pound a week. Gibson has not consumed a pound a month. Maclay's have been entirely without except Fuh Chau butter & occasionally supplies from us. Gibson is selling & giving away that which he has now received. It looks well & tastes well- but his conceit is against it & there is less trouble in controlling one's judgement than one's caprice. The fault of the article- for which it certainly is not responsible- is simply that it is not fresh. The Fuh Chau butter he will not eat because if is "white". The fact is we could not suffer if we were entirely butterless. It is an article for cold climates & nature has made no provision for it here- We neither crave it nor need it. Cows give milk- a thin watery fluid- I fancy- at least it is so when it reaches us- A small quantity is sufficient for tea & coffee & the natives wonder why we find it essential for these. Milk costs us about ten cents a day- about three pints perhaps nearly two quarts- abundance for bread- cakes- drinks &C. Jimmy's favorite beverage at meals is milk & water cold & mine of late is milk & water hot. Baby sips a little, but cannot be induced to use a bottle & tube constantly- She prefers the natural- If she lives till cool weather comes again- we will try to break off her necessary connexion with the Chinese nurse-

Mrs. Gibson is better- she is going to the hill inside the city to recreate for a few days & after that- down the river to one of the ships- lying at the anchorage- Called on Mr. Peet- He was at dinner with his three girls- The eldest about the age of Belle Darlington- the youngest about as big as our Willie. They are going to the mountain next week- Mr. & Mrs. Baldwin & family are up among the monks & so are the Hartwells. It is a lovely cool place 2000 feet above our present level. We must go up by & by- Mr. Peet talks of taking his girls to America about the beginning of winter. I hope Providence will open up the way for my children to go by some convenient opportunity. Perhaps with the Peets.

July 27th- Sunday

Baby was highly interested at breakfast with the performances of the cats under the table- The grey had his dish of meal & the little white, hers- By a sort of illusion common to more intelligent animals each thought the other's portion better & fairer than his own- This notion led to predatory excursions & predatory excursions led to sundry growls & spittings & scratchings at which baby was highly amused- This did not prevent her from calling for a piece of potato or meat to hold in her hand & suck & reaching for the napkin ring to throw at some convenient mark- She cries a good deal of late & with good reason- She is cutting teeth- is broken out with prickly heat & has a boil upon the right temple & another upon the upper tip of the left ear. They have discharged & are breaking up- good for the blood but uncomfortable customers- It is raining still & she is confined

159

to the house which she especially dislikes. The nurses have the trick of all nurses- playing upon her credulity to bring about their own ends- "Baby go walk!" "Anna go hill?" Of course- baby is ready- hot or not- for a ramble outside & leaps to the arms of the nurse only to be tugged up stairs vexed & deceived-

Mothers & nurses are responsible for an awful amount of the lying & deception that curse this wicked world of ours. Many a Jacob has been made party to the deception schemes of an ambitious mother & suffered twenty years banishment & States prison "hard labor" in consequence. I fancy a good deal of "original sin" & "old Adam" originates with the training of the first years of infancy. I am not sure either but that deception is as instinctive in such & as natural & necessary as in cats as a substitute for strength & as an offset for the arts by which we are environed.

I slept from 9 till 11 & felt refreshed. Went to church at the house of Mr. Peet- The "mother in Israel" was not there- Two voices have dropped out of sabbath songs- tuned doubtless to higher strains.

July 28th- Monday

Cloudy & cool- It has been a remarkable summer. June was an uncomfortable month to me- July has had not more than a week of hot weather all told. August is yet in store. The Sam Russel by which I intend to send this is reported ready for sea- My letters & Journals must go on board to-day. It is the first direct chance for America by ship for months- Several others will go shortly. She may sink & carry all our household experiences to the bottom of the sea. It will save "old eyes" if she does- I thought at first of retaining July for another opportunity- but a better way may not occur & my jottings may as well all sink or swim together- I am hourly sensible that the golden chain which bound my interests & affections to yours has been snapt asunder. That only a little silver link remains- so frail that the slightest touch of disease might part it & leave as we were of yore- Our universe is one of motion. The probability is that no two particles in it occupy the same relation to it & each other for two successive instants together. How then can we expect permanency in our relations. From the changeable we pass to the changeless- Even here- memory immortalizes mortality & imparts durability to the passing & transient. One of the brightest portions of my shifting panorama was that illuminated by the presence of our darling Anna. The brightness- like that of a painting by the old Masters- was enhanced by its solitariness & the darkness which surrounded it- It has dwindled to a star- Another guiding lamp to Heaven.

EPILOGUE

Anna Wentworth

Daughter of Anna and Erastus Wentworth

EPILOGUE

History demands conclusions. It is therefore incumbent upon the writer to bring the lives of each of our main characters to their natural ending in order to satisfy the curiosity of the reader and, too, to allow him to make a more complete evaluation of Anna and Erastus Wentworth and the influence, or lack of influence, that they might have had on those closest to them.

As the story ended with Erastus' final letter to his father-in-law, Joseph J. Lewis (June 15, 1858) we find Erastus comfortably settled in the Missionary community of Foochow. It is nearly three years since the death of his second wife, Anna, and he toys with the thought of a third marriage to one of the three single missionary women recently arrived in Foochow--but with little enthusiasm. He is secure in the knowledge that his two children, Jimmy and Anna are well cared for by their families in America, but is aware of the growing estrangement from them brought about by distance and time. News of Anna's brother and sister (Charlton and Joe) comes to him now second-hand from his son Jimmy. He complains to Joseph Lewis that even his correspondence has ceased to be regular. Altogether it is a sad letter from a lonely man who feels more and more forgotten by those once nearest and dearest to him.

It is not surprising, therefore, that a year later (October 3rd, 1859) Erastus embarked upon a third marriage. His bride was Phebe Elizabeth Potter, one of the three missionary women alluded to in his letter. A year later a daughter, Frances Caroline, was born but died soon after in Foochow.

In 1862 Erastus and Phebe returned to the United States where Erastus took up his first ministerial post in Troy, N.Y. Between 1862-1868 four of their six living children were born: Louis Miller (1862), Nettie Louise (1864), George Edmond (1866), and Ellen Saxe (1867).

The family then moved to Pittsfield, Mass, where their fifth child, Cornelia Converse was born in 1869. In 1871 they moved to Amsterdam, N.Y. where they stayed for only a year before moving to Cincinatti, Ohio where Erastus took up his new job as Editor of the Ladies Repository. Between 1869-1873 two more children were born but both died in infancy. In 1874 a daughter, Maggie Harris, was born. Shortly after the birth of this last child Phebe (Potter) Wentworth died leaving Erastus, now 61, with their six young children, the eldest being only 12 years old.

Erastus stayed on as editor of the Ladies Repository for two more years before retiring in 1876 at the age of 63. During his retirement he continued as a delegate to several Methodist Church Conferences, but gave up ministerial work, preaching only from time to time when the occasion demanded. He served on a committee for the revision of the Methodist Hymnal. Most of his time, however, was devoted to writing. His articles appeared in secular journals as well as church periodicals and covered a wide range of subjects.

In 1881 he moved his family to Sandy Hill, Washington County, N.Y. where he spent the remainder of his days. He died on May 26th, 1886.

His eldest son Jimmy, who was 15 when he sailed with his step-sister Anna and her Chinese nurse from Foochow to America, was parted from his sister after their arrival in Boston. The baby Anna went to her grandparents, the Joseph Lewis' of West Chester, Pennsylvania and one can assume that until his father returned from China five years later, Jimmy was sent to live with his grandparents, Erastus Wentworth (Sr.) and his wife Esther who were living at that time with their daughter Abby in Stonington, Connecticut. The boy whom Erastus had described in his diary of June 4th, 1856--as "impatient of scientific labor & though a good deal of a rote man will never- I begin to fear- accomplish anything which requires application", proved his father's prediction to be quite wrong. For in 1867, at the age of 26, Jimmy graduated from Albany Medical College with the degree of M.D. He died ten years later. In my husband's possession is a two volume Genealogy of the Wentworth family written by John Wentworth LL.D. of Chicago in 1870 for private distribution only, which Jimmy bequeathed to his step-sister Anna.

Mary Lewis expressed the excitement that she felt at the forthcoming arrival of her granddaughter from China in a letter written to her father, Charles Miner, dated March 9th, 1857: "Our last months letters from China were so long delayed that we began to despair of getting any by the March mail, but on Friday night they came and brought us the exciting news of our little darling having left China early in December and we may look for her almost any time. We shall expect certainly to hear of their arrival in Boston early next month. We shall have an anxious time until we hear of their safety. I will enclose to you parts of several letters that contain the most of the particulars concerning their preparations for the voyage and the vessel in which they sailed. They all came by the same mail, though written partly on the 25th of November and partly on the 9th of December. It is a great disappointment to me that her old nurse Ling Choah is not with her. Mr. Peet's daughters are little girls all under Mary Ellen's age and besides them the Doctor does not mention any other female on board the vessel and I am afraid the old Chinese woman who cannot speak a word of English will prove a poor nurse if the baby should be sick."

The excitement of the arrival of the baby was not restricted to the Lewis family alone as on April 14th, 1857 a West Chester newspaper reported the following:

A LITTLE TRAVELLER FROM A FAR OFF LAND–

On Thursday evening last the cars brought to this place a very precious freight indeed to some hearts in our midst. It was only a little child of two summers, but a peculiarly touching history was connected with it. Scarcely three years since a company of Christian Missionaries left these shores to carry the benign and embracing influence of our divine religion to the myriads of human beings who people the vast empire of China. One of that number was born in this village, and her name and person were as familiar to us all as "household" words. Shortly after she arrived at her destination, she gave birth to a little girl, and not very long after this happy event, the young mother was borne to the grave in a strange land, leaving to her desolate husband only this pledge of their mutual devotion. Tidings reached the homestead here that she had passed away, and the only bright spots on the dark outlines of the picture were, that she had died at the post of duty, and had left a little one that might in the future come back to console the hearts of the bereaved who gathered sadly around the hearth stone, which the mother had left, never more to return.

Months ago a vessel sailed from the shores of China, destined for our own favored land, and this child and a faithful Chinese nurse, were among its passengers. They were sent over the bosom of the broad ocean with the prayers of the Missionary father accompanying both. These prayers were neither unavailing nor unheard, for after a journey of months, in which were traversed half the circuit of the great globe we live on, the little girl is safely placed in the same home from which her mother went out a few short years since, full of hope and faith in her glorious mission. We need hardly state to this community that we refer to the child of the lamented Mrs. Anna Wentworth, the daughter of our

townsman, Joseph J. Lewis Esq. Much interest was felt
when it was known that the Chinese nurse and her charge,
which she had so carefully and so long protected, had
arrived in the evening car, and quite a concourse was
gathered there to see both child and nurse, the latter
appearing in the full costume of the Chinese, and looking
strange enough to our eyes, as she came forth curiously
arrayed and bearing the little girl in her arms."

Baby Anna and her Chinese Nurse

The warmth and stability of the Lewis house into which
the baby Anna was received was short-lived. The prophesy of
the dying mother in China about the future of her daughter became
a reality: "I know she will be well taken care of and better brought
up than I can bring her up, so long as my Mother lives, but I
think after a few years my Mother will be taken away. My brothers
and sisters will settle in life and have families of their own, and

she is a little <u>girl,</u> and as she grows up into woman-hood, she'll need a <u>Mother's</u> sympathy- and counsel".

Mary Lewis' delicate health deteriorated slowly and painfully after the arrival of her grandchild. Three years later, in 1860, she died. Anna was 5 at the time of her grandmother's death. The running of the household passed successively to the elder daughters until they too, married and left home. Anna clung tenaciously to the youngest of the Lewis children, Willie, (her aunt) who was only five years older.

After the death of his wife, Joseph J. Lewis entered whole-heartedly into politics as a supporter for the candidacy of Abraham Lincoln as President of the United States. Lewis had informed himself fully on Lincoln's character and had read all his speeches. Nurtured as he had been in the Quaker belief in the equality of all men, Lewis, like his father before him, had abhorred the idea of slavery in America and in Lincoln he saw the true embodiment of this belief. He published a sketch on Lincoln in a local newspaper which was extensively copied in other newspapers. In 1860 he was appointed as a delegate from the district to the National Republican Convention in Chicago. After the convention he continued writing articles and making speeches on Lincoln's behalf.

On March 2nd, 1863, two years after Lincoln had become President, Joseph J. Lewis received a letter from Colonel Forney inviting him to become Commissioner of Internal Revenue in Lincoln's Cabinet. He accepted the appointment and served the office with distinction. In May, 1865, a month after the President's assassination, he resigned the post leaving Washington for New York where he became a partner in his son Charlton's law firm which also included Hon. S. S. Cox.

In 1866 he married Mrs. Sarah Jones of New York, who died two years later. He remained with the law firm for three years before returning to Philadelphia where Joseph J. Lewis set up his own law firm. Among other commitments he took charge of the affairs of his son-in-law, Hon. Wayne MacVeagh during the latter's absence as United States Minister to Turkey. MacVeagh had married Letitia Lewis or Let as she was referred to in Anna's letters.

On June 5th, 1872, Joseph J. Lewis married Phoebe A. Brooks, widow of James Brooks Esq. That same year he returned to West Chester where he resided until his death in 1883 in his 82nd year.

During all this time Anna and Willie experienced a very unsettled life moving from one house to another as convenience dictated, without the permanence of either residence or mother relationship which both so sorely needed. In later years Anna confessed to having always felt like "the poor relation".

Whether she was invited by her father to come and live with his new wife and family after his return from China in 1862, is unknown. It seems likely that with his knowledge of her transient existence, he would have done so. Her refusal in those early years might have been due to her close attachment to Willie, the youngest of the Lewis children and the one real anchor in her young life.

In later years snobbishness would have played a large role in preventing her from up-rooting herself from the structured social life of Philadelphia with all of its demands, taboos, and superficialities for the simple life of a Methodist minister's family in "up-state" New York and cities further West. For Anna was by then well enmeshed in Philadelphia society and surrounded by relatives of not only local but national importance. She attended the fashionable DeLancey Street school in Philadelphia. Her grandfather (Joseph Lewis) was a prominent lawyer and Presidential Cabinet Minister. Her aunt, Letitia, had married Hon. Wayne MacVeagh, a distinguished lawyer and diplomat who served as United States Ambassador in Italy and Turkey. Another aunt, Josephine, had married Stephen Darlington from an old and well-established West Chester family. Another uncle (Charlton Lewis) was a wealthy lawyer in New York and author of many important historical works. Her grandmother, Phoebe Lewis, (Joseph Lewis' third wife) was herself "well-born" and might have exerted some influence on Anna's thinking.

Whatever the reason, it is known that she looked down with an air of superiority upon her father's family. This was revealed in later years when she told her son, Richard Park, of having met her step-sisters and brothers for the first time on a trans-Atlantic crossing and of having refused to speak with them. One finds it difficult to believe that she could have been the progeny of the humble, selfless Anna and of Erastus Wentworth who, above all, abhorred "sham" and superior airs in others.

But times had changed in America and Anna's life, more than any other, reflected those changes. The values of the earlier decades of the 19th century with their emphasis on religion and education were gradually being replaced from the mid-decades onward by a new dedication to the amassing of great wealth and with it the pursuit of pleasure. A new class of citizens had emerged --the industrial magnate--a man who owed very little to education but whose success was due to hard work, dedication, skill, inventiveness and most of all vision. Many of the early pioneers in industry were the sons of the immigrants and had served their apprenticeship in small businesses. Thus, from an early age, they had seen at first hand the material needs of the growing nation and upon reaching manhood had set about supplying those needs in their own factories; the iron ore, coal, steel, railroads, agricultural machinery, etc.

Having made their fortunes they then built their grand houses often in close proximity to the houses of other "new--moneyed" industrialists. "Millionaire's row" became a familiar term of expression by the local residents of the cities and of the older families who looked upon those grand edifices and their occupants with a decidedly "jaundiced eye". The relationship between the older families with their very different set of values and the clearly visible "nouveau riche" and their often ostentatious living was at best uncomfortable and at the least non-existent. The merger between the two did not take place until a generation later when the sons and daughters of the millionaires, having been schooled alongside the children of the older families, emerged upon the scene as a new hybrid, a mixture of old and new values far more acceptable to the older families whose values too, were changing. Success was largely measured by wealth and the millionaire sons and daughters of those early industrialists became a valuable commodity in boosting the declining fortunes of "respectable" families at home and titled families abroad.

In this setting we can more fully understand Anna's gnawing sense of inferiority in her position as the "poor relation" of the Lewis family.

For a time she seems to have toyed with the thought of pursuing an academic career, for at the age of 16 she left the DeLancey St. School and enrolled at the preparatory school at Vassar College. Two years later she was admitted to Vassar's freshman class. Although she remained at Vassar for only a year she was active in dramatics, music and was elected class poet.

On June 1st, 1882 Anna married Richard Gray Park, son of James Park, Jr. and Sarah (Gray) Park of Pittsburgh, Pennsylvania. The evening wedding took place at Anna's aunt and uncle's house, Mr. & Mrs. Stephen Darlington, of West Chester and was solemnized by the Rev. R. J. Carson assisted by the Rev. B. T. Jones of Westminster Presbyterian Church, the denomination to which her husband belonged (the Park family being of Scotch-Irish ancestry).

Whether Erastus Wentworth attended his daughter's wedding is not known, but it seems unlikely for if he had, he most certainly would have officiated at the service. Erastus was 69 at the time and was reported to have been in good health until shortly before his death in 1886. This suggests that the break between father and daughter was then absolute.

Richard Park's father, James Park, Jr., was a pioneer in the steel industry, having been the first to develop Bessemer steel in America of a quality equal to the best in Europe. His company, The Black Diamond Steel Works (later called James Park Brothers) had a greater capacity for the manufacture of crucible steel than any other in the world including that of the Krupp Works in Prussia. In later years the company was bought by Andrew Carnegie.

After a honeymoon in Montreal, the couple settled into their new home in Montclair, New Jersey--a convenient suburb to New York City where Richard Park managed a branch of his father's company. Four of their five children were born in Montclair, only three of whom lived to maturity.

Anna's financial situation had now dramatically changed from her oft referred to "poor relation" status in the Lewis family to that of the wife of a millionaire. In 1890, at the age of 39, Richard Park retired from business altogether and moved his family to West Chester where they bought a large town house, another in Philadelphia and in 1895 built a palatial country house on the highest hill-top on their several hundred acres of farmland two miles outside of West Chester which they named Cloverly Farm.

Like so many wealthy matrons of the day, Anna's life was divided into three compartments: domestic, social and charitable duties. While her husband attended to the management of the farm and the finances of the family, Anna supervised the large staff of servants, the bringing up of the children and the myriad of problems connected with the running of three houses.

On the social side she was a member of the Acorn Club and the National Society of Colonial Dames in Philadelphia, attended Friday afternoon concerts at the Academy of Music and during the summer months at Cloverly Farm entertained extensively at week-end parties with the guests sometimes staying for a week or two on that large estate which included a 9 hole golf course, tennis courts, gaming rooms and even a full length bowling alley, not to mention the riding and shooting parties in the cooler autumn months. As an accomplished pianist herself, she often entertained her guests in the large "music room" at Cloverly accompanied by talented musicians from the region. Alcoholic beverages were never served in the Park household as Richard Park had taken the Oath of Temperance.

Anna's knowledge of her mother's devotion to Christianity was not forgotten, however. Although soon after her marriage she left the Methodist Church and became an active member of Holy Trinity Episcopal Church in West Chester, she became a regular member of the Sunday School teaching staff of that church. She supported many poor families both black and white in the town and assisted many young men and women in obtaining higher degrees in education by relieving them of the burden of finance. That she was held in high esteem by the townspeople is attested to by the number of black and white children who were named for her. She found The Wentworth Home in West Chester in memory of her mother which exists to this day. The Home cares for elderly Christian women of meager circumstances.

In 1912 two of their three children married. Richard G. Park, Jr. married Ellen Nixon Graham, daughter of Mrs. Peter Graham of Chestnut Hill, Philadelphia, and Helen Miner Park became the bride of William R. Breck of New York. Five years later their third child, Sarah Gray Park married Hazen Morton Chase of Gardiner, Maine. Sarah died a year later only days after giving birth to a healthy baby boy. The tragedy was deeply felt by both parents and the scar remained with Anna for the rest of her days.

Tragedy succeeded tragedy as only a year after the death of this favorite daughter Anna's husband died suddenly of a stroke on December 28th, 1919.

Now a lonely widow Anna sought comfort from her two remaining children and seven grandchildren. For awhile she took a house in Washington close to the Richard Park family. Later she lived near to the Breck family in Rosemont (a suburb of Philadelphia). For several months of the winter she stayed in hotels in Santa Barbara, California or in Atlantic City, New Jersey. But her summers were spent at Cloverly Farm. The Park and Breck families alternated each year in spending their summers with her at Cloverly.

The Brecks lived next door to my family in Rosemont and their youngest child Billy (only ten days older than myself) was my childhood playmate. Therefore, when the Brecks went to Cloverly I, too, was invited to come along. In this way I came to know Anna Park in the latter years of her life. Most of that time she was bedridden with a nurse in attendance day and night as she suffered painfully from angina.

She was a smallish woman with snow-white hair, a sallow complexion and darkly circled eyes, an outward evidence, no doubt, of the pain she suffered from almost continuously.

Each morning I was summoned to her bedside at which time I was asked to give an account of what plans Billy and I had for the day. I remember feeling very uncomfortable in her presence as if being "called down" by a strict school-teacher. Like most children of ten or eleven we never planned our day but instead did whatever we thought of at the moment- therefore I found it necessary to concoct a new story every day to satisfy her curiosity.

In retrospect I realize now that perhaps her only means of contact with those staying in her house was occasioned by her "summons". For although she commanded respect from her family, she lacked the necessary warmth to draw them to her voluntarily. This, no doubt, added to her already established sense of insecurity. My husband recalls a tragic scene in his childhood when she pleaded with him to tell her why he liked his other grandmother better than herself.

One can only speculate on how different Anna Park's life might have been had she been given the security of a normal mother-father relationship or if her grandmother, Mary Lewis had lived to give her the continuing love and support during those impressionable years of her childhood.

Anna Park died at Cloverly Farm on November 10th, 1933 at the age of 78. Her life spanned three eras of American history: the waning years of religious revivalism, the high water mark of the Victorian era, and the beginning years of the "modern" era. We see her most at home in the Victorian period with its focus on luxury, comforts and superficialities, but not without the consciousness of that earlier era. In imagining an encounter between Anna in her adult years and her parents, Anna and Erastus

Wentworth, one can feel quite certain that neither would have found enough in common to sustain more than a polite hello and goodbye.

Polly Park